International Corporate and Investment Banking – Practice and Law

institute of
financial services

International Corporate and Investment Banking – Practice and Law

Mark Largan

Institute of Financial Services
IFS House
4-9 Burgate Lane
Canterbury
Kent
CT1 2XJ
United Kingdom

T 01227 818649
F 01227 479641
E editorial@ifslearning.com
W www.ifslearning.com

Institute of Financial Services publications are published by The Chartered Institute of Bankers, a non-profit making registered educational charity.

Typeset by John Smith
Printed by Antony Rowe Ltd, Wiltshire

ISBN 0-85297-696-8

ifs institute of financial services

Preface

This book has been specifically written to complement the Institute of Financial Services' new option module 'International Corporate and Investment Banking – Practice and Law' which forms part of the BSc/ACIB in Financial Services.

International Corporate and Investment Banking – Practice and Law provides all the essential elements relevant to individuals working within corporate or investment banking, from the principles of private international law, through the structure of loan agreements to mergers and acquisitions.

The underlying theme throughout this book is to approach the subject from a structural point of view by focusing on the documentation requirements of loans and various financial instruments as well as highlighting the legal risks that financial institutions face on transactions in both the UK and abroad, and the ways in which financial institutions can mitigate that risk.

The advent of the FSA and the enactment of the Financial Services and Markets Act 2000 along with the Enterprise Act 2002 has changed the acquisition and merger landscape. Europe too has become a significant factor with the EU Merger Directive and the EU Regulation on Jurisdiction (Regulation 44/2001). The issue of future European Monetary union for the UK is also considered form a legal standpoint. Wherever possible up to date legal cases have been cited.

I am grateful to both Paul Raby and Nigel Clayton for their suggestions to the coverage of the book and to Marie Smith and her colleagues at the Institute of Financial Services for their support and guidance.

Mark Largan
August 2003

Acknowledgements

All extracts taken from past *Corporate Banking – Practice and Law Examiner's Reports* were authored by Nigel Clayton. The author and The Institute of Financial Services are grateful to Nigel Clayton for his agreement to reproduce these extracts.

Contents

One

Conflicts and choice of law

1 Private international law: an introduction

Private international law or conflict of laws has been defined as: 'That branch of law that deals with cases in which some relevant fact has a connection with another system of law on either territorial or personal grounds, and may, on that account, raise a question as to the application of one's own or the appropriate alternative (usually foreign) law to the determination of the issue, or as to the exercise of jurisdiction by one's own or foreign courts'.

Or, put more simply, an international loan contract will obviously involve two or more different countries, each with its own legal system. No contract can exist in a legal vacuum and conflict of law principles determine which country's law will govern it. Note this will not necessarily be the enforcing forum, ie the country's courts that hear any dispute in the contract.

The possible laws, which may be involved in an international loan contract, are:

(a) law of the borrower's country;

(b) law of the lender's country;

(c) law of the market, eg London eurodollar market;

(d) law of a neutral country;

(e) public international law.

The parties normally expressly choose which of these laws will apply to their contract. This governing law is known as the proper law or *lex causae*. The proper law (also known as the governing law) is thus the law that governs many matters affecting a contract. The principles involved in determining which law will govern the contract in particular if none is expressly chosen are known as conflict of laws or private international law.

2 Objective of choosing the proper law

The legal and practical purpose of an express choice of law clause is to seek to control or, at the very least, bring some degree of predictability to the agreement. The contractual authority and capacity of the borrower and his representatives may be interpreted by applying the chosen proper law (although the law of the borrower's country of residence is often applied to these matters). The interpretation of clauses and words in the agreement will be a matter for the chosen proper law as will the availability of remedies, eg acceleration on an event of default. Also relevant are the application of exchange control and withholding tax regulations. The degree of predictability will be brought to the following issues.

(i) The validity, enforceability and interpretation of all legal documents evidencing and constituting the underlying banking transaction, for example in a syndicated loan, the syndicated loan agreement, in Euro Commercial Paper Programme, the Euro Commercial Paper Programme Agreement, the issuing and paying agency agreement, the global note and the deed of covenant or deed poll.

(ii) The legal rights and obligations of the various parties to the financing transaction in question.

(iii) The extent to which other systems of law (other than that of the proper law) will affect the transaction.

In the absence of such an express choice of law the financing transaction in question may be subject to and be affected by a number of legal systems. This may include, in particular, the law of the place where the relevant documents are executed, where the borrower is incorporated or where litigation is ultimately commenced. Each such law may interpret the financing transaction, and the rights and obligations that arise differently.

3 The legal systems that may impinge upon an international law contract

These are as follows:

(a) the proper (or governing) law of the contract (*lex causae*);

(b) the laws of the countries of residence of each of the parties (*lex domicili*);

(c) the law of the country whose courts will hear a dispute on the contract (*lex fori*);

(d) the law of the place where the contract is entered into (*lex loci contractus*);

(e) the law of the country where the contract is to be performed, eg place of payment (*lex loci solutionis*);

(f) the law of the currency used (*lex monetae*);

(g) the law of the country where any security for the loan is sited (*lex situs*).

The law of the place of residence of the borrower will determine the status, power and authority of the borrower and its representatives and may also determine the effect of exchange control regulations (*lex domicili*). The *lex fori* will determine everything to do with court procedure and formalities, eg witnessing of signatures in the agreement. The *lex fori* may also affect the essential validity of the contract if it refuses to enforce it because it offends its public policy requirements, or it conflicts with a directly applicable statute of its own (eg exchange control), or it involves an illegal act at the place of performance.

NB: Section 72 of the Bills of Exchange Act 1882 provides that interpretation of the issues of drawing, endorsement and acceptance of a bill are governed by the *lex loci contractus*.

4 Factors in choosing the proper law

Factors influencing the parties' choice of law are:

(a) non-legal factors, eg familiarity, patriotism, xenophobia!

(b) the desire for certainty and predictability may lead to a lender choosing his own law or to unify *lex causae* and *lex fori*;

(c) commercial orientation of the legal system and its political stability;

(d) the lender may wish to insulate himself from the borrower's law and the risk of future changes in it, which will affect his contract.

4.1 The concept of insulation

In the case of *Kahler v Midland Bank* (1950) HL ' the proper law, because it sustains, may also modify or dissolve the contractual bond.'

Insulation is the desire by lenders in so far as possible to insulate the law applying to the agreement (the proper law) from political interference by legal changes effected in the borrower's country, particularly if the borrower is the government of the country. Hence it is preferable to choose a governing law, which is external to the borrower.

This conclusion is drawn from the widely held doctrine that the proper law applying to the agreement is the law as it exists from time to time, as held in the case of *Re Helbert Wagg* (1956) Ch 323, if the law changes then the parties may be bound by the change. In this case a German moratorium law required a German borrower to make loan repayments under a loan contract governed by German law to a government agency in Berlin in German marks instead of pounds sterling.

A contrasting case to that of Helbert Wagg was the case of *National Bank of Greece SA v Metliss* (1958) AC 509, HL, a Greek decree reduced the interest rate on bonds issued by a Greek bank and subject to English law. Held: the Greek law was disregarded and the borrower was liable to pay arrears of interest. Thus the English governing law insulated the contract from changes in Greek law.

Limits to insulation

There are limits to insulation, which can be therefore summarized as follows.

(a) Local enforcement: local courts may ignore the choice of a foreign proper law.

(b) Aspects governed by local law: some areas will be non-choice including, for example, property or insolvency.

(c) Exchange controls may be imposed by another state.

5 Contracts (Applicable Law) Act 1990

This Act enacts the Rome Convention (1980), the Luxembourg Convention (1984) and the Brussels Protocol (1988) into English law with regard to choosing a proper law. The Rome Convention governs private international law in all the EU countries.

5.1 The purpose and application of the Rome Convention

1. Continuation of efforts to unify private international law throughout the EU.
2. Continuing to follow in the field of jurisdiction and enforcement by the previous Brussels convention that will be discussed in the next unit.
3. The convention applies to contracts in any situation involving a choice between the laws of different countries, whether or not those countries are EU member states.
4. The Primary Rule by Article 3 is that a contract is governed by the law chosen by the parties. This is known as the freedom of party autonomy. If there is no choice then contracts will be governed by laws of the country with which the contract is most closely connected.

   'A contract shall be governed by the law chosen by the parties. The choice must be express or demonstrated with reasonable certainty by the terms of the contract or the circumstances of the case. By their choice, the parties can select the law applicable to the whole or a part only of the contract' (Article 3(1)).
5. The convention is concerned only with the law applicable to contractual obligations. It does not impact on areas of local law or limitations of the proper law as already discussed.

By Article10 of the Rome Convention, the applicable law (proper law) will govern the interpretation of the loan, the performance (repayment) of the loan, the breach of the loan including damages, and the limitation period applicable to bringing claims for breach of obligations under the loan.

5.2 Limitations of choosing a proper law

The Rome Convention reaffirms the principle that choice must be bona fide, legal and not contrary to public policy that confirms previous English case law on the subject in that the English courts will not uphold an evasive choice of law. This was held in the case of *Vita Food Products Inc v Unus Shipping Co Ltd* [1939] AC 277, PC and also that of the House of Lords in *Miller v Whitworth Street Estates* [1970] AC 583 whereby a choice of law must be bona fide and legal.

If there is no express choice of law contained in the agreement the general position at common law will infer a choice of law from a jurisdiction or arbitration clause unless there are compelling indications to the contrary, which is discussed in detail below in section 6. Under the Rome convention if there is no express choice Art 4(1) states that the contract will be governed by the law of the country to which it is most closely connected.

5.3 Mandatory rules

Article 7(2) provides that nothing in the convention shall restrict the application of the rules of law of the forum in a situation where they are mandatory. Mandatory areas will, for example, include land law, insolvency. Also there is the rule that courts will not enforce contracts that are illegal at their place of performance.

5.4 Conclusion

The Rome Convention does not change the existing approach of the rules of private international law except that it is probably more important to state expressly in all contracts (except cheques, Bills of Exchange, promissory notes) the law by which they are governed.

6 Applicable law where there is no stated choice of law

In English law, the courts will look first to see if the parties have made an express choice of law. If not, they will seek the tacit or implied choice. The fact that the parties have chosen a country's courts as the forum raises a strong inference that the implied choice of law is that country's law.

Article 4(1) of the Rome Convention provides that, where the parties do not expressly choose the law that applies, the term loan will be governed by the law of the country with which it is most closely connected. There was a clear distinction to be made between the proper law that applies to loans and the proper law that applies to security taken by a lending bank[1].

Article 4(2) of the Rome Convention goes on to provide a presumption that the test of closest connection will be the country where the party that is to carry out the characteristic performance of the contract is based. This is of course payment, as was held in the cases of *Sierra Leone Telecommunications Co Ltd (Sierratel) v Barclays Bank plc* (1998) and *The Bank of Baroda v The Vysya Bank* (1994)[1].

Article 4(2) of the Rome Convention also sets out certain rebuttable presumptions; in particular, in the case of a company which is to effect the characteristic performance of the contract, the place of residence of the company or where its central administration is located[1].

Further, if a severable part of the contract is more closely connected with another country, then that part of the contract (the severed part) may exceptionally be governed by the laws of another country[1].

Professor Phillip Wood, *Law and Practice of International Finance* expresses the view that in a lending contract, the characteristic performance is the repayment by the borrower, and hence the residence or central location of the company would determine the law that applies[1].

By Article 4(5) the presumptions, including that in Article 4(2), can be disregarded if, looking at all the circumstances, it appears that the contract is more closely connected with another country[1].

NB: The proper law must be ascertained by reference to the time the contract was made and all events after that are irrelevant. *Armer Shipping Co Ltd v Caisse Algerienne d'Assurance et de Reassurance* (1981) CA. The contract cannot exist in a vacuum until something happens to determine the proper law.

NB: Incorporation of law is a different matter in that, eg the definition of a subsidiary company may be expressed to be by reference to the English Companies Act 1985 whilst the proper law is New York. Such an incorporated piece of law does not alter with subsequent amendments of the statute unlike proper law.

Figure 1.1

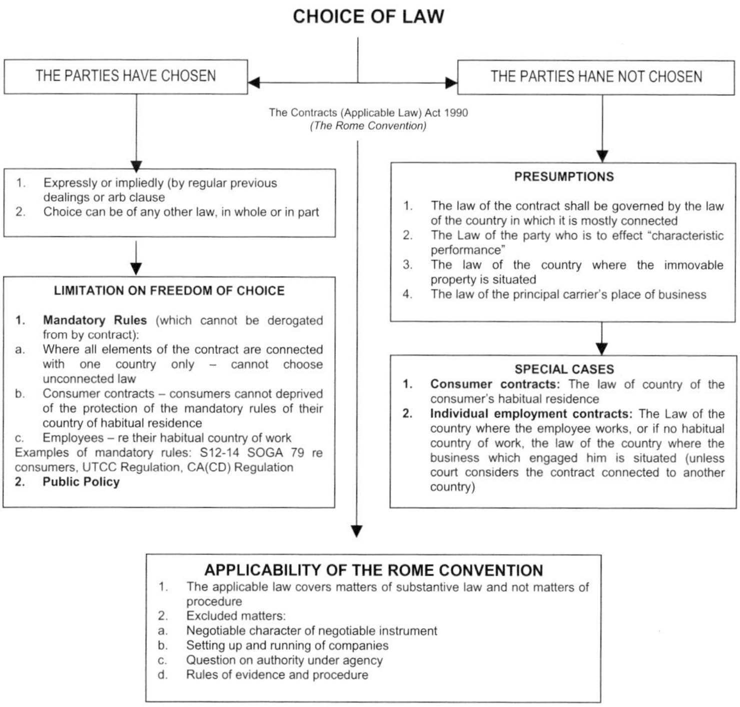

6.1 The position in New York

In New York the courts have applied a range of criteria to decide the proper law; these are:

(a) centre of gravity doctrine, similar to 'closest connection';

(b) policy interests doctrines now absorbed into the Conflicts Restatement which enshrines seven of these, viz, the needs of the different legal systems, the relevant policies of the forum, the relevant policies of other states and their relative interests in the outcome, protection of justified expectations, basic policies underlying the particular field of law, predictability of result and the ease of application of each law.

6.2 The Calvo doctrine

Some South and Central American states apply the 'Calvo doctrine' to international sovereign contracts whereby their law prohibits the submission of their sovereignty to any external law or jurisdiction.

7 The scope of proper law

The proper law will govern the essential validity of the contract (whether it is enforceable), the interpretation of it (ie words and phrases used in it), its effect (ie what are the obligations of the parties) and discharge of it (ie have the parties performed the contract, eg the effect of a moratorium).

7.1 Essential validity

The essential validity is where the substance of the obligation to matter in the contract itself and meaning of words used and contractual terms will be governed by the proper law.

7.2 Discharge

The question of whether there has been an effective discharge by performance etc will be determined by the proper law. This is particularly important due to proliferation of moratorium legislation that seeks to extinguish contractual obligations: *Kahler v Midland Bank* (1950).

7.3 Illegality

A contract that is illegal by its proper law cannot be enforced in England or one that is contrary to English Public Policy. A contract that is illegal in the place of performance cannot be enforced in England if English Law is proper law. There is a distinction between contracts that are illegal at the outset and those where the illegality arises.

8 Matters not governed by the proper law

The proper law is not of universal application because procedural questions are governed by the law of the place where proceedings are brought (the *lex fori*), ie whether courts have jurisdiction, laws of evidence. Availability of a pre-judgement order, ie Mareva injunctions, (a freezing order which will be discussed in detail in the next unit) will be determined by the *lex fori* as would the availability of legal remedies to enforce any claim. Any question of immunity will also be determined by *lex fori*.

8.1 Status and capacity

This is the law of the institution's domicile (*lex domicili*), ie country of incorporation. For corporations these apply to their powers as to whether the corporate can enter into legally binding commitments.

8.2 Formal validity

This is where a contract has to be sufficient to comply with the formalities of the proper law, but a contract will be formally valid if it meets the laws of the place where the contract is made (*lex loci contractus*) even if it does not meet that of the proper law.

9 Documentation provisions

The choice of law clause is simple, typically: 'this agreement shall be governed by and construed in accordance with English law'. This expressly covers matters of both validity and interpretation, unnecessary in fact, *Re Helbert Wagg & Co Ltd* (1956).

A double jeopardy clause may be included, allowing the lender to cancel the agreement if it becomes illegal for him to continue it, eg a London bank has an agreement governed by New York law which becomes illegal under English law.

Attempts to stabilize the proper law are probably ineffective as every contract must have a proper law and it must be allowed to change.

The choice of law will generally be dictated by the lender who will prefer an external law, probably his own or in the case of a syndicate the residence of the organizers. English and New York law are universally popular choices.

International agency lenders, eg World Bank, tend to exclude municipal laws and opt for public international law.

10 The legal implications of the euro in the UK

The legal framework for the introduction of the euro is governed by two European Council Regulations. The first Regulation was introduced under Article 235 of the Treaty of Rome, as amended by the Treaty on European Union signed in Maastricht in February 1992. The Article 235 Regulation applies to all EU Member States whether or not they participate in Economic and Monetary Union ('EMU').

10.1 Continuity of contracts

The principal legal issue in the Article 235 Regulation concerns continuity of contracts.

Under English law, a contract normally remains in full force and effect until both sides have performed all of the obligations that they originally undertook.

There was some debate as to whether contracts might be frustrated or terminated as a consequence of the introduction of the single currency and the loss of corresponding national currencies that would constitute legal tender.

However, contracts expressed in a participating national currency and governed by English law will remain valid and enforceable notwithstanding:

(i) the introduction of the euro; and

(ii) the withdrawal of the national currency units in which the debt was originally expressed

English law therefore affords no basis for the termination or frustration of such contracts. The EU Commission allayed any concerns over the question of continuity by the introduction of the Article 235 Regulation, which by Article 3, provides as follows:

> *'The introduction of the euro shall not have the effect of altering any term of a legal instrument or of discharging or excusing performance under any legal instrument, nor give a party the right unilaterally to alter or terminate such an instrument. This provision is subject to anything which parties may have agreed.'*

The Article 235 Regulation is directly applicable in all Member States, whether or not they will be adopting the euro. The wording reproduced above must therefore be treated as part of the domestic contract law of the UK. So far as contracts governed by English law are concerned, Article 3 of the Article 235 Regulation entirely disposes of the continuity of contracts question.

The Article 235 Regulation does not alter the law in non-EU jurisdictions. If the contract in question is governed by the laws of a state outside the EU then the continuity question would be governed by the law applicable to the contract as a whole. In such a case the Article 235 Regulation would not form part of the domestic system of contract law of the state concerned.

10.2 Documentation

'Euro clauses' are now included in financing and other documentation. The language is normally in the form of change of currency provision and the effect of EMU on future payment provisions under contractual agreements. For example, ISMA has published an Annex to the standard form master repurchase agreement. The provisions include continuity of contract, changes to the definitions of 'business day' and 'equivalent securities' and payment netting. IPMA is also developing redenomination, reconventioning and payment working for issues denominated in national currencies.

Of particular interest is the initiative developed by ISDA for a multilateral protocol agreement. It enables parties to an ISDA master agreement to agree amendments to outstanding contracts with other signatories without the individual amendment of all outstanding deals. Amendments cover continuity provisions, price sources, payment netting, EMU definitions and bond options. The protocol is discussed further in a later unit on Swaps.

11 Introduction to the EU Directives

Banking has for many years been an international business, not least as a result of its role in financing international trade. On a global scale there can be little doubt that the regulators' ability to supervise internationally active firms is deficient. The existence of different accountancy standards, insolvency law and hugely variable standards among many national regulators create a far from ideal background. Coupled with this the growth of financial markets into the underdeveloped worlds and the emergence of information systems such as the Internet mean that interdependence, and thus systemic risk, grows daily bigger.

While the process of international regulation has begun at least in Europe through various directives it would be foolish to imagine an overnight liberalization of financial services. Politics, protectionism and national pride will continue to slow this process down.

Among the most pressing issues confronting financial services regulators is the need to develop practical arrangements to supervise an increasingly global industry. Unsurprisingly, regulators are involved in a game of catch up – trying to impose effective regulation on firms who already have global groups, branches and above all global risks.

In 1974 the Basle Committee on Banking Supervision was established by the G10 central banks and the initial focus of its work was to define the role and responsibilities of home and host supervisors of internationally active banks. Its key success has been in the development of capital adequacy rules that set down minimum requirements for internationally active banks. The securities industry has the International Organization of Securities Commissions (IOSCO) of which the regulators of some 70 countries are members. More recently the world's derivatives regulators have agreed to cooperate to share information through the Windsor Declaration and the Boca Raton agreement. These initiatives are the basis of the beginnings of international information sharing and standards setting, a process being actively supported by G7 nations that culminated in the European single market in financial services becoming a reality in 1995, when a number of European Directives finally came into force.

To understand the impact of these directives it is important to understand some of the background. Under the European Community rules financial services business is deemed to be conducted by two principal groups – banks and investment firms. For the banks (or credit institutions) the major changes necessitated in preparation for the single market were included in the Second Banking Coordination Directive enforced in 1993. For investment firms the key piece of legislation that led to the creation of a single market was the Investment Services Directive that came into force on 31 December 1995.

The purpose of both Directives was to create a business environment in which European financial institutions of whatever type may operate throughout the region without the burden of having to be separately authorized in each member state and without being bound by various and different capital adequacy regimes.

11.1 Summary of main EU Directives to date

1989 Undertakings in collective investments in transferable securities has enabled certain collective investment schemes to be sold throughout Europe.

1993 Second Banking Coordination Directive – which created a single market for banks throughout the European Economic Area (EEA is comprised of EU states plus Norway, Iceland and Liechtenstein).

1994 Insurance Directive – created a single market for insurance.

1996 Investment Services Directive ('ISD') – created a single market for investment firms throughout the EEA. Only the UK, Ireland, Netherlands, Spain, Norway, Sweden, Belgium, Finland, France, Italy, Denmark and Germany have implemented the ISD.

1996 Capital Adequacy Directive – created uniform set of financial requirements for banks, securities and investment firms.

It should be noted that the various Directives that have introduced the idea of passporting do not do away with the ability of the various member states to have different laws from one another. However, if a state chooses to have different and more demanding regulations, these regulations must satisfy the so-called 'general good' criteria. Broadly, these criteria outlaw rules or laws that discriminate against businesses from other member states and which are overly restrictive. Furthermore, where differences exist, such differences should be justifiable in the public interest. Consequently, in the context of financial services, most authorized UK investment businesses will find it possible to use their UK authorization to provide investment services elsewhere within Europe, without the need to be re-authorized. Notwithstanding this apparent freedom, it is still necessary for the passporting business to comply with certain local regulations if such regulations are in the 'general good'.

12 The EU Capital Adequacy Directive (CAD)

The CAD is part of the single-market regime and sets out the minimum standards of capital adequacy with which both investment firms and banks doing investment business must adhere to. The purpose of the CAD is to develop common rules of capital adequacy in respect of both credit institutions and investment firms when they engage in direct competition with one another. Since the directive applies to both banks and investment firms the regulations differentiate between the trading book and the non-trading book. The items that comprise the non-trading book will include those concerned with traditional banking such as lending, whereas trading book items will be those that involve positions in financial instruments for short-term trading purposes.

12.1 The consequences of the CAD

The CAD makes a number of important changes; these are as follows.

Consolidated supervision

Under CAD financial supervision is applied on a consolidated basis, thereby providing regulators with a complete picture.

Home states are entitled to enforce regulations that exceed the minimum standards established by the CAD – a concept known as super equivalence.

Financial resources

The CAD applies two measures to a firm's capital which are an initial and further capital requirements. Investment firms at all times must meet a level of initial capital of one of three levels. These are as follows:

€50,000	providing that the firm does not hold client money or securities and does not deal on its own account or underwrite;
€125,000	provided the firm does not deal with its own account or underwrite;
€730,000	for all other investment firms.

Already authorized firms that do not satisfy these requirements will be eligible for transitional arrangements – 'grandfathering' – that will allow them to remain in business.

13 EU Investment Services Directive (ISD)

The Investment Services Directive is an important part of the European Community's single-market programme and became effective 1 January 1996. The directive gives a common passport to all securities firms within the community (with a limitation in Greece, Spain and Portugal where the directive was planned to come into effect on or after 1 January 1999). The guarantee of investor protection will lie in a licence to trade that will be granted by the local regulator. The ISD is however silent on a number of important issues such as solicitation and marketing. Consequently, passported firms may need to market in accordance with a plethora of domestic laws.

Therefore, a firm may obtain authorization in its home state, for example Denmark, and then wish to open a branch or cross-border sell in the UK. It will then apply for membership of the appropriate UK regulator. The UK regulator will not be able to refuse it membership because it is already deemed to be fit and proper elsewhere in the EEA. Once authorized by the local regulator the firm will be bound by the local conduct of business rules. This will be a major advantage for those firms that have a network of European offices or which conduct cross-border business. The table below outlines the basic split of responsibilities.

Many member states have good reason to fear inwardly passported firms from states with a highly developed financial services sector such as the UK and accordingly some states, notably Italy, will use this to protect their domestic business.

HOME	HOST
AUTHORIZATION	CONDUCT OF BUSINESS
FITNESS AND PROPRIETY	(in host state)
CAPITAL ADEQUACY	
CLIENT MONEY	
CONDUCT OF BUSINESS	
(within home state)	

There are a number of important issues that stem from this directive, not least among them being the fact that the client money rules will comprise part of the prudential regulation conducted by the 'home' regulator.

An earlier worry was one of regulatory arbitrage in which firms might set up in the easiest jurisdiction within the EEA and then outwardly passport. This, as yet, does not appear to be happening.

A further concern relates to the ability to discipline 'passported' business. At present the ultimate sanction is the withdrawal of authorization, thereby removing the ability of the firm to trade. While the situation would appear to be that the UK regulators are able to use the full range of disciplinary powers open to them, there is a conflict here.

If the UK expels a 'passported' firm then it is implicitly questioning the fitness and propriety of the firm. This would mean that the UK regulator is contradicting the home state regulator. If this is not possible then the UK regulator would only have the sanction of fines, which does not create a 'level playing field' between UK and non-UK firms. There is also little reason to have confidence that the EU Commission will act effectively to police miscreant states because many states still have laws that are in contravention with the 1960 Treaty of Rome.

14 The Second Banking Coordination Directive (2BCD)

The Second Banking Coordination Directive (2BCD) is similar to the ISD but relates to banking activity. Once again, the concept is that the home state authority may grant the passport to the firm to operate throughout the EEA.

The directive is based on the German model of the 'universal bank' and therefore extends to cover more than straightforward banking activities. The passport will cover:

(a) trading in securities;

(b) participation in securities issues;

(c) advice with regard to corporate finance activities such as take-overs and mergers; and

(d) portfolio management.

This passport is available only to *credit institutions and to financial institutions* as defined in the directive. The limitations on the definitions in the directive led in part to the ISD because many firms in direct competition with the passported banks would not themselves fall within the definition of credit or financial institutions and would therefore not be able to obtain the passport. With the introduction of the ISD investment firms are now able to compete on the same basis as the banks.

The 2BCD came into effect on 1 January 1993 and since that date a number of overseas banks with Financial Services and Markets Act 2000 authorizations have been allowed to trade on the basis of their home state authorization, subject only to the local rules of the UK.

Once again there is a potential problem with regard to enforcement in that the authorization granted by the home state is basically the test of fitness and propriety, therefore limiting the ability of the UK regulators to expel 'unfit' businesses.

15 European Commission Communication on the Second Banking Coordination Directive

In 1995, the European Commission published a draft communication on the freedom to provide services under the Second Banking Coordination Directive (2BCD). The draft communication set out the views of the Commission as to the circumstances in which notification and regulation of cross-border services under the 2BCD (ie those not provided through an overseas branch) should take place. The Commission suggested that a credit institution that is subject to the provisions of the 2BCD should notify such services where it proposes to 'canvass' an overseas investor. The view of the UK authorities is that the 'canvassing' test is not appropriate, and is not supported in the text of the 2BCD or in Community law generally.

The view of the UK authorities is that firms should notify in respect of activities that are carried out within the territory of another member State but where those activities fall short of the establishment of a branch. This would apply, for example, to the transaction of business through agents or travelling salesmen. Notification should also be made where a firm holds itself out as being willing to provide remote services (eg telephone-based dealing) to clients in another EEA state.

Notification would not be required in other circumstances, such as in the event of occasional, unsolicited telephone request from overseas.

The UK authorities have also expressed concern that any decision relating to the treatment of cross-border services under 2BCD must not be considered in isolation, but must be addressed consistently, and in parallel, in the banking, investment services and insurance sectors.

16 The Basle Committee on Banking Supervision

The Basle Committee was established by the central bank governors of the G10 countries at the end of 1974, following serious disturbances in international currency and banking markets, including the failure of a German bank, Bankhaus Herstatt, part way through the trading day. The committee is comprised of members from Belgium, Canada, France, Germany, Italy, Japan, Luxembourg, the Netherlands, Sweden, Switzerland, the UK and the USA. The committee is best known for its work on Capital Adequacy. In 1988 it published the Basle Capital Accord, which established a measurement framework and minimum standards that are followed not only in all member countries, but in virtually all other counties with internationally active banks.

The committee is also responsible for the Basle Concordat, which has helped to define the respective roles of home and host country supervisors in the supervision of internationally active banks. This framework was developed into a set of minimum standards in 1992.

The committee's conclusions have no legal force, but rather represent broad supervisory standards, practices and guidelines which individual authorities use to implement detailed arrangements best suited to their own national circumstances. The key objectives of the committee are to strengthen international cooperation by improving the quality of banking supervision worldwide, and to ensure that no foreign banking entity escapes supervision.

16.1 An outline of the Basle Concordat

The minimum standards of the Concordat are as follows.

1. All international banks should be supervised by a home-country authority that capably performs consolidated supervision.
2. The creation of a cross-border banking establishment should be subject to the prior consent of both the host and home supervisor.
3. Home supervisors should be able to gather information from overseas establishments.

4. If the host supervisor believes that any of these standards are not met it can impose restrictive measures or prohibit the establishment of banking offices.

17 EU Post-BCCI Directive

The Post-BCCI Directive, so-called because it sprang from concerns arising from the BCCI case, officially amends a number of existing financial services Directives, among them the ISD, was implemented in 1996.

The Directive requires that in order for ISD firms, banks and insurance undertakings to be authorized, their relationship with any other group members should not prevent effective supervision of the authorized entity. Accordingly, the Directive obliges regulators to require firms to provide information to ensure that this requirement can be met. It also expands the bodies with which regulators can exchange information for this purpose. It requires auditors of both an authorized entity and a group member to report to regulators where they become aware of breaches of regulations or matters affecting the continuous functioning of a regulated firm, or propose to qualify the accounts of such a firm.

18 The EU Money Laundering Directive

In 1991, the European Union adopted Council Directive 91/308 on prevention of the use of the financial system for the purpose of money laundering. This Directive must be implemented by all member states. In part, the impetus for the directive was the removal of obstacles to free movement of capital and freedom to supply financial services that was to come about upon completion of the European internal market. The Directive provides that all European Union member states should ensure that all financial and credit institutions located within the national member states should implement certain internal procedures and controls.

The aim of those internal procedures is threefold:

1. **Deterrence** – to prevent credit and financial institutions being used for money laundering purposes.
2. **Cooperation** – to ensure that there is cooperation between credit and financial institutions and law enforcement agencies.
3. **Detection** – to establish customer identification and record-keeping procedures within all financial and credit institutions which will assist the law enforcement agencies in detecting, tracing and prosecuting money launderers.

The Directive and subsequent UK legislation applies to all firms and individuals authorized to conduct investment business under the Financial Services and Markets Act 2000, as well as to other financial institutions.

The Directive envisages that these provisions will enable the financial sector to play a powerful role in combating money laundering and, consequently, criminal activity. Additionally, it foresees that regulation of this kind will maintain public confidence in the soundness and stability of the European financial system.

For some years, there has been UK legislation dealing with the laundering of terrorist funds and the proceeds of drug trafficking. In the implementation of the European Council Directive, the UK has extended the existing legislation to cover the laundering of proceeds of any criminal conduct. In addition, obligations have been imposed upon the financial sector to ensure that it fulfils the provisions of the Directive.

Notes

1. Paragraphs reproduced from ***ifs*** Examiner's Report, May 2000 (Corporate Banking – Practice and Law).

Two

Jurisdiction

1 Introduction

In essence, jurisdiction means the ability of a court to hear a case. Predictability and certainty flow from knowing in advance which court will hear any dispute. The lender may be obliged for practical reasons to sue in the borrower's country but not if the borrower has assets abroad or a reciprocal enforcement convention applies. An express forum selection clause will have the advantage of conferring jurisdiction on external courts that would not otherwise be able to hear the case. This provides the lender with an additional forum from which to choose, thus the term 'forum shopping'.

2 Factors influencing the choice of jurisdiction

The choice of jurisdiction is broadly the same as for choice of law. The relationship between the forum and governing law is important because many of the objectives behind the express choice of law will fail if courts either refuse to recognize the choice of law, or recognize it only insofar as it is consistent with local law. The ability to insulate is of paramount importance to lenders, as is the choice of forum.

2.1 Insulation

As discussed in the previous unit the use of an external governing law helps to shield the obligations from adverse legislation introduced by the government of the borrower's country. But those courts could ignore the proper law or apply it only if it is consistent with the local law, eg a moratorium on external indebtedness.

2.2 Forum and governing law

Lenders must be confident that any judgement obtained can be effectively enforced. The location of borrower's assets (or use forum whose judgement will be recognized and enforced in the asset's jurisdiction). It is a summary procedure to prevent assets being removed out of the jurisdiction, eg by Mareva Injunctions, which are freezing orders over all assets. The Mareva is an indispensable weapon in the banker's armoury, ie *Hill Samuel & Co v Littaur* (1985).

2.3 Standard of the courts

The chief factors are: competent judiciary, familiarity with commercial transactions, immunity (this will be dealt with in a later unit), geographical convenience.

3 The English systems of jurisdiction

3.1 Introduction

In England there are two totally different systems for the basis of jurisdiction. Firstly, there are the original or traditional bases of jurisdiction that are contained in the Civil Procedure Rules that apply to non-EU countries and then there are the Rules that apply to contracting states under various EU Regulations or Conventions, referred to as the Brussels Convention.

There are three regimes that now apply in Europe, the main one being the EU Regulation on Jurisdiction (Regulation 44/2001) often known as Brussels II which came into force in March 2002; the Brussels Convention on Jurisdiction and Enforcement of Judgments in Civil and Criminal Matters 1968, and the Lugano Convention of 1988.

If the country concerned is a contracting state under either the EU Regulation on Jurisdiction or the Brussels or Lugano Conventions, the general or special base of jurisdiction will apply. The Brussels and Lugano conventions are the strictest regimes in Europe and so compliance with those is the safest position (they were the principal regimes before the new EU Regulation and so jurisdiction clauses can remain largely unchanged). In the text the European position on jurisdiction will be described as Brussels II , Brussels I and Lugano Conventions. If the country is not a contracting state then either the presence, submission or extended/discretionary base of jurisdiction will apply.

4 Jurisdiction where defendant domiciled in contracting state under EU Regulation on Jurisdiction (Regulation 44/2001) Brussels II, 1968 Brussels Convention or 1988 Lugano Convention

4.1 Introduction

The Civil Jurisdiction and Judgments Act 1982 & 1991, (CJJA) gives effect in UK to the Brussels and Lugano Conventions on Jurisdiction and Enforcement of Judgments in civil and commercial matters of 1968 and 1988 respectively. The countries covered by the Brussels I and Brussels II convention are Austria, Belgium, Denmark, Finland, France, Germany, Greece, Ireland, Italy, Luxembourg, Netherlands, Portugal, Spain, Sweden and the UK. The Lugano convention extended the Brussels convention to Iceland, Norway, Poland and Switzerland.

Therefore providing a court has jurisdiction over a defendant domiciled in another convention country, service on the defendant out of England may be effected without leave of court. If a defendant is domiciled in a non-convention country then service abroad needs leave of court.

Domicile is also defined by the CJJA as effective if an individual or company has a substantial connection with UK. Loan agreements should contain jurisdiction clauses because this affords the greatest degree of predictability. Under Brussels II there is an important exception to the domicile rule where the parties agree which courts should have jurisdiction, and this is discussed further in section 8.3.

4.2 Main provisions of the Brussels I and Brussels II Conventions

Application

The Conventions apply to all persons domiciled within any contracting state, irrespective of their nationality. They do not apply to revenue, customs or administrative matters. There are a number of rules in the Brussels Conventions to determine jurisdiction. There are a number of possible alternatives, because there are a number of rules. The Brussels Convention does not expressly state which rule takes precedence to another rule where the application of the rules conflicts.

Article 2 is generally the starting point of the Brussels Convention. This provides that a person (an individual or a company) shall be sued where they are domiciled. This would therefore be where the borrower is domiciled. This is the main provision of the Convention.

In relation to a contractual matter, article 5(1) of the Brussels Convention provides that the matter will be determined according to the place where performance of the obligation is to be carried out. There are a number of general contract cases which apply this test such as *Boss v Boss* (1996) CA, and *Agnew v Lansforsakringbolagens AB* (1997) CA. In the context of a lending obligation it is suggested that performance is the place where repayment is to take place. This could be in England, where the person is domiciled or the country where the borrower is domiciled. If the first option is chosen, it would produce a different result from the rule above.

Article 5 also provides that a party is to be sued in tort (or delict wrongful infliction of harm) at the place where the harmful event occurs. Parties are allowed to agree where proceedings can be brought, and exclusively or partially exclusive jurisdiction clauses are allowed by Article 17.

Articles 21 and 22 of the Brussels Convention provide a third rule. This provides that the country that will have jurisdiction is the country where proceedings are brought first, by either the borrower or the lender[1]. In a situation where there are simultaneous actions pending in England and in a foreign jurisdiction between the same parties and involving the same or similar issues this is known as the doctrine of 'lis alibi pendens'. Under the Brussels/Lugano conventions only the first court in a contracting state in which cause of action was filed, shall have jurisdiction and any other court of another contracting state shall decline jurisdiction. However, the Brussels Convention is not retrospective, *Davy International Ltd v Voest Alpine Industrieanlagenbau GmbH* (1999).

In England the English courts will no longer be authorized to accept jurisdiction over defendants domiciled in a contracting state on the mere grounds that a defendant maintains assets in the UK or that he temporarily resides there.

There are three articles of particular application, although their exact scope is not entirely clear[1].

Article 6(4) of the Brussels Convention covers contractual matters, where the contractual claim could be combined with an action against the same defendant, in matters concerning immovable rights in property. This is wide enough to cover the inclusion of security given, whether directly in the loan, or separately as part of a debenture, executed separately. In such a situation, the place where the security (property) is located would be the country that has jurisdiction.

By Article 16(1) of the Brussels Convention, where proceedings are brought whose object(s) concern rights in immovability property, then the country in which that asset is situated will have jurisdiction. Where this rule applies, domicile is disregarded. This article supports the earlier article discussed above[1].

However, if the proceedings are simply related to the loan, rather than the security given for that loan, then Article 16(1) will not apply, *Jarrett v Barclays Bank plc* (1996)[1].

Article 24 covers the bringing of proceedings as a protective measure in one state, even though another state has jurisdiction to deal with the substance of claim. If borrowers sought to deal with, or unlawfully sell, an item of immovable property, then the bank could take protective measures in that country even if another country had jurisdiction. However, enforcement proceedings would be proceedings going beyond protective measures, *Banque Cantonale Vaudoise v Waterlily* (1997).

4.3 Recognition and enforcement of foreign judgments under the Brussels I, Brussels II and Lugano Conventions

Under the CJJA 1982 &1991, which incorporates the Brussels and Lugano Conventions, all judgments rendered in a contracting state must be recognized in the other contracting states without any special procedure. Judgments rendered in a contracting state and enforceable in that state shall further be declared enforceable and enforced in another contracting state upon application by a party. This will be discussed further in the next unit.

5 The bases of jurisdiction under the Brussels I, Brussels II and Lugano Conventions

5.1 Introduction

In the absence of a jurisdiction clause convention provides a general basis of jurisdiction that applies when the defendant is domiciled in a contracting state. There are consequentially the following bases of jurisdiction under the conventions:

a. ***General jurisdiction*** – Articles 2 and 4 to prevent a plaintiff from forum shopping and provide that individuals or corporations domiciled in a contracting state should, whatever their nationality, be sued in the courts of that state.

b. ***Special jurisdiction*** – where a defendant is being sued in a contracting state in which he is not domiciled over matters of contract or tort.

c. ***Exclusive jurisdiction*** – there are certain circumstances in which courts of a particular contracting state will have exclusive jurisdiction regardless of domicile. These cases are as per Article 16:

   (a) property;

   (b) corporations, ie insolvency.

5.2 Jurisdiction clauses for convention countries

Jurisdiction clauses in loan agreements where one of the parties is domiciled in a convention country will be drafted in such a way so as to select the courts of a contracting state. This will exclude other contracting states and will, additionally, select the courts of a non-contracting state that will undoubtedly be non-exclusive. Thus has the effect of allowing lenders to bring proceedings in a number of different jurisdictions. This is illustrated in Appendix 1 of this unit.

6 The traditional bases of jurisdiction (applies only to non-Convention countries)

6.1 Introduction

There are three traditional bases of jurisdiction that apply only to non-convention countries which are Submission, Presence and the discretionary/extended base of jurisdiction. There is also the concept of 'Long Arm Bases of Jurisdiction'. These are now discussed below.

6.2 Express submission

The English courts will have jurisdiction over a contractual dispute if the defendant voluntarily submits to the jurisdiction of the English courts. However, it must be possible to serve process on the defendant within the jurisdiction of the English courts with leave of court to serve process abroad. Submission is usually effected by an express submission clause within the loan agreement that may be an exclusive or non-exclusive jurisdiction clause.

A borrower would prefer an exclusive jurisdiction clause to prevent forum-shopping by the lender.

The US courts will generally respect an exclusive jurisdiction clause if there was no undue influence applied, The *Breman v Zapata Off-Shore Corpn* (1972). The NY General Obligation Laws of 1984, Chapter 421 provide for the automatic acceptance of exclusive jurisdiction clauses choosing New York courts in contracts of a value of not less than $1 million.

The English courts will generally respect the clause and grant a stay of proceedings to the defendant. They will not if a plaintiff can show a 'strong cause'. In deciding whether this has been shown, the courts will look at all the circumstances including the balance of convenience of calling evidence in each forum, what the *lex causae* is, the connections of each party to each country, whether the defendants are merely seeking a procedural advantage, whether the plaintiffs would be prejudiced by a stay in being deprived of security for their claim, of effective enforcement, be time-barred or unlikely to get a fair trial, *The El Amria* (1981) CA affirmed in *The Sennar* (1984) HL.

A lender will normally insist on a multiple jurisdiction clause, typically specifying two or more alternative forums and declaring these to be non-exclusive thus leaving a wide choice at the time of default. The English courts may grant a stay of proceedings if an action has begun abroad or it may (rarely) order the cessation of the foreign proceedings by injunction. They have become increasingly ready to grant a stay. Where a parallel action abroad is already pending the plaintiff 'must establish by cogent evidence that there is some personal or juridical advantage that would be available to him only in the English action that is of such importance it would cause injustice to him to deprive him of it', *The Abidin Daver* (1984) HL.

The question of whether a court will exercise jurisdiction whether or not there is an express clause conferring it is known as 'basis of jurisdiction'.

6.3 The presence base of jurisdiction

A defendant in England can always be served with legal process unless he is domiciled in an EU contracting state (see later) and it is the service of process within the jurisdiction that effectively provides the basis of jurisdiction.

Presence:

(a) Individual – any physical presence in England.

(b) Company – if registered with the companies registry, or it has a place of business is sufficient.

(c) Presence of Assets – some jurisdictions, eg Germany/Austria.

(d) Carrying on business.

A company registered in England is deemed to be present in England wherever it does business, service at its registered office being effective.

6.4 Foreign companies with a place of business in England

A foreign corporation which establishes a place of business in Great Britain must register as an 'overseas' company with the Registrar of Companies, section 691 of the Companies Act 1985 and must provide the name and address of a GB resident to accept service. If no such person exists, process may be served at any established place of business in GB. If the foreign corporation has not registered in GB it may be served at any place where it carries on business. This must be a fixed and definite place of business where business has been carried on for a sufficient time – maintaining an exhibition stand for nine days was sufficient in *Dunlop*

Pneumatic Tyre Co Ltd v A/G Cudell & Co (1902) CA. It is sufficient if the corporation carries on business through an agent locally as long as it is the corporation's business, not the agent's. The test is – does the agent have authority to make contracts? *Saccharin Corpn Ltd v Chemische Fabrik A/G* (1911) CA or *Okura & Co Ltd v Forsbacka Jernverks A/B* (1914) CA where contracts had to be approved. The transaction does not need to have been effected through the place of business or agent in England. *A/S Dampskib Hercules v Grand Trunk Pacific Ry of Canada* (1972) CA. Mere presence in England of a director of the corporation is insufficient, *The Theodohos* (1977), or of an associated company, unless it qualifies as an agent.

There is a right of action against a defendant who submits to the jurisdiction of the court by commencing a related action or by appearing to defend the action, but not if he appears solely to contest the court's jurisdiction under the Civil Procedure Rules. By giving prior agreement to the jurisdiction of the English court (whether express or implied), the defendant concedes an automatic right of action against him on the relevant contract. If he has appointed an agent to receive service of process on his behalf the action can be affected even if the defendant is abroad at the time of service under the Civil Procedure Rules. If no agent has been appointed, the courts leave to serve the writ out of the jurisdiction is required under the Civil Procedure Rules Part 6.

6.5 The extended and discretionary base of jurisdiction

If the defendant is not present in England and does not submit to the jurisdiction of the English courts then the courts may exercise discretionary power under Order 11, of the Rules of the Supreme Court but it is discretionary and is exercisable only in appropriate cases.

The English courts may therefore exercise jurisdiction based on transaction connections if the contract was (a) made in England or (b) was made by or through an agent trading or residing in England on behalf of a principal or (c) is governed by English law Civil Procedure Rules Part 6. Regarding (a), note the effect of the postal acceptance and telephone/telex acceptance contract rules. Regarding (b), 'by or through an agent' means the agent need not have authority to make contracts but merely sends them for acceptance. In addition the Civil Procedure Rules Part 6 extends the court's jurisdiction to cases where there has been a breach of the contract in England. Failure to make payments of interest would therefore confer jurisdiction only if the payments should be made in England under the contract. The Civil Procedure Rules Part 6 grants jurisdiction when a tort is committed in England. Relevant torts include negligent misstatement by a managing bank, or a negligent misrepresentation inducing a lender to enter into a contract, eg in a prospectus.

The court has jurisdiction if the tort is committed in England, which may not follow if the misrepresentation is communicated from abroad to someone in England. The

Civil Procedure Rules Part 6 gives the court jurisdiction if an injunction is sought to restrain the defendant from doing something in England, eg creating a charge over assets in England contrary to a negative pledge covenant. This is not applicable to a 'Mareva' injunction, *The Siskina* (1979) HL. Under the Civil Procedure Rules Part 6, jurisdiction is conferred where an action has been properly begun against another defendant and the foreign person is a necessary or proper party to be joined as co-defendant. This might include a guarantor or joint borrower.

6.6 Long-arm bases of jurisdiction

Long arm is whereby courts can claim jurisdiction merely where one of the partners has some connection with the country of the courts. The presence of assets of a borrower within the territory is sufficient to grant jurisdiction. In the extreme there is the position in Germany (Article 23 Construction) and Austria where there is the Hotel bedroom slipper base of jurisdiction where the French skier Jean Claude-Killy was subject to jurisdiction on the basis of a pair of slippers left behind in an Austrian hotel. This would not be so in England/France but Scotland does accept jurisdiction on the basis of local assets.

Most legal systems have 'long-arm' rules whereby quite tenuous connections with the country can lead to the power to hear a case but this is limited by the court's discretion as to whether it will exercise that power. The criteria applied by any particular country's courts as to the first of these questions can be any of the following:

(a) Consent – if the defendant appears to defend himself but not merely to contest the jurisdictional issue.

(b) Plaintiff connections – more popular with the civil law countries, eg France – the residence of the plaintiff is sufficient to start an action against a foreigner.

(c) Defendant connections – preferred by the common law systems – although the connection may be transient, eg *Grace v MacArthur* (1959), or indirect, eg trading through an agent or associated company.

(d) Transaction connections – where the contract has connections with the country concerned. Adopted by England and the USA with limits.

(e) Asset connections – restricted to some continental European states, known as the 'toothbrush' jurisdiction. Most countries permit a pre-judgment attachment, however, limited to the extent of assets within the jurisdiction.

English law: Actions *in persona* may be instituted by service of a writ against a defendant who is within the jurisdiction or who has a representative or office that is. With leave of the court a defendant may be served with a writ anywhere in the world. A merely transient presence by the defendant is sufficient, *Maharanee of Baroda v Wilderstein* (1972) CA. An individual foreigner trading within England can be served and any partnership carrying on business in England can be served in England and this constitutes automatic service on all the partners wherever they are now contained within the Civil Procedure Rules).

Agent for service: submission is effective only if it is possible to serve process on defendant and it is therefore common for parties (normally a borrower) to appoint an agent for service within the English jurisdiction. If English courts are forum and if such an agent is present in England the borrower is deemed to submit.

NB: All the above bases of jurisdiction are at the court's discretion.

6.7 The position in New York

New York law: Consent to the action by appearing to defend it is sufficient. Foreigners present in the jurisdiction are subject to its courts only if the 'minimum contacts' rule is satisfied otherwise the action would be unconstitutional. In the example of an external corporation doing business in a state, this was established when the corporation had no office there and merely solicited orders through salesmen there and sold products there, *International Shoe Co v State of Washington* (1945). A mailbox representative of an airline was sufficient for the New York courts in *Bryant v Finnish National Airlines (1965) Volkeswagenwerk AG of Wolfsburg* (1972). The New York courts seem more ready to view a local associated company as a branch of an overseas parent, *Taca International Airlines v Rolls-Royce of England* (1965) and *vice versa* in *Published Administrator v Royal Bank of Canada* (1967).

Transaction connections are less likely to confer jurisdiction, however. In *Hanson v Denckla* (1958) local law being the governing law was insufficient without 'minimum contacts'. Section 302(a)(i) of the New York Civil Practice Law and Rules confers jurisdiction over a defendant who in person or through an agent 'transacts any business within the state'. Asset connection jurisdiction in New York has ceased to apply without at least 'minimum contacts'.

7 Restrictions on jurisdiction

7.1 The doctrine of *forum non conveniens*

Related to the topics discussed above is the doctrine of *forum non conveniens* whereby courts of one country will decline to hear a case if another country's courts can more conveniently hear it and may grant a stay of proceedings to the defendant whether or not an action has begun in the other country. Assuming no jurisdiction clause applies, and no current action in another court the English court will grant a stay if:

(a) the defendant satisfies the court there is another forum he is amenable to and which can do justice at substantially less inconvenience or expense, and

(b) the stay would not deprive the plaintiff of a legitimate personal or juridicial advantage, *MacShannon v Rockware Glass Ltd* (1978) HL.

The court must balance the interests of both parties in reading a decision, *The Abidin Daver* (1984) HL. Where there is already an action pending in another country which is a natural and appropriate forum, a parallel English action will be allowed only if the plaintiff can establish by cogent evidence there is some personal or juridicial advantage available to him only in the English court that is of such importance it would cause injustice to deprive him of it.

It has been assumed above that the plaintiff initially has an automatic right to sue due to the presence of the defendant in England if that is not so, he faces the additional burden of obtaining the court's leave to serve the writ out of the jurisdiction. If the English court's jurisdiction is based on 'long-arm' rules which are not mutually applicable the discretion will be exercised against the plaintiff unless he can show justice cannot be obtained in the foreign forum or only at excessive cost, delay or inconvenience, *Amin Rasheed Shipping Corpn v Kuwait Insurance Co* (1983) HL.

Forum non conveniens has long been an established principle in US courts, *Gulf Oil Co v Gilbert* (1947) in which the competing interests to be balanced were listed:

(a) the plaintiff wishing access to his own courts,

(b) the defendant not wishing to be sued externally,

(c) the availability of witnesses, and

(d) public interest in keeping cases away from congested centres and in unifying *lex causae* and *lex fori.*

In *Piper Aircraft Co v Reyno,* the courts would not allow an action in the USA where the main reason was the more favourable prospects for the plaintiffs. N.B. The English decision in *British Airways Bond v Laker Airways Ltd* (1984) HL where the court declared its right to stop an action in a foreign court if it was 'unconscionable'.

NB: The EU Judgments Convention, to be implemented by the Civil Jurisdiction and Judgments Act 1982, Article 17 will provide that a chosen (exclusive) forum in the EU must be used first by the plaintiff.

7.2 *Lis alibi pendens*

This is where there are simultaneous actions pending in England and in a foreign jurisdiction between the same parties and involving the same or similar issues (*lis alibi pendens*). Jurisdiction clauses are liberally drafted to allow this but English courts may stay the proceedings, stay the foreign ones or require a plaintiff to select which proceedings to pursue. *Re The Christiansborg* (1885).

The court exercises discretion with great caution but the traditional approach was to refuse a stay of proceedings unless a defendant could show that allowing both actions was oppressive, but this is now liberally interpreted by courts since *MacShannon v Rockware Glass* (1978).

7.3 Where Brussels I , Brussels II or Lugano Conventions apply

Under the conventions all subsequent courts shall decline in favour of jurisdiction of the first court. However, the conventions only apply where the conflict of jurisdictions is between those of contracting states. Where the conflict is between a contracting state and a non-contracting state, the UK courts retain jurisdiction to stay proceedings on the grounds of *forum non conveniens* as held in the case of *Harrods (Buenos Aries) Ltd* [1991] 3 WLR, CA.

Under Brussels II there is an important exception to the domicile rule where the parties agree which courts should have jurisdiction. Under Brussels II the provision on jurisdiction clauses for the benefit of one party has gone completely. Instead Brussels II provides that if the parties give jurisdiction to the courts of a member state, that jurisdiction will be exclusive unless the parties agree otherwise. Therefore, if parties want to confer non-exclusive jurisdiction, they should be able to set out expressly what they intend. This is not the case with Denmark or with those countries covered by the Lugano Convention.

7.4 Exclusive jurisdiction clauses

Banks prefer non-exclusive clauses because this results in freedom of action in choosing the appropriate forum in which to bring proceedings. Borrowers though face possibility of a multiplicity of suits in various jurisdictions, one of which may be hostile.

On exclusive jurisdiction clauses it is generally that where a contract provides for a foreign court to have exclusive jurisdiction an English court will stay proceedings brought in England in breach of such a clause, but the plaintiff will be allowed to proceed if he can prove that it is just and proper for the English proceedings to continue.

Article 17 of the Brussels Convention (applicable only to contracting states) provides that if one or more of the contracting parties are based in a contracting state then they can agree an exclusive jurisdiction clause whereby disputes will be governed by one jurisdiction. The effect of such a clause was confirmed in the case of *Kurz v Stella Musical Veranstalungs Gmbh* (1991).

In another case of *Banque Cantronalle Vaudoise v Waterlily Maritime Inc* (1997), the borrower (but not the bank) submitted to the jurisdiction of the English courts. This was also upheld as valid. In addition the bank also reserved itself the right to bring proceedings in the courts of any other country. This was also upheld as valid.

Exclusive has a wider meaning than its normal meaning. It means more than one jurisdiction, which will usually be drafted so as to give complete discretion to the lending bank.

Where there is an exclusive jurisdiction clause, case law establishes that such a clause will take precedence over the 'first seized' rule in articles 21 and 22 (ie jurisdiction will be governed by the agreement of the parties and not where proceedings are first brought), *Bank of Scotland v SA Banque Nationale de Paris* (1995)[2].

7.5 Floating jurisdiction clauses

These permit one or more parties to select the country whose courts will have exclusive jurisdiction and are becoming increasingly common in international contracts. A number of jurisdictions are selected at the outset usually by the lender but advantageous for the borrower because he will know proceedings will not be instituted in a hostile country. The validity of floating choice of forum will be determined by the proper law and if English law is proper law such a clause will be deemed valid and may be given effect.

But such clauses can be a problem as to predictability of result are often accompanied by floating choice of law clauses which may be struck down as invalid.

8 Arbitration

Few bankers perceive arbitration clauses as being suitable for international loan agreements. There is an exception where loans are granted to sovereign borrowers because many will not submit to jurisdiction of a foreign court. Banks may prefer to submit disputes to arbitration rather than risking proceedings to the sovereign government's local courts. It may be appropriate in the case of a sovereign borrower who is restricted by the Calvo doctrine and it is popular for political reasons with the World Bank, because it is neutral.

The English Arbitration Act 1996 allows parties to exclude any right of appeal to the courts and even if this is not incorporated the right is limited. Such finality is not popular among bankers in case of a rogue decision by an arbitral body.

8.1 Advantages of arbitration

(1) Privacy of proceedings

(2) Expert adjudication

(3) Flexibility and speed

8.2 Problems of arbitration

(1) Limited power of enforcement that the arbitral tribunal may exercise.

Enforcement is very important to a bank and therefore any weakening of this position is serious.

(2) Effectiveness of any arbitral award will be influenced by the type of award rendered by the tribunal.

(3) The problem of arbitration is that to offer any sort of realistic alternative to litigation the award ultimately obtained must be binding on all parties.

Most banks will therefore prefer to leave any subsequent dispute in the hands of any appropriate court which would hopefully be in a position to effectively enforce any decision made in favour of the lending bank.

A general advantage of arbitration is the availability of expert adjudication but loan contracts do not generally demand an understanding of technical facts beyond normal commercial principles at which judges are competent. Equally, the privacy of the arbitration hearing is no advantage if the publicity would encourage the defendant to settle. Access to a speedy summary judgment may be lost in a simple case if the case has to go to a full hearing first, because this will be a condition precedent of enforcement proceedings. Experience has shown arbitration bodies to be less predictable than courts and the right to use the court as a forum is usually lost. It may be harder to enforce a judgment if the arbitration was a neutral country and enforcement must be external, although the 1958 New York Convention on Recognition and Enforcement of Foreign Arbitral Awards, ratified extensively (including UK), may assist.

The International Centre for Settlement of Investment Disputes (ICSID) has over 80 signatories, the main exception being the Calvo doctrine states. It can hear disputes involving a member state and a private entity. The state must consent to the arbitration in the loan agreement, the parties can express this to be non-exclusive jurisdiction, but the state party can insist on the exhaustion of municipal remedies first. If no express choice is made, the proper law is that of the contracting state. Enforcement provisions are good and a public policy defence is expressly not available.

There have been three recent cases concerning the enforceability of an arbitration award, where the issue has been whether its enforcement is contrary to English public policy.

In *Soleimany v Soleimany* (1999) a father and son conspired to break Iranian revenue laws and export controls by the son exporting carpets and the father selling them in England. There was a dispute between the father and son as to how the proceeds of this scheme should be divided. The father and son agreed to submit their dispute to the Beth Din, which applied Jewish law. Under Jewish law, the illegality of the scheme was not relevant. The Beth Din made an award in favour of the son, who sought to enforce the award in the English courts[3].

The Court of Appeal would not allow the son to enforce his award on the basis that he was seeking to enforce an illegal contract. There was still illegality despite the fact that there was an arbitration award[3].

In *Westacre Investments Inc v Jogoimport-SDPR Holding Co Ltd* (1999) Westacre (W) was appointed as a consultant to assist a Yugoslavian government body, FDS, to sell military equipment to Kuwait. W's fees were guaranteed by a Yugoslavian private bank, UB. W did not receive its fees and commenced arbitration proceedings against FDS and UB in Switzerland[3].

FDS and UB alleged, in the arbitration proceedings, that W had bribed various influential Kuwaitis. This was rejected and an award was made in favour of W. W sought to enforce the award in the English courts[3].

The Court of Appeal would allow W to enforce his award. The arbitrators had rejected the allegations of bribery. In consequence the agreement was not affected or tainted by any illegality[3].

In *Omnium de Traitement et de Valorization SA v Hilmarton Ltd* (1999) Omnium de Traitement et de Valorization SA (OTV) contracted with Hilmarton Ltd (H) that H should approach certain Algerian public servants so that OTV could obtain a public contract within the Algerian law which prohibited the use of intermediaries in such situations[3].

Although OTV was awarded a contract with the Algerian government, it paid only half the agreed fees to H. H took its dispute with OTV to arbitration in Switzerland as provided in its contract with OTV[3].

As a matter of Swiss law, the fact that Algerian law was breached did not make the contract unlawful. The Court of Appeal accepted that this approach was different from English law which would render such a contract unlawful and would have the effect that any judgment obtained for its breach could not be enforced in the English courts[3].

The Court of Appeal in *Omnium de Traitement et de Valorization SA v Hilmarton Ltd* (1999) considered the Westacre decision (discussed above). In particular, it applied a principle derived from that case that the English courts are not concerned with the underlying contract but, rather, the enforcement of the award[3].

The Court of Appeal in *Omnium de Traitement et de Valorization SA v Hilmarton Ltd* (1999) also considered the earlier Court of Appeal decision of *Soleimany v Soleimany* (also discussed above) which was regarded as simply the illegal smuggling of carpets out of Iran. The Court of Appeal in *Omnium de Traitement et de Valorization SA v Hilmarton Ltd* (1999) were of the view that English law would never enforce an award involving such illegal smuggling, because this was contrary to English public policy at common law[3].

The Court of Appeal in *Omnium de Traitement et de Valorization SA v Hilmarton Ltd* (1999) considered that the breach of Algerian laws, on the facts before it, which merely did not allow for the use of intermediaries and did not involve corruption or illegal practice, was in contrast to the facts of *Soleimany v Soleimany.* The consequence was that the Swiss Arbitration award could be enforced in the English courts[3].

9 Legal opinions

9.1 Introduction

As can be seen from the forgoing discussion on choice of law and jurisdiction the unfamiliarity with another law often necessitates taking a legal opinion from a lawyer who is familiar with that law. A legal opinion relates to the documents as entered into by the borrower and the lender and states the validity and enforceability of the documents in the state in which they were executed.

The law is the domestic law of the jurisdiction of the lawyer who is giving the legal opinion. The comfort is local and not universal. The legal opinion does not give comfort as to future changes in law. The objective of legal opinions is that they cover matters of law only and not matters of fact.

9.2 Conditions precedent

Legal opinions are commonly required as a conditions precedent to draw-down. The legal opinion does not affect the commercial terms or negotiations between the parties.

9.3 Jurisdiction

Usually there is more than one jurisdiction in relation to which it may be desirable to obtain a legal opinion. There are:

(a) the borrower's place of incorporation;

(b) the jurisdiction of the proper law of the loan agreement;

(c) if funds are being disbursed in other jurisdictions;

(d) where security is given in any relevant jurisdiction.

9.4 Liabilities of the lawyer giving an opinion

Lawyers will restrict responsibility to the addressees of the opinion and it is only they who may rely upon the opinion.The opinion may also state that it may not be relied upon by assignees of the lender or any sub-participant.

Despite this disclaimer some other person may seek to hold him responsible. Liability will to a large extent depend on jurisdiction.The position at English law is as follows:

(a) The lawyer is responsible for accuracy of opinion and if directly instructed by the lender there is a contractual responsibility, but in a syndication the contract will be with the agent unless addressed to all the banks.The lawyer will be negligent for any inaccuracy.An opinion is an opinion not a guarantee because the lawyer is not an insurer.

(b) His duty will lead him to point out any pitfalls in the documents, any legal risks. He will set out his qualifications, assumptions etc.

(c) If the opinion is given by the borrower's lawyer as for example with respect to the laws of the borrower's domicile then the lawyer will have a responsibility in the law of tort to the lenders. This responsibility is that he must not be negligent and again qualifications assumptions will limit this responsibility.

(d) Third parties re investors or assignees would not have a claim in contract so they would seek to establish a claim in tort based upon a failure to take reasonable care in the legal work done by the lawyer but it is a long shot, although the *Hedley Byrne & Co v Heller* (1964) extended the tort of negligence but this may not in itself be relied upon.

9.5 Limitations of legal opinions

Insofar as the limitations of legal opinions is concerned you should be aware of the following issues:

(a) The fact that the opinion should cover matters of law only not matters of fact.A legal opinion will often state that certain facts have been assumed and lenders will need to bear in mind when reading the opinion that this is the case because the onus is upon them to check the assumed facts or to take the risk that the assumptions are not correct.

(b) The opinion will normally speak only for the laws of one particular jurisdiction and since it is common for more than one jurisdiction to be involved it may be necessary to take more than one opinion.

(c) The liability on the giver of the opinion rests in contract with the party to whom the opinion has been given and in tort subject to the limitations on liability that follows from the line of cases established by *Hedley Byrne and Co*

Ltd v Heller (developed more recently in the line cases following *Caparo v Dickman*) and will depend to a large extent on whether a duty of care exists between the giver of the opinion and the party who has suffered loss in respect of the negligent misstatements contained in the opinion.

(d) Opinions are often based on a large number of assumptions and these assumptions have to be carefully considered by the party seeking to rely on the opinion.

(e) Having set forth the matters that are expressly given as part of the opinion lawyers giving the opinion will then set forth the qualifications to which their opinion is subject and these qualifications will again have to be carefully considered by the party relying on the opinion.

Finally, the opinion will speak only at a given moment in time and any changes in law in the future may well affect the transaction. The opinion will therefore be relied upon only to the extent of its terms as at the date that it is given. It will not give continuing comfort as to the terms set out therein.

9.6 Structure of a legal opinion

A legal opinion can be divided into four parts that are as follows.

(1) Outline of transcripts and documents.

(2) Assumptions that the lawyers have made on matters of fact concerning the transaction.

(3) The actual matters upon which the lawyers are opining.

(4) Qualifications and exceptions.

The first part of the opinion will list the documents that the lawyer has seen and those upon which he will be opining upon. The second part of the opinion will list the assumptions that the lawyers have made on matters of fact concerning the transaction.

If the form of any proposed legal opinion is agreed at an early stage before the form of the underlying transaction has been settled, it will help to raise any legal issue that might cause difficulties. But in addition a party to the transaction might well be asked to warrant and covenant as to a particular set of facts that the lawyer is unable to cover in his opinion. A legal opinion will often state that certain facts have been assumed and lenders will need to bear in mind when reading the opinion this is the case since the onus is upon them to check the assumed facts or to take the risk that the assumptions are not correct.

9.7 Matters upon which the lawyers are opining

The matters that are opined upon which may establish, *inter alia,* that the borrower is duly incorporated and empowered to enter into the relevant transaction. Detailed opinions in this regard will flush out whether there are any particular constitutional/limiting authorities which will need to be addressed in the terms of the underlying documentation should they arise. Clauses dealing with authority will also highlight whether there are any contractual restrictions (for example negative pledges) that might prevent the creation of security interests in favour of the lenders. Again requesting a legal opinion which in the first instance would focus on completely unfettered powers on the part of the borrower would highlight any potential risks and act as a form of due diligence.

Opinions covering the applicability of withholding taxes, exchange controls, stamp duties and other taxes etc, will also highlight any possible risks in relation to the imposition of such taxes which might affect the commercial return in the transaction expected by the lenders. Once again this process would act as a form of due diligence and enable appropriate clauses to be drafted in the terms of the underlying documentation to minimize the risks involved.

Opinions covering actual pending or threatened litigation, the ranking of the obligations of the borrower in terms of them being *pari passu* with other unsecured creditors and the efficacy of relevant choice of law clauses will also identify whether it is necessary to incorporate terms in the underlying documentation (particularly in the representations and warranties and covenants to address some of the issues which have arisen in the negotiation of the legal opinion).

9.8 Qualifications included within legal opinions

There are qualifications that are incorporated within the legal opinions, which may have the effect of limiting the efficacy of certain clauses to be found in underlying agreements and the ability to enforce the terms of those agreements in local courts as to certain matters. Once again although it will not be possible to draft round all of the qualifications that might be incorporated within the opinion the listing of the qualifications themselves will highlight the potential risks to the lending bank and any steps that might be taken to minimize those risks by additional diligence. Qualifications that are likely to be included in legal opinions are as follows:

(i) enforceability of default interest clauses;

(ii) enforceability of currency indemnity clauses;

(iii) ability of local courts to stay proceedings if concurrent proceedings are being brought elsewhere;

(iv) enforceability of conclusive certifications by the bank;

(v) availability of specific performance in local courts;

(vi) potential for rights to be limited by bankruptcy/liquidation proceedings;

(vii) possibility of certain claims becoming statute barred;

(viii) potential problems with illegality and public policy within local jurisdiction;

(ix) limitations on the exercise of discretions;

(x) limitation on clauses relating to severalty.

10 Summary: Choice of law and jurisdiction

10.1 Key points and revision for the examination

Choice of law and jurisdiction are separate topics. Unfortunately, students confuse them. Remember that the choice of law is a separate decision from the choice of jurisdiction. It is perfectly possible to have a choice of law that is French law, but a choice of jurisdiction that is the English courts.

However great care must be taken, because any choice of law can be struck down if it is not bona fide and legal, or if it is evasive or contrary to public policy under the Rome convention as enacted in the Contracts (Applicable Law) Act 1990. Likewise a choice of jurisdiction can also be struck down by the courts on the grounds of, for example, *forum non conveniens*, on the basis that there is a more appropriate forum. This would be the case where there is a lack of connecting factors to the choice of jurisdiction.

Also remember that just because you have chosen a jurisdiction does not mean that the courts of another state cannot reach out and grab jurisdiction. This is of course the 'Long-arm base of jurisdiction' that arises out of a court claiming jurisdiction in the case where there may only be the most tenuous connection.

Please refer to the following tables which summarize the learning you have done and the following points in the text.

The most important reason for incorporating both choice of law and jurisdiction clauses is to bring predictability to the proposed transaction to the extent that one is able to apply a system of law with which one is most familiar to as many aspects of the transaction as possible. The most effective way in which this can be achieved is by selecting both the system of law that governs the substantive aspects of the transaction (the proper law of the contract) and the courts that will have jurisdiction to resolve any disputes that may arise in respect of the transaction.

In terms of certainty with regard to choice of law you should describe how the choice of law governs many aspects affecting a contract, namely essential validity of the contract and its discharge.

Also identify those important issues like status and capacity, formal validity, and the currency of contractual damages that are not governed by the proper law should be mentioned and the way in which the proper law of the contract will be determined under English rules of private international law.

Also describe precisely how private international law differs from domestic law and the various features of an international banking contract that may be governed by different systems of law.

Remember to distinguish, for example, between the proper law of the contract which may govern the substantive aspects of the contractual documentation with those matters that are not governed by the proper law of the contract, namely procedural questions which would under English rules of private international law be governed by the law of the place where proceedings are ultimately brought (the *lex fori*), the formal validity of an international banking contract, which would normally be governed by the law of the place where the contract is made (the *lex loci contractus*), the status and capacity of the parties to the contract which would be determined/governed by the law of the place where the parities are domiciled (the *lex domicili*) and the question of illegality which, following the decision in the Allied Arab Bank case, is governed by the law of the place where the contract is to be performed (the lex loci solutions).

Jurisdiction – summary

You should focus on the ability to bring proceedings in a jurisdiction with which one is familiar in terms of the remedies that will be available in the jurisdiction and the assets of the borrower against which enforcement will be sought.

In the event that it is necessary to bring a claim on an international banking contract the ability to enforce that claim effectively against assets within an appropriate jurisdiction that provides, for example, procedures to freeze the assets to prevent dissipation will be most important. The identification of an appropriate jurisdiction clause, particularly where that is linked to speedy process being obtained against the relevant party, will be critical in ensuring that the banker's rights are maintained and freely available to be enforced against the borrower.

The systems of jurisdiction have been discussed above but are summarized as follows:

Convention	Countries	Bases of Jurisdiction	Details
EU Regulation on Jurisdiction – Regulation 44/2001 (often known as Brussels II)	All EU countries with the exception of Denmark (the contracting states)	General	The general base of jurisdiction applies where the defendant is domiciled in a contracting state.
		Special	Where the defendant is not domiciled in a contracting state, but where an action is being taken in a contracting state such as enforcing a judgment.
Brussels Convention on Jurisdiction and Enforcement of Judgments in Civil and Criminal Matters 1968	Denmark	General	As above
		Special	As above
Lugano Convention on Jurisdiction and Enforcement of Judgments in Civil and Criminal Matters 1988	Iceland, Norway, Poland and Switzerland	General	As above
		Special	As above
UK Civil Procedure Rules	All other countries	Presence Submission Extended/ discretionary	

Notes

1. Paragraphs reproduced from ***ifs*** Examiner's Report, May 2000 (Corporate Banking – Practice and Law).
2. Paragraphs reproduced from ***ifs*** Examiner's Report, May 2000 (Corporate Banking – Practice and Law).
3. Paragraphs reproduced from ***ifs*** Examiner's Report, October 2000 (Corporate Banking – Practice and Law).

Three

Sovereign immunity

1 Meaning of sovereign risk

(a) Doctrine of sovereign immunity – originally that a sovereign could never be sued in a foreign court, *De Haber v Queen of Portugal* (1851). There has been an erosion of immunity as states increasingly undertook commercial acts.

(b) A sovereign borrower is in charge of its legislature and can therefore alter the proper law or *lex fori* to its advantage. Also it may expropriate assets forming security or annul the loan contract, impose withholding taxes, impose moratorium or quotas of debt repayments, or exchange controls (recognized under 'Bretton Woods' in external forum).

(c) No bankruptcy machinery for states, although they do become insolvent so no provision for *pari passu* distribution of available assets.

(d) Calvo doctrine – constitutional prohibition on adoption of foreign law when a state is party to contract.

Most legal systems now permit domestic proceedings against a state, English Crown Proceedings Act 1947 – no enforcement, however.

The restrictive theory of immunity is now universally applied, ie no immunity if a state acts commercially.

2 Position at English common law

It is a principle of public international law that a foreign sovereign state cannot be sued in the English courts unless it has submitted to the jurisdiction of the English courts: *De Haber v Queen of Portugal* (1851). For many years this was an absolute immunity until the 1970s when courts began to recognize a distinction between acts of government and commercial acts. Immunity only applied to acts of government as a result of the case of *Trendtex Trading Corpn v Central Bank of Nigeria* (1977), CA, in which it was held that there was no sovereign immunity for a defendant who declined liability on letters of credit it issued because it was not an arm of the state and this was a commercial act.

The restrictive theory of immunity was confirmed in the case of *I Congreso del Partido* (1981) HL, affirmed the commercial act exception and established that a governmental decree cannot transform a commercial act into a governmental act, (suspension of trade with Chile imposed by Cuban government).

3 State Immunity Act 1978

This Act has three themes: (a) no immunity when a state acts commercially, (b) distinguish between immunity from action and immunity from enforcement, (c) distinguish between central departments of a state and state off-shoots. The act applies only to contracts formed after 1978. Before then, or if the Act is expressly excluded, common law is applied.

In section 1 of the Act there is the general rule that the State is immune from the jurisdiction of the courts of the UK, subject to certain exceptions outlined at point 3.1 below. Remember the question as to whether the state is immune and if not does a UK court have jurisdiction?

The Act defines 'state' as any foreign state outside the UK including governments and government departments excluding state entities and parts of a federal state. It recognizes immunity, then provides exceptions to it.

3.1 Exceptions to immunity from jurisdiction/action

(a) section 2 of the Act – if a state submits to jurisdiction, including by prior written consent by a person having power to contract on behalf of the state. NB: waiver of immunity is not sufficient.

(b) if proceedings relate to a 'commercial transaction', defined as:

- any contract for the supply of goods or services;

- any loan or other transaction for the provision of finance and any guarantee or indemnity in respect of any such transaction or of any other financial obligation;
- any other transaction or activity into which a state enters or engages otherwise than in exercise of sovereign authority.

(c) various other specific exceptions.

Constituent states are immune only if acting in the exercise of sovereign authority and in the same circumstances the state would have been immune. There is a similar rule for separate entities, defined as distinct from the executive government and capable of suing or being sued.

Section 9 removes immunity from a state that has agreed to arbitration, so far as court proceedings relate to the arbitration.

Exceptions to immunity from enforcement:

(d) prior written consent, either partial or general, section 13(3),

(e) where the property to be seized is used or intended for use for commercial purposes, section 13(4).

In *Alcom Ltd v Republic of Colombia* (1984) HL it was held that a bank account used for the day-to-day running of the embassy was not property used for commercial purposes even though sometimes it was used for commercial purposes; it would have to be almost exclusively so used to lose immunity. Therefore an embassy's bank account can be the subject of garnishee proceedings only if it is was exclusively used for commercial purposes. There is some doubt whether this case applies only to embassy accounts or whether it extends general accounts also.

In the unreported case of *Camdex International v Bank of Zambia (No 3)* (1998) the discussion of which is by William Blair QC in *The Legal Status of Central Bank Investments under English Law,* Vol 57 (1998) CLJ 374. In this case the Court of Appeal considered that the Bank of Zambia must be free to use its foreign exchanges in accordance with its duties as central bank. If the funds of the Bank of Zambia were the subject of successful garnishee proceedings, one debtor would be preferred to other debtors. The court did not want this, so the garnishee proceedings did not succeed[1].

Separate specific consent is required for injunctions (including 'Marevas') and specific performance. Property of a Central Bank is deemed to be governmental. NB: the remedy of set off is always available, because it does not require a court order.

Service of writ: if no agent appointed in UK, requires leave to serve abroad through Foreign and Commonwealth Office, with a two month delay before return. NB: there is total immunity for diplomatic premises under the Diplomatic Privileges Act 1964.

4 Immunity from enforcement

The state may not be immune from jurisdiction, but enforcement is another matter. The general rule is that the Act excludes all available measures of enforcement (injunctions, specific performance etc.) unless an exception applies as follows:

(a) If the state gives written consent (which may be mitigated or limited).

(b) Against property if it is used for commercial purposes.

ie a distress warrant, garnishee order, or charging order may be obtained but never injunctions or specific performance because non-compliance would be contempt of court involving arrest, fine, imprisonment, or sequestration.

There is the problem of seizing property in proving purpose of funds, ie bank accounts, as in the case of *Alcom Ltd v Republic of Columbia* (1984) discussed above and again below. If any funds were for immunized purposes then the whole fund is immunized unless it is proved it is entirely for commercial purposes.

Another illustrative case is *Standard Chartered Bank v International Tin Council* (1986). This case concerned the International Tin Council (ITC) which was an international organization that can be given immunity from suit and enforcement under the International Organisations Act (1968).

The ITC was given immunity from jurisdiction and enforcement unless it expressly waived such immunity. The ITC sought to rely on this immunity when sued by the bank who had loaned it £10 million. In the loan agreement the ITC submitted irrevocably to English jurisdiction and the court dismissed the application of immunity.

5 The position of sovereign immunity in the USA

In the USA the law is the Foreign Sovereign Immunities Act 1976 that also affirms sovereign immunity then provides exceptions. It defines foreign states to include political subdivisions, agencies and instrumentalities of state if they perform government functions.

Exceptions to immunity from jurisdiction/action:

(a) express or implied waivers or immunity, eg submission to US jurisdiction.

(b) where action is based on acts with US connections, viz:

- commercial activity carried on in the USA by a foreign state;
- an act performed in the USA connected to a commercial act of a foreign state; and

- commercial activity outside the USA by a foreign state having a direct effect in the USA, eg *National American Corporation v Federal Republic of Nigeria* (1978) – letter of credit breached which was payable through a New York bank to a New York beneficiary.

Exceptions to immunity from enforcement:

(a) immunity expressly or impliedly waived,

(b) property concerned is used for the commercial activity upon which the action is based,

(c) enforcement relates to judgment declaring rights based on international law,

(d) enforcement follows a claim where no immunity from jurisdiction was available (applies to agencies and instrumentalities only, ie no extra immunity from enforcement for these entities).

Pre-judgment attachments are available only if there is an express and specific waiver and the assets are used for commercial activity in the US. No restriction on other injunctions and specific performance.

Service: any express arrangements will be respected, otherwise answerable within 60 days.

General immunity for central banks.

6 Documentation provisions

The relevant clauses in the loan agreement in England are:

- express submission to jurisdiction of English courts;
- appoint an agent for service within the UK (not the Ambassador);
- express consent to issue of any enforcement process;
- express consent to issue of any pre-judgment process, eg 'Mareva';
- separate submissions and consents required from central bank; and
- the above may be appropriate for a private borrower in case it is later nationalized.

The exact wording and format of the clauses is illustrated in Appendix 1 to this unit, to which you should now refer.

6.1 The clauses in the USA

- Express waiver of immunity from jurisdiction of US courts;
- express submission to jurisdiction of specific US courts;
- agreed procedure for service, appoint agent, not Ambassador;
- express waiver of immunity from pre-judgment process;

- express waiver of immunity from enforcement; and
- express waiver of objections to venue.

NB: separate waivers are required from the central bank.

6.2 Conflict issues

The Acts presumably respectively apply to all actions brought in the UK and USA irrespective of the proper law of the contract but can insert a clause that all waivers will be construed in accordance with the *lex fori*.

Insert representations and warranties (discussed in detail later in this book) to the effect that the contract is a commercial act, linked to event of default. Such a clause may raise an estoppel against the borrower from raising a defence of governmental act.

6.3 Act of State doctrine (USA)

Respect internal acts of another country, eg *Allied Bank International* (1985) – loans to Costa Rican banks, suspension of debt repayments by government decree. Act of State doctrine and principles of comity (courtesy) require respect of a decree, but on appeal, it was held that debts payable in the USA and comity was not appropriate in this case, so Act of State did not apply.

7 Particular risks in relation to sovereign immunity

7.1 Changes in the Law of State in question

(Private) corporate borrowers may be affected by changes in law of the borrower's state either introduced by a state borrower to protect itself or by the state to protect private borrowers, ie moratoria, reductions of interest rates, cancellation of maintenance of value clauses. Also for private borrowers there are withholding taxes, confiscation, expropriation, interference by government, and discrimination.

If a state attempts to change its laws to excuse itself from breach or change the nature of its obligations, then whether this is effective is a matter for the proper law of the contract. This was illustrated in *RV International Trustee* (1937) where a change in the proper law (New York) was held to be effective to abrogate certain gold clauses in a British bond issue.

Also where an agreement was governed by German law a change in the proper law requiring repayment in German currency was effective to override contractual provisions for sterling repayment in London.

7.2 Insulation

These reasons illustrate the need for lenders to insulate themselves from changes in the law of the borrower's state by expressly choosing another choice of law. If proper law is not that of the state in question then the general rule is that changes in its law have no legal effect on the loan agreement.

This is general but there are problems of legal immunity from suit or the practicalities of enforcement, as illustrated in the case of *National Bank of Greece v Metliss* (1958) which was discussed previously.

7.3 Exceptions to the general rule

(1) Regardless of proper law, an English court will enforce a mandatory domestic law of the UK.

(2) If English law is proper law an English court will recognize and defer to laws imposed in the place of performance.

(3) If there is a knowing attempt to evade laws of a foreign friendly country public policy may prevent recognition of an agreement.

(4) Where property is concerned English proper law defers to the law of the *lex situs*.

(5) Certain procedural remedies.

(6) *Lex domicili* may apply, such as if a state abolishes a lease of entry.

(7) Statute of Limitation.

(8) Exchange controls.

7.4 Summary

This is a topic that still seems to confuse students and there are two aspects to Sovereign Immunity, namely immunity from jurisdiction and immunity from enforcement. The positions with regard to different institutions are summarized below.

Body/ institution	Transaction	Immunity from Jurisdiction	Immunity from Enforcement
Sovereign/ government	Government	Yes	Yes
Sovereign/ government	Commercial	No	Yes
State body/ quango	Government	No	No
State body/ quango	Commercial	No	No
Central Bank	Government	Yes	Yes
Central Bank	Commercial	No	Yes

It is important to note that under English law the definition of Sovereign applies only to the head of state and the direct organs of government. Sovereign immunity does not apply to Local Authorities or to Quangos (quasi autonomous national government organizations).

This approach is not the same in other countries, notably in the USA, where some Quangos and local authorities may have sovereign immunity. This is why a legal opinion must always be taken when dealing with the law of other states.

Although other state bodies under English law may not enjoy immunity you must remember the special position of central banks. Central banks, irrespective of whether they are immune from jurisdiction or not, are always immune from enforcement unless otherwise waived.

If therefore a state changes its laws to, say, change the terms of its obligations or to discharge them, whether this is effective is a matter for the proper law of the contract. If the proper law is that of the state in question then a change in the law is effective. The general rule is that if proper law is not that of the state in question then changes in that law have no legal effect on the contract, although problems of enforcement and mandatory areas of local law remain.

It is important to recall the limitations of the proper law (which were covered earlier) as:

a) regardless of the proper law, courts will enforce mandatory domestic/local law, ie property, insolvency;

b) if English law is proper law an English court will recognize and defer to laws imposed in the place of performance;

c) contrary to public policy or attempts to evade the laws of a foreign friendly country.

d) In the case of property – English proper law defers to the law of the state in which the property is situated and thus may recognize expropriation subject to some limitations.

e) If a state abolishes a legal entity, these are matters for the law of the domicile.

f) Exchange controls may be recognized.

8 Expropriation of property outside the state

The general rule is that expropriation is ineffective, as illustrated in the case of *Banco de Vizcaya v Don Alfonso de Borbon y Austria* (1935).

This is where the London branch held bonds/securities deposited by the King of Spain who was subsequently declared a traitor and all his property expropriated. The London branch was required to surrender property but the courts decided that the King was entitled to the property not being in Spain and not subject to Spanish jurisdiction. Also confirmed in *Bank Voor Handle Nv v Slatford* (1953). There is the question of ambulatory property, ie ships, aircraft, but the rule here is that they cannot be expropriated in an English port. Also many cases the *situs* of a debt is held to be the place of performance (ie payment), eg *International Corporate Ltd v Besser Manufacturing Co Ltd* (1950). The place of payment was England and when non-payment occurred the place of breach was where payment should be made (that being so English courts have discretion under the Civil Procedure Rules.

In *International Corporate Ltd v Besser Manufacturing Co Ltd* (1950), the place of payment was England and when non-payment occurred, the place of the breach was where payment should be made (that being so the English courts had jurisdiction). The above cases are all cases where the contract provided for payment in a particular place.

In the case of *Ralli v Compania Naviera Sota v Aznar* (1920) the contract was governed by English law, but provided for payment in Spain. A change in Spanish law affected the amount payable and an English court would enforce only the amount so limited as that owing in the place of performance. English law therefore defers to the law of the place of payment of a debt. The *situs* of the debt is the place of performance and where English law is the proper law it defers to the law of the place of performance.

9 Expropriation inside the sate

All moratoriums will be determined by the proper law of the contract, but in cases where the moratorium is of property then it depends where the property is situated.

9.1 If property is inside the state

The general rule is that English law recognizes an expropriation of property within the territory of the state at time of expropriation as held in the case of *Luther v Sager* (1921).

A more important case is that known for short as the *Rumasa* case. The case concerned a Spanish company that controlled shares in other companies including (i) an English company (W & H) which had licences from a Jersey company and (ii) a Dutch company. The Spanish government expropriated shares in the Spanish company and thus obtained control over all those companies. However compulsory acquisition, held the court, was universally recognized and an English court would recognize the foreign acquisition even if produced effects outside Spain.

9.2 Act of state doctrine

As already discussed the US courts will not review or question any act of state done by a state and having effect within its own jurisdiction. It does not apply if the state expropriates property outside its own borders. This is illustrated in two US cases that concerned the *situs* of a debt held to be a place of payment. Three Costa Rican banks issued promissory notes under central bank direction to Allied Bank payable in New York. In 1981 Central Bank of Costa Rica suspended all external debt payments and made it illegal to pay the promissory notes. Allied Bank sued and the New York courts held that as the property was outside Costa Rica it was outside Act of State Doctrine.

A contrasting case is that of *Brak v Bancomer,* a US case, where Dollar certificates of deposit were issued by Bancomer but were held in Mexico – Bancomer was nationalized and prohibited from paying. Braka sued but Act of State Doctrine applied. These cases are illustrative of the current contradictory position.

9.3 *Libyan Arab Foreign Bank v Bankers Trust* (1987)

In this case, President Reagan (in 1986) issued two executive orders that purported to block bank accounts in the USA or American banks abroad. The Libyan bank sued in London for the return of their deposits that the London branch has frozen. The English courts held that the US orders were of no effect because the *situs* of the deposit was in England and thus subject to English law of which there was no such freezing order in effect.

10 Recognition of states

The following principles apply:

(a) Unrecognized states cannot sue or be sued in English courts and that government acts and laws of such unrecognized states cannot be recognized in an English court.

(b) Recognition is a political process whereby the Foreign Secretary issues a certificate as to whether a state is recognized by Her Majesty's government. It recognizes states not governments (Foreign Corporations Act 1991).

10.1 State entities

Immunity given to entities that are separate from the state is less significant as regards both jurisdiction and enforcement. In the US case of *Mellinger v New Brunswick Development Corpn* (1971) it was held that the entity was not a separate entity from government, and so immune.

In the *Trendtex* case (1977), which has already been discussed, the Central Bank of Nigeria was held to be a separate entity and all central banks have immunity from jurisdiction. The general rule is that the separate entity is not immune from jurisdiction generally and certainly not for commercial acts. It will thus be immune only if the state itself would be immune in a non-commercial transaction. It can of course submit to jurisdiction.

10.2 Immunity from enforcement

The general rule is that if the entity is not immune from jurisdiction then the entity is not immune from enforcement.

10.3 Central banks

Central banks are a separate entity and it has the same immunity from enforcement but not jurisdiction as a state. (Otherwise central banks would not maintain reserves the in UK.) A central bank's property is not to be regarded as being for commercial purposes so enforcement is possible only if it consents to enforcement by the use of a de-immunizing clause.

Appendix I

Extract from loan document

25.2 :Any communication from any party to any other under this Agreement shall be effective when actually received. Any such communication may be sent by telex or telefax or left at the address required by Clause 25.1 or sent by post (by airmail if to another country) postage prepaid and addressed to the addressee at that address. Any communication sent by telefax shall be confirmed by letter delivered or despatched by post as aforesaid within 24 hours of the despatch of the telefax (but failure to send or receive such confirmation shall not prejudice the effectiveness of the telefax communication).

25.3 :All communications and documents to be delivered under this Agreement shall be in the English language or shall be accompanied by a certified English translation.

26. This Agreement may be signed in any number of counterparts, all of which taken together and when delivered to the Agent shall constitute one and the same instrument. Any party may enter into this Agreement by signing any such counterpart.

27.1 :This Agreement shall be governed by and construed in accordance with English law.

27.2 :The borrower agrees that should any party bring any legal action or proceeding (together 'Proceedings') against it in respect of this Agreement in the courts and in the circumstances specified in Clause 27.3 (or in the courts of Sweden) no immunity from such Proceedings or from execution of judgment shall be claimed by or on behalf of the borrower or in respect of its assets, the borrower hereby irrevocably waiving any such right of immunity which it or any of its assets now has or may hereafter acquire. The borrower consents generally in respect of any Proceedings in the courts and in the circumstances specified in Clause 27.3 (or in the courts of Sweden) to the High Court of Justice, in England.

27.5 :The Agreement, waiver and consent by the borrower in Clauses 27.2 and 27.3 do not apply to:

(a) the borrower's title to or possession of property used for the purposes of a diplomatic mission, or

(b) property which is, or is intended to be, used in connection with a military activity and

(i) is of a military character, or

(ii) is under the control of a military authority or defence agency, or

(c) except to the extent permitted by Swedish law, an assets situated in Sweden, or

(d) (for the avoidance of doubt) any property held in the name of Sveriges Riksbank,

and in addition Sveriges Riksbank is and shall be treated as being separate from the borrower for all purposes in connection with this Agreement and shall not be responsible for the obligations of the borrower under this Agreement and no Proceedings shall be capable of being brought against Sveriges Riksbank or its assets in connection with this Agreement.

AS WITNESS the hands of the duly authorized representatives of the parties hereto the day and year first above written.

Without prejudice to the foregoing execution of this Agreement by the parties hereto, each of:

hereby expressly and specifically confirms its agreement with the provisions of Clause 27 of this Agreement for the purpose of (a) Article I of the Protocol annexed to the Convention on jurisdiction and the enforcement of judgments in civil and commercial matters signed at Brussels on 27 September 1968 and (b) Article I of the Protocol No. I annexed to the Convention on jurisdiction and the enforcement of judgments in civil and commercial matters opened for signature at Lugano on 16 September 1988.

Notes

1. Paragraphs reproduced from ***ifs*** Examiner's Report, May 2000 (Corporate Banking – Practice and Law).

Four

Enforcement of foreign judgments

1 Introduction

The lender may obtain a judgment against the borrower in the lender's country's court. To what extent can he follow the borrower's assets into the borrower's country or elsewhere? There is never automatic enforcement abroad, and the local courts have to be involved to some extent. This will involve one of three alternative processes:

(a) the lender starts a fresh action locally,

(b) the lender sues locally as a simple debt due, or

(c) the lender relies on a reciprocal enforcement convention with the local country.

2 Starting a fresh action locally

Starting a fresh action locally is clearly the most cumbersome approach and a fresh hearing on the merits may even produce an opposite result. This can be useful perhaps to get a judgment in a different currency. The English Civil Jurisdiction and Judgments Act bars any action in England if the plaintiff has already won abroad unless it is not enforceable or not recognized in England. Even if he lost abroad he may well be barred by the doctrine of issue estoppel, *The Sennar* (1984) HL.

The local court may recognize the foreign judgment and thereby accept it as evidence of a debt due, which avoids a fresh hearing on the merits. A reciprocal enforcement convention enables the lender to move directly to enforcement procedures locally without the need to obtain any judgments there.

3 Recognition versus enforcement

Judgment can be recognized by a court without being enforced, but if a court enforces a foreign judgment it must first have recognized that judgment. Recognition on its own may be valuable, eg a foreign court's declaration of proprietary rights. Recognition on its own is a defensive process that acts as a shield to block fresh proceedings being commenced in a foreign jurisdiction when judgment has been obtained elsewhere.

Recognition and enforcement of foreign judgments, whether or not under a convention, is likely to be subject to the following conditions:

(a) The court of origin had competent jurisdiction, often a double test, viz in its own terms and in the local court's terms. However, express submission by the defendant may well be conclusive. English law is that the foreign judgment will be recognized if its jurisdiction was sufficient within the English rules, other than English long-arm rules. Consent, submission or carrying on business in the country concerned are sufficient. NY courts are more likely to recognize a foreign judgment based on long-arm jurisdiction, eg selling through a local distributor: *Somportex Ltd v Philadelphia Chewing Gum Corpn* (1971).

(b) The defendant is not entitled to sovereign immunity locally. English law: section 31 of the Civil Jurisdiction and Judgments Act 1982.

(c) That the original court would recognize a corresponding judgment of the enforcing court. This doctrine of reciprocity is not applied by English or NY law.

(d) That the original court was competent to hear the case, for example the English Civil Jurisdiction and Judgments Act 1982 provides that a foreign judgment obtained in contravention of an exclusive jurisdiction clause will not be recognized in the UK and English conflict rules are applied to determine the issue of contravention.

(e) That the original court provided a fair trial. The English law declares 'natural justice' to include fairness of a hearing and impartiality of judges. Any fraud in the hearing by witnesses or judges will permit an English court to reopen the case and rejudge it on the merits. US law makes a distinction between intrinsic (eg perjury) and extrinsic (eg bribing a witness) fraud. Only extrinsic fraud will invalidate the original court's decision.

(f) Another feature of English natural justice is adequacy of notice of a hearing. However, if a defendant has agreed to submit himself to the foreign court's jurisdiction, he cannot complain of lack of due notice so long as the court's procedural rules were followed, *Vallee v Dumergue* (1840). Nor can he complain of the court's rules of evidence. US law has clearly defined principles of 'due process'.

(g) The judgment does not conflict with local public policy principles. In *Israel Discount Bank of New York v Hadjipateras* (1984), CA the court declared its power on policy grounds to refuse enforcement of a New York court's judgment on a guarantee, where undue influence was raised, but declined to do so when the defence had not been raised in New York.

(h) The judgment is for money. No enforcement will be available of an injunction, eg to restrain disposal of assets.

(i) The judgment is not based on a tax claim: *Government of India v Taylor* (1955), HL. Also the Protection of Trading Interests Act 1980 limits the enforcement of multiple damage actions based on anti-trust laws.

(j) The judgment is final and conclusive. In English law it is generally possible to seek enforcement even if avenues of appeal are still available in the foreign court but the defendant may be granted a stay of execution if he shows an appeal will take place.

(k) The foreign judgment does not conflict with a local judgment on the same issue. Thus the lender plaintiff should not initiate multiple actions for this reason as well as the risk of a stay due to *lis alibi pendens*.

In English law, so long as the applicable conditions are satisfied, the court will not re-examine the merits of the case even if a blatant error in applying English law took place. NY courts generally do not re-examine. However, many European countries will.

English courts can give judgment in foreign currency and may convert foreign judgments into sterling.

There are a number of circumstances in which an overseas judgment will not be enforced in the English courts. Some of the major situations are considered below[1].

1. Where the original court that decided the case did not actually have jurisdiction to decide it. In this situation the English courts will not recognize the original decision, and therefore will not enforce it[1].

2. Where the overseas judgment is obtained contrary to rules of natural justice, *Adams v Cape Industries* (1990). The concept of natural justice was construed widely so that a judgment by a United States court that awarded damages on a total basis without considering the particular position of particular individuals, was considered contrary to natural justice and would not be enforced in the English courts[1].

Natural justice includes other situations, including some procedural irregularity in the obtaining of the overseas judgment. In *Desert Sun Loan Corpn v Hill* (1996), the defendant, a former partner in a partnership, instructed his own American lawyers to defend a claim on a guarantee. The guarantee was entered into by all the partners. Another partner, acting for the partnership, accepted liability for all the partners without the defendant partner's agreement. Judgment was entered against all the partners in an Arizona court in the USA. This judgment was not enforced in the English courts. The Court of Appeal was of the view that there was a 'triable issue' on whether the defendant had voluntarily submitted to the jurisdiction of the American court. Since there was a triable issue, the plaintiff corporation could not obtain summary judgment (immediate judgment) in the English courts on this guarantee[1].

However, if the defendant simply decides not to argue a particular defence, such as undue influence, in the overseas court, then the defendant cannot raise undue influence as a defence in the English courts. Thus a plaintiff was able to enforce, in the English courts, a judgment of the USA court in New York regarding a guarantee signed by the defendant in the US, where no defence had been raised in the actual hearing of the action in the US, *Israel Discount Bank of New York v Hadjipateras* (1983). There was no breach of the rules of natural justice. This principle was confirmed in *Fennoscandia Ltd v Robert Clarke* (1999)[1].

Where a party has submitted to the jurisdiction of an overseas court as regards a particular claim, that party will be taken to have submitted to its jurisdiction as regards claims arising out of the same subject matter, and also related claims, *Murthy v Sivajothi* (1999)[1].

3. Where the judgment is obtained by fraud. However, fraud must be proved. Where the allegation of fraud is unsuccessful, the judgment will be enforceable, and this exception will not apply, *Owens Bank Ltd v Bracco* (1992) Privy Council. A loan was made by the plaintiff bank to the Bracco company. This loan was not repaid, and the plaintiff bank sued the Bracco company[1].

   The first defendant B was the director of this company, and the second defendant was the company itself. B alleged that the loan documents were a forgery, and the Bracco company claimed that in any case B did not have authority to enter into this transaction. These defences were originally rejected by the St Vincent Court. The defendants appealed to the Privy Council, which concluded, as a matter of law, that a defendant would have a defence to the enforcement of a judgment, because there was fraud which he could not have discovered with reasonable diligence. There has been subsequent litigation of this matter in *Owens Bank v Etude Commerciale SA* (1995), and *Owens Bank Ltd v Bracco (No 2)* (1994). The principle that a foreign judgment obtained by fraud will not be enforced in the English courts was confirmed in *Masters v Leaver* (1999)[1].

4. Where to recognize the judgment would be contrary to the public policy of the common law[1].

5. Where the English courts are asked to enforce a judgment other than a money judgment[1].

6. Where the English courts would be enforcing another country's tax laws. This principle, at common law, was confirmed in *QRS 1 ApS v Frandsen* (1999). Furthermore, this rule was not overridden by article 1 of the Convention on Jurisdiction and the Enforcement of Judgments in Civil and Commercial Matters[1].

4 Methods of enforcement

4.1 Position at English common law

A judgment creditor cannot enforce the foreign judgment directly in England but must bring an action in England.

4.2 Enforcement under statute

This occurs where the common law position is qualified, and the requirements before an English court will recognize or enforce a foreign judgment are as follows:

1. Foreign court acted with jurisdiction.
2. Defendant is not entitled to sovereign immunity locally (section 31 of the Civil Jurisdiction and Judgments Act 1982).
3. Original court was competent to hear the case (Civil Jurisdiction and Judgments Act 1982, section 31). Provides that a foreign judgment obtained in contravention of an exclusive jurisdiction clause will not be recognized in England.
4. Not contrary to natural justice.

   If not English court could reopen the case and rejudge it on the merits.
5. Defendant received notice of the foreign proceedings.
6. Judgment not contrary to public policy in England.
7. Judgment is for money. No enforcement will be available of an injunction, eg to restrain disposal of assets.
8. Judgment is not based on a tax claim: *Government of India v Taylor* (1955).
9. Judgment not obtained by fraud.

10. Non-conflict with local judgment (section 4 of the Foreign Judgments (Reciprocal Enforcement) Act 1933).

4.3 The statutes

There are five UK statutes providing reciprocal enforcement of foreign judgments:

(a) provides for reciprocal enforcement of the judgments of superior courts of most Commonwealth countries (not Canada) and a few others. Judgments are registered and then have the same force as judgments of an English court;

(b) provides for a similar registration system in respect of many European states and includes judgments of inferior courts;

(c) the Civil Jurisdiction and Judgments Act 1982 and 1991 are designed to implement both of the above This is discussed in detail below;

(d) provides for recognition of EEC state judgments against the UK; and

(e) provides for enforcement of judgments of Scottish and Northern Ireland courts.

The USA has a 'full faith and credit' clause in its constitution whereby judgments in one state may be enforced in another so long as 'due process' is observed. Some states, including NY, have enacted a permitting enforcement of foreign judgments on the same principle as those of other US states. NY requires the plaintiff to sue on the judgments; a summary process is available.

4.4 Advantages of reciprocal enforcement conventions

The general advantages of a reciprocal enforcement convention are:

(a) jurisdiction – a judgment can be registered whether or not the defendant is present at the time;

(b) procedure – simpler and quicker;

(c) no review of the merits;

(d) no defence of denial of fair trial available;

(e) no defence of lack of reciprocity available.

4.5 Relationship between jurisdiction and choice of law clauses

The proper law of the contract determines the interpretation of the jurisdiction clause. If the basic contract is void, the clause will fail but not if the contract is only voidable. The *lex fori* and not the proper law will determine whether the addressed court's jurisdiction is ousted by a clause. The proper law determines whether a Calvo doctrine is effective.

A suitable clause (from a lender's view) would provide for the borrower's submission to the non-exclusive jurisdiction of two or more specified courts and appointing an agent within each of the jurisdictions to receive service with an agreement to appoint a substitute agent if the first ceases to be available. A consent to the mailing of process to the borrower's address abroad may be useful in avoiding any debate on 'due process'. Express waivers of right to object to venue will prevent arguments about which courts in a country should hear a dispute and an express waiver of a *forum non conveniens* objection may assist. Sovereign borrowers should be asked to make the appropriate waivers and submissions and this topic will considered in the next unit.

5 Judgment and enforcement under 1968 Brussels Convention and 1988 Lugano Convention

Civil Jurisdiction and Judgments Act 1982 and 1991 are designed to implement both of the European Judgment Conventions. The countries covered by the Brussels convention are Belgium, Denmark, France, Germany, Greece, Ireland, Italy, Luxembourg, Netherlands, Portugal, Spain and the UK. The Lugano convention extends the Brussels Convention to Austria, Finland, Iceland, Norway, Sweden and Switzerland.

The Conventions provide a system of enforcement against a non-convention domiciliary whereby a court judgment in any member state can be automatically enforced in any other even if its jurisdiction was 'long-arm' and meanwhile pre-judgment attachments are available throughout the contracting states. Where the defendant is an EEC domiciliary the plaintiff is bound to sue in any contracting state court that the parties have agreed shall have exclusive jurisdiction although he may sue in non-contracting states courts specified in the agreement.

5.1 General features of the Conventions in relation to enforcement

The essential features of the conventions in relation to the enforcement of foreign judgments are as follows:

(1) More liberal than other reciprocal conventions in that it covers both monetary and non-monetary judgments.

(2) Also not restricted as to whether court acted with jurisdiction.

(3) Also includes specific performance/injunctions so is useful in enforcing non-monetary obligations under loan agreements.

(4) Enforcement applies to all judgments within its scope whether or not such judgments are against persons domiciled or resident in a contracting state.

(5) Not subject to general considerations – allows judgments given in one contracting state to run freely throughout the convention countries.

NB: Defendant need not be domiciled in a contracting state. Although the Conventions relates to persons domiciled in a contracting state this restriction does not apply to enforcement of judgments. So judgment against defendant will be enforced throughout the convention countries as per Article 26 Convention, without any special procedure being required. In the UK an action under the conventions is by way of registration pf the judgment at the High court as per section 4 of the Civil Jurisdiction and Judgments Act 1982.

5.2 Advantages of enforcement under the Brussels and Lugano Conventions

(a) Jurisdiction – a judgment can be registered whether or not the defendant is present at the time.

(b) Procedure simpler and quicker.

(c) No review of the merits.

(d) No defence or denial of fair trial available.

(e) No defence or lack of reciprocity available.

5.3 Refusal of recognition

Under Articles 27/28 of the Brussels and Lugano Conventions provide that a judgment shall not be recognized where it is:

(1) Contrary to public policy.

(2) Judgment was rendered in default and the defendant was not duly served notice.

(3) Judgment irreconcilable since it conflicts with a judgment between the same parties rendered in the state in which the recognition is sought.

(4) Conflicts with provisions of Lugano/Brussels Convention.

6 Freezing orders

A freezing order, formerly known as a Mareva injunction, is a summary procedure to prevent assets fleeing the jurisdiction, now known as third party orders, and comes from the case of *Mareva Compania Naviera SA v International Bulk Carriers* (1975). A Mareva injunction is an indispensable weapon in the bankers armoury as demonstrated in the case of *Hill Samuel & Co v Littaur* (1985). It is comparable to the Doctrine of Saisie Conservatoise (Provisional attachment) used in France. It is important to understand that applications may be made to the courts of a contracting state for a Mareva as may be available under the law of that state even if under the conventions the courts of another contracting state have jurisdiction.

For example if a defendant is domiciled in Germany then plaintiff can take proceedings in Germany but also apply to English courts for a Mareva preventing the defendant from removing assets in England prior to judgment.

Under section 25 of the Civil Jurisdiction and Judgments Act 1982, extra-territorial freezing orders can be granted in England where proceedings have been or are to be commenced in a contracting state. This was demonstrated in the case of *Republic of Haiti v Duvalier* [1989] 2 WLR 261. In this case a Mareva injunction was granted in England as there were assets there, even though proceedings were not contemplated in England but in France, and service outside the jurisdiction is permitted as long as proceedings are within contracting states.

Notes

1. Paragraphs reproduced from ***ifs*** Examiner's Report, October 2000 (Corporate Banking – Practice and Law).

Five

Exchange controls

1 Introduction

The issue of exchange controls is very important in cross border financial transactions and it arises in changes of the proper law. They help a government to exert some influence and control over the value of their currency, by either restrictions on trade or by direct intervention in the market.

To be an exchange control it must be: a direct control on the financial aspects of a transaction, controlling the movement of currency, property or services, to protect exchange resources of a country.

UK exchange controls were abolished in UK from 1979. The UK has adopted IMF provisions on making of payment/transfers for current international transactions without IMF approval.

2 Types of exchange control

There are three types of exchange control:

(a) restrictions on resident national borrowing in foreign currency;

(b) deposit requirements obliging borrowers to pay a percentage to their central bank;

(c) prohibitions on access to domestic capital markets by foreign borrowers.

Enforcement is usually primarily by fines and other criminal-type sanctions but the effect on a loan contract is to render it illegal and therefore void or unenforceable or at least to modify it, *Re Helbert Wagg & Co Ltd* (1956), payments in inflation-ravished German Marks were held to be an effective discharge of the agreement to pay in sterling after a German Government moratorium in 1933; the proper law was German. Any attempt to enforce in the courts of the country that imposed the control is doomed to failure. *Boissevain v Weil* (1950) HL. The result is a windfall gain for the borrower. The lender's only change is an action in an external forum. Even this remedy is restricted by the effect of the IMF Bretton Woods Agreement of 1944.

Where Bretton Woods does not apply, the courts will give effect to the regulation if it emanates from the proper law of the contract unless it is 'oppressive or discriminatory' – *Re Helbert Wagg* (1956); the rule is similar in the USA where in *French v Banco Nacional de Cuba* (1968) the courts recognized a Cuban regulation which was considered to be 'within the limits of international legality'. The Act of State doctrine was also invoked. If the proper law is external, the control may have no effect on the contract, *Kleinwort Sons & Co Ltd v Ungarische Baumwolle Industrie AG* (1939) CA, similarly in the USA: *Lann v United Steelworks Corpn* (1938).

If a new control in the place of payment renders payment there illegal, the English law is that payment will not be enforced, *Ralli Bros v Compania Naviera Sota y Aznar* (1920) CA. The US courts have adopted the fairer solution of shifting the place of payment, *Pan American Life Insurance Co v Blanco* (1966).

Article VII, section 2(b) of the Bretton Woods Agreement provides 'exchange contracts which involve the currency of any member and which are, contrary to the exchange control regulations of that member maintained or imposed consistently with this Agreement shall be unenforceable in the territories of any member'. An exchange contract involves a contract to exchange the currency of one country for the currency of another country.

The phrase 'exchange contracts' has been the subject of litigation. The English courts preferred a narrow definition of it in *Wilson, Smithett & Cope Ltd v Terruzzi* (1976) CA where an Italian sought to avoid payment to English metal dealers. Where cheques are used to exchange currencies, it will be by an exchange contract as held in the case of *Mansouri v Singh* (1986). However, in *United City Merchants (Investments) Ltd v Royal Bank of Canada* (1982) HL the court refused to recognize a sale of goods contract insofar as it was designed to exchange Peruvian currency for US$. The arrangement can be (i) genuine sale, and (ii) an exchange of currency where the sale price was inflated in order to allow an exchange of currencies to take place. The genuine sale was upheld by the court, but the exchange of currencies beyond the commercial sale price was an 'exchange contract'.

The above cases confirm the 'narrow' approach of the English courts to the interpretation of 'exchange contract', and also followed by the US courts. The New

York courts have favoured the narrow construction of the Article in *Banco do Brasil SA v AC Israel Commodity Co* (1964) and in *J Zeevi & Sons Ltd v Grindlays Bank Uganda Ltd* (1975) where a letter of credit was held not to be an exchange contract. An earlier approach, now not followed and which was overturned by the above cases, was that any contract that affected a country's exchange resources fell within the definition of an exchange contract, as in the case of *Sharif v Azad* (1967). This approach is known as the 'wider' approach and has been followed in the French courts, the Luxembourg courts, and some earlier decisions of the German courts.

A number of cases have confirmed the requirements for currencies to be exchanged in order for there to be an exchange contract contrary to the Bretton Woods Agreement. If funds are merely transferred form a bank account in a country which is a signatory to the agreement, and which has exchange controls, then that mere transfer of funds will not be an exchange contract as held in the case of *S v A Bank* (1997) and *Ispahani v Bank Melli Iran* (1997). In the case of *Ispahani v Bank Melli Iran* (1997), the court took the view that the setting up and crediting of a bank account in London of funds transferred from Bangladesh, did not involve any exchange of currency and therefore not an 'exchange contract'[1].

3 Documentation provisions

(a) Specify a currency and place in a country unlikely to impose exchange controls, eg Dollars in New York.

(b) Insert the following provisions into the documentation which include:

   (i) that it is a condition precedent to the draw-down of the loans that all necessary exchange control consents in the borrower's country have been obtained for the borrowing and for payments of both interest and capital. The agreement will thus not be effective until the consents are forthcoming. If the consents cannot be obtained before draw-down comfort letters will have to suffice. Consents may not be granted in advance for non-scheduled prepayments of capital;

   (ii) a currency transfer undertaking from the borrower's central bank which agrees to sell to the borrower the necessary foreign currency for the due payments and to allow it to remit them to the lender and to ensure sufficient foreign currency is available for the purpose. This gives the lender a direct contractual relationship with the central bank that does not occur with consents issued to the borrower. It is appropriate in the case of loans to state-related bodies. The currency transfer agreement is in effect a contract rendering the central bank liable for default. The central bank under UK law is not immune from jurisdiction but its assets have special immunity unless it consents to execution against those assets. Therefore enforcement may be impossible;

(iii) covenants linked to an event of default in respect of the initial obtaining of consents and maintenance of consents throughout the duration of the agreement. Therefore a right to accelerate if consents cease to apply, probably self-defeating;

(iv) a double jeopardy clause permitting the lender to call for prepayment if it becomes illegal for him to maintain the loan while the proper law of the contract does not recognize that illegality;

(v) a currency indemnity clause providing for the conversion of any foreign currency judgment award as at the working day preceding judgment and an indemnity for the lender if he suffers a loss on the conversion, expressed as an independent clause not to merge on judgment.

NB: English courts can make awards in foreign currencies: *Miliangos v George Frank (Textiles) Ltd* (1976) HL. New York courts do not and may convert currency as at the day of default.

Other methods by which lenders protect themselves could include the following.

- Provision for repayment to be made in a currency likely to be free of exchange control problems.
- Obtain central bank consents from the borrower's state covering repayment. Such consents could be obtained in advance of draw-down and included in the documentation as a condition precedent.
- If advance consents cannot be obtained, the opinion of the relevant authority could be sought as to the likely result of a future application for unblocked funds to repay the loan and a commercial judgment made by the lender on the reply.
- A currency transfer agreement could be obtained from the central bank in the borrower's state.
- The documents could contain an express warranty to cover the provision of all necessary currency to repay the loan and interest. The lender could obtain legal opinions from the borrower's state to cover the likely problems of exchange control.
- The loan document could include currency indemnity clauses dealing with local rules concerning payments. Such clauses could indemnify the lender for any conversion losses resulting from exchange control impositions.

4 Summary

In examination questions on exchange controls you should discuss generally the impact of exchange control restrictions/regulation and the impact that this will have on the ability of the borrower to make payments with foreign exchange. You should also discuss the conflicts of laws implications of exchange control restrictions.

In terms of limiting the impact of exchange controls the following issues should be covered:

(a) to provide that the loan agreement required payment in a currency and country which is not likely to impose exchange controls;

(b) obtaining appropriate central bank and/or treasury consents in the state in question which provides that foreign exchange will be made available;

(c) obtaining a currency transfer agreement from the central bank or appropriate central body in the state in question whereby it will undertake to sell to the relevant borrowers sufficient currency to repay the various facilities entered into by borrowers;

(d) finally the imposition of appropriate warranties, covenants and events of default covering changes to the exchange control protection incorporated within the documentation.

Notes

1. Paragraphs reproduced from ***ifs*** Examiner's Report, May 2000 (Corporate Banking – Practice and Law).

Six

Structure of loan agreements

1 User benefits

- Medium-term commitment by the lender means, that the borrower has certainty of funds when required, which may be an essential consideration to the borrower, depending on his needs, eg property developers need the assurance of funds to see the project through to its conclusion, and the point where cash will be generated.
- It may be available either in revolving or straight loan form, to suit the borrower's need and the purpose of the facility.
- It is flexible as to the purpose, and particularly useful simply as a 'standby' facility in the event that other, perhaps cheaper, alternatives are unavailable to the borrower at the time funds are required.
- When drawings are made, the rate of interest on the fixture is based on short-term inter-bank rates that are generally lower than medium-term rates.
- The facilities are 'committed' by the bank, which guarantees to provide funds in the currency in which the facility is denominated, usually for periods up to 12 months.
- There is great flexibility in the facility in that rollovers for other than the 'standard' inter-bank periods of one, three and six months can be arranged.
- Drawings can be made in a wide range of currencies.
- Other lending centres (usually abroad) can be incorporated into the facility.

- The facilities can be tailor-made to the funding requirements of the borrower.
- The option to draw by means of (sterling) bankers acceptances can be written into the facility.

The facility can be used as a 'standby facility' in support of borrowing from other sources or to meet unforeseen contingencies.

1.1 User limitations

- Short-term interest rates may have increased significantly at the time a company is obliged to borrow.
- Currencies and fixture periods beyond 12 months are subject to availability. However, banks will usually commit to provide a specified range of currencies and can indicate the current availability of longer-term fixtures.
- The bank may wish to restrict the number of currencies drawn at any one time.
- Where the full amount of the loan is drawn in currency, and the sterling (or base currency) equivalent at the time of rollover, is higher than the amount of the facility the excess will have to be repaid – usually only if it is more than 5% of the facility amount.
- Care needs to be taken with:
  - value dates (same day for domestic sterling, spot, ie two business days ahead for eurocurrencies);
  - whether interest is calculated on a 360-day (usually for eurocurrencies) or a 365-day year;
  - the frequency of interest payments, which is likely to produce higher costs on an annual basis;
  - any other fees and expenses payable which increase the overall/true cost of borrowing.

In the case of the bank it will receive a margin and fees for providing the loan. However, the problems that face the bank will obviously include default or restructuring of the borrower. Also the bank may face the erosion of its margin from a variety of factors that may include the application of increased costs or as a result of a market disaster. It is up to the loan agreement to incorporate provisions to protect the bank that will be discussed below.

2 Loan documentation

The loan document will incorporate many clauses such as the choice of law and jurisdiction clauses, have already been discussed in previous units. This unit looks at the principal clauses within a loan agreement that are as follows.

2.1 Facility type

The loan will either be a term loan or revolving facility that is, usually, of a committed nature, although a 'repayment on demand' clause may be specified in the agreement. The amount of the facility will be stated and how the loan can be drawn down either as a single sum known as a bullet or in tranches or revolving.

2.2 Currency

Such 'market-rate linked' facilities are available in most currencies (naturally, subject to availability) and in most major financial centres around the world. Multi-currency facilities are also available. This type of facility provides the borrower with access to a nominated range of currencies. At the time of draw-down of an amount required, the borrower simply nominates the currency he requires, which must be within the nominated range agreed at the outset.

2.3 Term/maturity

A medium-term loan will usually be for a period of seven years but may be longer or shorter. Each draw-down will be for a specified 'rollover' period (sometimes called 'fixture' period) – usually one or three months; in exceptional cases six, or a maximum of 12 months. Some banks may allow draw-down on an overnight or seven-day period, although this is quite unusual as part of a committed medium term LIBOR loan facility.

2.4 Repayment

The repayment clause will be self-explanatory and simple providing that repayment in a term loan being repaid by instalments or in a single amount known as a bullet. In the case of a revolving facility there is no formal repayment programme agreed; the facility 'limit' will be set and the borrower will be allowed draw, repay and redrawn throughout the agreed term. However, the LIBOR loans involve an element of repayment, since each is, effectively, repayable at maturity of its respective rollover period, eg a tranche of £1 million drawn down today on a one-month fixture will be repayable in one month's time. This is where the expression 'rollover' comes from, since it is quite usual for 'repayment' to come from a new draw-down for a further period.

2.5 Pricing

Fees

There is an arrangement fee, and a non-utilization fee, in respect of undrawn balances. The former is paid up front and subsequently, on renewal; the latter is assessed retrospectively, annually or half-yearly.

Interest

There are three elements involved. First, there is LIBOR, and this will be the prevailing rate at the time of draw-down, which is fixed throughout that period. Second, a margin will be agreed at the outset, and this will apply for the term of the facility. The margin will depend on the borrower's standing and the lender's perception of the risk involved. The final element will be any mandatory costs levied by a central bank or a regulator. The Financial Services Authority levies a fee of £48 per £1m of deposits for authorized deposit-takers in the UK, or for banks outside the EEA but which have UK branches, and £16 per £1m of deposits from banks which have branch in the UK, but are incorporated in another part of the EEA.

Such fees that are levied by the FSA on a bank will be passed on to a borrower as 'mandatory costs' and this will be done by using a prescribed formula that will be put into the loan agreement.

2.6 Restrictions on purpose

Generally loans are usually stated as being for general corporate purposes and specific purposes are not usually stated except in rescheduling and project finance. There would of course be the general problem of policing in the case of having a specific purpose for the loan. Lending for an illegal purpose is also rare. The only restrictions in England would be those contrary to section 151 of the Companies Act 1985 in prohibiting financial assistance to a company to purchase its own shares. There may be the problem however of ultra vires in some jurisdictions (ie the company acting outside of its power).

The Companies Act 1989 has virtually removed the concept of ultra vires acts from the perspective of the company's creditors. A person dealing with a company in good faith should therefore not be concerned with the company's constitution.

2.7 Prepayment

The repayment clause will be self-explanatory and simple providing repayment by instalments or in a single amount known as a bullet. Prepayment clauses will be more complex, perhaps providing for notice to be given in advance, for such notice to be irrevocable and for the application of prepayments that will usually be in inverse chronological order to the borrower's commitments so the effect is to shorten the life of the loan. A premium may be charged to compensate the lender for the loss of his investment, English law insists it must not be 'unconscionable', *Multiservice Bookbinding v Marden* (1978). If the loan is secured there is an additional requirement that there be 'no clog on the equity of redemption', but in the case of corporate loans the criterion is almost as limited. A similar principle applies to a clause forbidding prepayment. If nothing is said about prepayment it would be difficult to imply a right to do so. Corporate debentures may not be prepaid without an express right being conferred on the borrower.

Payment clauses will specify the time and place of payment (in their absence, the debtor must 'seek out his creditor'). Place of payment will be a powerful factor in determining proper law in the absence of an express clause and will give an English court jurisdiction under the Civil Procedure Rules – breach of contract in England. Loan agreements do not normally commit the borrower to borrow but instead confer an option to the borrower to do so.

3 Conditions precedent

3.1 The purpose of conditions precedent

The purpose of conditions precedent is to provide a 'list' of certain conditions that must be satisfied by the borrower (normally in form and substance satisfactory to the lending bank) before the lending obligation can be triggered.

3.2 The content of conditions precedent

The various conditions normally cover the following matters:

(i) appropriate legal opinions and constitutional documentation which seek to ensure that the loan and any security, is valid and binding on the borrower in accordance with its terms and that the borrower has the power and all necessary authorizations to enter into the agreement;

(ii) that no events of default have occurred during the period between execution and draw-down under the agreement; and

(iii) the representations and warranties continue to be true in all material respects.

3.3 Legal effect of the conditions precedent

The legal effect of conditions precedent will depend upon how they are legally construed. It will be necessary to determine whether they are true conditions precedent, ie they constitute a contingent condition or they are simply promissory conditions. If they are promissory conditions there is a valid and binding agreement from the moment the agreement is executed and neither the borrower nor the lender can withdraw without incurring potential liability for breach of contract. If they are contingent conditions it will be possible for the lender to 'walk' away from the transaction in the event that the conditions are not satisfied. An important consideration in determining the legal nature of conditions precedent will be whether their satisfaction is outside the control of the contracting parties. In revolving facilities conditions precedent may require to be satisfied prior to each and every draw-down thereunder.

A bank is entitled to waive a condition precedent inserted entirely for the bank's benefit and enforce the contract against the borrower as if the condition had been omitted, *Bennett v Fowler* (1840).

The potentially problematic conditions precedent for a borrower are those where a third party is involved such as accountants reports, licences, legal opinions.

4 Representations and Warranties

4.1 Purpose of the representations and warranties

The purpose of the representations and warranties is to provide a right on the part of the lending bank to terminate the agreement and accelerate repayment prior to maturity or alternatively in appropriate circumstances, where the warranty is fundamental to the entire contract, the entire agreement may be null and void (for example, where the borrower has no legal capacity to borrow in the first place). Representations and warranties endeavour to provide for misrepresentations in the event of inaccuracy. Therefore may enable lender to cancel commitment and accelerate loan since linked to event of default.

4.2 The content of the representations and warranties

Representations and warranties can be broken down into various groupings. The first group are very similar to the conditions precedent in that they require the borrower to represent and warrant that it has legal status and capacity etc. to enter into the underlying loan agreement (and any security arrangements in respect thereof) and that all relevant authorizations and permissions have been obtained in order to enable the borrower and/or any guarantor to enter into a contract which is legally valid and binding.

The representations will require the borrower to represent and warrant that all of the obligations as set out in the underlying documentation constitute legal valid and binding commitments and that the performance of the borrower's obligations will not violate any provisions contained in its constitutional documents.

The second group of representations and warranties relate to the financial and business position of the borrower and/or any related guarantor. Such representations cover the accuracy of all financial statements and information submitted to the lending bank and in addition cover such matters as 'no litigation' and 'no material adverse change'. Such warranties are an attempt to reflect a position where the lending bank is requiring the borrower to maintain the lending bank's understanding of its financial and business position as represented in the discussions that preceded the execution of the loan agreement.

4.3 The legal effect of the representations and warranties

A misrepresentation inducing a breach of contract may entitle the lender to rescind the contract and obtain damages. Such a misrepresentation that becomes a warranty may entitle the lender to repudiate for breach of contract and damages. English contract law distinguishes the fundamental conditions, breach of which leads to the right to repudiate and the less important warranties, breach of which gives a right to damages only. A lender will seek to effectively give himself the right to repudiate for breach of any warranty by the event of default clause. This may not assist recovery if the breach was as to validity, eg the ultra vires nature of the borrowing or breach of exchange controls.

An acceleration of the loan agreement for breach of representations and warranties is provided by linking them to the events of default clause. In the context of international banking transactions, the contracts can normally be immediately accelerated by virtue of the linking of the breach of the representation and warranties to the events of default clause.

The borrower may also be stopped from pleading absence of capacity or absence of authorization if appropriate representations and warranties are given (see *Janred Properties Ltd v ENIT* [1989] 2 All ER 444).

4.4 Environmental concerns

Environmental issues are of increasing concern to banks: quite apart from any civil liability like adopting a nuisance, banks should be aware of the onerous legislation such as the Environmental Protection Act 1990. This Act and the Environmental Act 1995, introduced a licensing system for specified 'polluting' processes, as well as powers to provide various bodies to enforce clean up of polluted sites. Primary responsibility rests with the polluter. However innocent owners or occupiers may be held liable if the person with primary responsibility cannot be found. In the USA the concept of lender liability is well established and a bank could find itself liable for clean-up costs.

As a result of these environmental risks banks are increasingly requiring an expert's report if the borrower conducts a high risk business. At a very minimum a bank will usually require a borrower to represent and warrant that it is in compliance with all applicable environmental laws and has obtained and complies with any licences that may be necessary for its business.

4.5 The evergreen clause

In the event that the loan agreement is of a revolving nature, the representations and warranties are often given 'evergreen' effect by a mechanism that requires them to be repeated upon each draw-down date.

5 Covenants

5.1 The purpose of covenants

The primary objective of covenants, when taken together, is to ensure the continued soundness of the loan facility being advanced to the borrower and to provide the lender with certain 'inside' information on, and limited control over, the business of the borrower.

5.2 The legal effect of covenants

Strictly speaking covenants are deeds but in this context the word means those promises the borrower makes as to his future behaviour and performance aside from the central obligations to repay. There is something of a blur however, between covenants and evergreen warranties. The extent of covenants will increase with the risk of the loan and mostly relate to a corporate borrower. They may seek to preserve the borrower's identity, eg prevent mergers and dissolution due to non-payment of taxes or to preserve equal ranking of the lender's claim, such as the negative pledge covenant and *pari passu* clause which are discussed below.

The most important covenant made by the borrower is, of course, the borrower's promise to repay the loan and this promise is reinforced by additional covenants many of which provide a monitoring or policing function.

5.3 Financial covenants

Financial covenants are frequently included in loan documentation and are designed to protect the lender's position should the borrower's credit-worthiness be deemed to deteriorate. Such covenants that often take the form of ratios require a flow of financial information from the borrower to the lender that enable the lender to monitor the borrower's financial health. Such covenants are given 'teeth' by linking them to an event of default clause in the event that the covenant is breached.

In relation to financial covenants it is necessary to require that the borrowing entity maintains a specified level of financial performance to ensure that it will be able to meet its payments of interest and repayments of principal as and when they fall due. The minimum levels incorporated into financial covenants represent the levels at which the borrower should have no difficulty in meeting its payment and repayment obligations. They will also function as an early warning device to the lending banks.

Financial information covenants will also provide the lending banks with an ability to monitor the borrower's compliance with the financial ratio covenants and will hopefully ensure a maximum level of disclosure of financial information which will enable the lending bank not only to determine compliance but also generally monitor the borrower's financial and business position.

5.4 Examples of financial covenants

The financial covenants will include financial ratios such as debt-equity ratios, a net worth minimum, a current ratio (the ratio of current assets to current liabilities), a working capital minimum (current assets less current liabilities), a ratio of interest payable to net profits, and a restriction of dividends and other distributions. There may also be restrictions on borrowings and the incurring of contingent liabilities and various financial ratios.

5.5 Other covenants

(i) **Contra-disposal clause** This is a clause where the borrower undertakes not to sell a material portion of its assets without seeking the consent of the bank. The problem is in defining material and it is usual to have a threshold – 20%, to avoid working capital disposals. The clause could however be absolute. Disposal for value is key but bank could have power to ratify all disposals. Disposals could be used for reduction/settlement of loan and in some loan documentation this may well be mandatory. In short there is therefore the dilemma of having flexibility as against the problem of materiality. The covenant will hopefully control the substantial disposal of revenue generating assets and may also consist of controls on the amount of dividends that may be distributed. A clause prohibiting or restricting the distribution of profits if ratios are breached. It is a clause that is strenuously resisted by corporates. Companies may try to maintain dividends but some banks could disagree.

(ii) **Anti-merger covenants** will attempt to maintain the identity of the borrower and may include specific reference to key personnel on the board of the borrower who are deemed critical to the financial well being of the borrower.

(iii) **Asset quality covenants** which include obligations to repair and insure, restrictions on the leasing of assets, on the making of investments in and loans to third parties, and on capital expenditure and various financial tests.

(iv) **Preservation of business covenants** which include restrictions on substantial changes in business and restrictions on substantial acquisitions of companies or businesses. It is possible to impose restrictions on what a company can do by reference to its constitutional documents (ie its memorandum and articles of association).

(v) **Excessive growth covenants** in this area include restrictions on mergers and the making of investments, limits on borrowings and capital expenditures and restrictions on substantial changes of business.

(vi) **Monitoring covenants** that include an obligation to provide financial information and accounts together with certificates as to compliance with the loan agreement and the absence of any events of default.

(vii) **Identity of borrower covenants** that will include restrictions on amalgamations, undertakings to pay various corporate taxes, various obligations to maintain corporate status in good standing and to renew corporate charters where necessary.

There is the general difficulty in monitoring any of the above-mentioned covenants and also the need to link such covenants with the events of default clause for the purpose of enforcement/acceleration of the loan.

6 The material adverse change clause

An alternative to ratio covenants is a continuing material adverse change clause that typically provides that it shall be an event of default if there is any material adverse change in the financial condition of the borrower that the lender reasonably determines may impair the ability of the borrower to perform its obligations. Such a clause is obviously much less precise in its application and will not provide a monitoring function in the same manner as that provided by financial covenants that require a regular flow of financial information to be given to the lending bank.

7 The negative pledge

The negative pledge is a fundamental covenant and is an attempt, in the context of an unsecured loan, to prevent the borrower from creating security in favour of third-party creditors that, if created, would prejudice the position of the unsecured lending bank.

The negative pledge covenant is designed to prevent the borrower from subordinating the unsecured lender's position by granting security to other creditors. The secured lender may wish to remain in a superior position. A useful by-product may be the restricting of ill-advised borrowing when the borrower's financial position deteriorates. It is not a security as it does not give an unsecured lender any priority or any special rights in a liquidation nor is it even foolproof in its operation. It is less appropriate, but not entirely so, in the case of sovereign loans.

The negative pledge clause has been held not to be anti-competitive and not contrary to Articles 81 and 82 of the Treaty of Rome in the case of *Oakdale (Richmond) Ltd v National Westminster Bank* (1997). The court of appeal held that a debenture is necessary to protect the commercial interests of banks and that funds would not be available if banks were not able to have such clauses inserted into their loan agreements. Therefore European Union law does not impose any limitations upon the negative pledge clause. Also the fact that as a corporate loan is made between two commercial organizations, the Unfair Contract Terms in the Consumer Contracts Regulations 1994 do not apply since one of the parties must be a 'consumer'.

The clause should be drafted carefully to include all the known types of charge, regarding mortgages, assignments, pledges, liens and hypothecations, adding 'any other security interest, encumbrance or arrangement having the effect of security'. The prohibition may be extended to security given by subsidiaries, to prevent the subsidiary guaranteeing the parent's unsecured debt and down-streaming assets to the subsidiary which then gives a secured loan. It is more difficult to prohibit the various title financing schemes such as title retention, hire purchase, leasing, sale and repurchase, sale and leaseback (where the 'lender' retains or acquires title to an asset), because the borrower should be allowed the freedom to act in a normal commercial manner. Even a prohibition on granting security may be over-restrictive and therefore certain relaxations may be expressed:

(a) the borrower may be allowed to give security if the lender receives equivalent security;

(b) some security interests may be freed, eg charges on after-acquired property mortgaged on purchase, substitutions, liens arising by operation of law;

(c) a general exemption of charges granted to different types of creditor than the lender may be conceded, or a 'basket' exemption calculated on a percentage of net worth.

7.1 Alternative forms of the negative pledge

The negative pledge may be drafted in such a way as to create either:

(i) equivalent security namely a clause granting security equal/identical to that granted in favour of a third party creditor; or

(ii) an automatic security clause which attempts to create in favour of the bank an automatic security interest in the event that the negative pledge clause is breached.

There is the problem of the automatic security negative pledge clause under English law and, in particular, whether such a clause in order to be effective would require registration under the terms of section 395 of the Companies Act 1985.

Thus such a provision is of doubtful effect in English law as it would be fraught with potential barriers such as being void for want of registration (although agreements to charge are not registerable under section 396 of the Companies Act 1985, or being void as a fraudulent preference under the rules in section 617, or priority may be lost, eg in a charge over land. However, specific performance of an agreement to create a charge is available at the court's discretion, and automatically if over land (*Hoermann v Hodges* (1983)).

Courts in the USA have been more accommodating to the lender, in *Commercial Co v New York NH and HRR* (1919) a bond issuer in breach could not create a valid mortgage and in *Kaplan v Chase National Bank* (1934), the lenders were granted a rateable charge.

7.2 Tortious liability of third parties

A third party who accepts a charge from the borrower knowing it is in breach of the covenant may, under English law, be liable in damages for the tort of procuring a breach of contract but the charge would be unaffected. Again, US courts have protected the initial lender by rendering the new charge subject to an equitable lien in favour of the lender: *Coast Bank v Minterhout* (1964).

Whether this works in practice depends on the registration provisions and would depend to a large extent on the precise wording of the negative pledge and the manner in which it was breached. According to Ross Cranston in *Principles of Banking Law,* the better view in England is that registration of the floating charge with its negative pledge does not constitute notice to the later chargee as in the case of *AIB Finance Ltd v Bank of Scotland* (1994).

7.3 Tortious liability in constructive trust

The concept of a constructive trust arise where a third party knew or should have known of the existence of a negative pledge that covered the assets now being taken as security. If a third party has (actual or constructive notice) of the assets caught by the negative pledge he may be liable for a breach of trust if it could be shown that he should have known of the breach.

7.4 The pari passu clause

The *pari passu* clause will simply be an undertaking by the borrower that its obligations to the lender rank equally with his other present and future obligations. Naturally he must be allowed an exemption for preferential claims, eg employees' remuneration and taxes.

8 General problems of covenants

There is the general difficulty in monitoring any of the above-mentioned covenants and also the need to link such covenants with the events of default clause for the purpose of enforcement/acceleration of the loan.

There is the problem of defining ratios and parameters for example in the definition of borrowings as to whether it should exclude short-term debt or include items such as leasing. There is also the problem in the case of financial ratios in that accounting practice differs in various countries.

One also needs to consider circumstances in which the above mentioned covenants may be restrictively drafted and may thereby impose unnecessary restrictions on the borrower's business which would have the effect of triggering a breach under the covenants on regular occasions. Although some banks may deem such restrictive covenants to be desirable in order that they are able to control the acceleration device at a moment's notice it may be undesirable in reality since the covenants would not fulfil one of their intended purposes as outlined above. However, covenants which are loosely drafted may fail to provide the early warning signs which are so often sought by the lending bank and may mean that when a loan is ultimately accelerated the borrower has either already gone into insolvent liquidation or alternatively all of its valuable assets have been secured in favour of third parties.

Consequently, there is a fine dividing line between appropriately drafted covenants which give the necessary degree of control to the lending banks on the one hand but do not unduly restrict the nature of the borrower's business on the other. The bank will want to be in a position to act where there is time to rescue a situation.

9 Miscellaneous clauses

The following clauses are designed to protect the bank against ways in which a lending banks' margin might be eroded.

9.1 Market disaster clause

A market disaster can occur from the inability by the bank to fund in the appropriate currency and the inability by lending banks from obtaining relevant quotations upon which a calculation of interest can be made. Such a disaster could apply to the reference banks who are identified in the documentation as the givers of relevant quotations or in respect of the screen facility from which the rates are obtained. The alternate interest rate setting mechanism is usually done by reference to the identification of reference banks, alternative screen facilities and finally by the calculation by the lender of the appropriate rate that should be applicable upon some mathematical formula that can be incorporated within the terms of the interest rate setting clause.

9.2 Increased costs

This is a clause which protects against increased costs, a protection against erosion of the bank's return.These could include central bank reserve requirements, special taxes, capital adequacy rules the capital adequacy requirements of the Basle Convergence Agreement and the EC Own Funds Directive.

Such liquidity requirements may impost costs on the bank which are attributable to the loan but which are not reflected in the cost of funding deposits.

The typical increased costs clause that will take into account, in particular, any increase in the underlying cost of funds that will have the effect of eroding the lending banks' margin. There is the difficulty in calculating the capital cost of a transaction and therefore any increase thereto. One must also consider reserve requests and liquidity costs and the recent changes in relation to capital adequacy requirements that are discussed in detail later in this book. Finally, there is also the practical difficulty of allocating certain costs to particular loans and the commercial acceptability of passing on some costs, eg cost of increases in the lending bank's equity base because of capital adequacy rates and therefore the difficulty of enforcing such a clause.

9.3 Illegality clause

This is a clause to protect the bank against the situation in which the lending becomes illegal, such as in the case of trading with the enemy or where there are freezing or blocking orders in force.

9.4 Currency indemnity

There is the fact that in some jurisdictions judgments for foreign currency debts are converted into local currency and this may lead to a loss for the lending bank in the event that the local currency depreciates.

9.5 Default indemnity

This clause covers the need for the borrower to cover losses (including breakage costs) resulting from the occurrence of any event of default or acceleration of the underlying facility. The clause may also be necessary for the following scenarios:

(a) by the application of exchange control restrictions which may limit or prevent entirely the payment by the borrower to the bank of its margin and potentially other amounts;

(b) by legal impediment which limits, for example, the application of certain rates of interest to a facility in a default situation. In England there is some concern that default interest clauses might be construed as penalties that would not be enforceable.

9.6 Withholding taxes

Withholding taxes are taxes levied at source on the payer on interest. The borrower deducts tax and accounts to his taxing authority. They serve as a tax collection device and are particularly effective in collecting from non-resident recipients. A lender will normally throw the burden of the tax onto the borrower, making the loan more expensive for him.

The lender will wish to include a tax indemnity or grossing-up clause in the documentation whereby the borrower agrees to make payments free of tax deductions unless he is compelled to deduct tax. In which case, he agrees to indemnify the lender in respect of the deductions and he further agrees that he will pay the due taxes before penalties become payable and on his own account.

The mere agreement to make payments free of deductions may not be effective if the borrower's law is the proper law, so an additional indemnity obliges the borrower to separately indemnify the lender if he does not receive the full amount.

The alternative grossing-up clause obliges the borrower to increase payments to the lender so that, after deduction of tax, the lender receives the agreed amount. The difference between the indemnity and grossing-up clauses is that in the former the borrower pays on his own account, whereas in the latter he pays more interest to the lender who has his tax liability discharged for him by the borrower. The indemnity is preferred as the grossing-up can lead to a deemed higher level of income receivable by the lender and a consequent tax downside in calculating his domestic liability when tax credits are applied.

10 Force majeure

There is, at the time of writing (2003), a trend to include some sort of force majeure clause that was previously only included in project finance agreements as a rule. A force majeure clause will be incorporated into an agreement to deal with the situation in which parties to an agreement consider performance of their obligations, is through no fault of any party, no longer possible. A 'force majeure' clause attempts to define those circumstances. Previously these were considered to be natural disasters and war but now it is terrorism that is the concern. A force majeure clause might provide that the obligations under the contract be suspended until the circumstances have passed, or that the contract be immediately terminated. In either case, however, there will not usually be sanctions on either party since, by definition, there is no blame. Previously loan agreements other than project finance had avoided the use of force majeure clauses preferring instead to rely on the increased costs, illegality and material adverse change clauses. The current view of global terrorism is now starting to change this mindset.

Seven

Syndicated facilities

1 Definition

A syndicated facility is one that is provided to a single borrower by a group of lenders. It enables very large sums to be accessed, which would otherwise not be possible through a sole lender.

2 General facilities

2.1 Introduction

The syndicated loan market has seen a deal of recent activity as corporates seek the flexibility to gain access to very large amounts – often to satisfy quickly medium- to long-term committed requirements.

2.2 Example of use

There are a number of typical uses of syndicated loans (see the sub-subsections headed 'Amount' and 'Purpose', below). In the main, though, a syndicated loan will be used where the amount required is too large for one bank to provide and where other markets are unsuitable – usually, owing to the need to arrange funds speedily. Also, compared with other means of raising finance, syndicated loans are flexible as to maturity and, to a degree, currency availability. Syndicated finance features very strongly in project finance, where the syndication has two key benefits:

- it provides access to the large sums required;
- it spreads the risks between a group of lenders, rather than be concentrated on one.

2.3 Purpose

The purpose is to provide medium- to long-term finance on a committed basis to cater for a range of needs as follows.

- Bridging finance, pending clearance/rearrangement from another source.
- Large capital expenditure transactions.
- High-value acquisitions.
- High-value permanent, medium- to long-term committed working capital needs.

Syndicated facilities may be used to cover a range of maturities, including short-term needs, up to financing of long-term projects – say, to 20 years, subject to availability of funds. Most lenders are, certainly, happy with terms of 10–15 years.

2.4 The parties to a syndicated loan

The parties involved in an agreement will be the borrower/s, the managing bank/s, the agent's bank/s and the participants. The borrower and manager, who prepares the information package, face possible liability as publishers of material intended to attract investment finance under fraud control legislation and liability to the participants for misleading them. An offer letter is drafted by prospective lead managers to the borrower bidding for the award of the mandate, ie to be selected to lead-manage the deal.

The borrower typically appoints a managing bank (and sometimes co-managers under a 'lead manager') to whom he grants a mandate setting out the financial terms of the proposed loan and authorizing the manager to arrange syndication. The manager prepares an information package on the borrower and the loan that is sent to potential participants. The manager negotiates more precise terms and makes a separate (and several) loan up to his commitment but each loan is on the same terms. Once the loans have been advanced an agent bank is appointed from among the participants (possibly the manager) to organize payments and act as administrator.

2.5 Responsibilities of the lead manager

There are some key parties involved with the focal role assumed by the lead manager. We shall look at the sequence of events a little later but, at this stage, we shall take a look at the responsibilities of the lead manager.

- He acts as the intermediary between the 'lenders' and the borrower.
- He coordinates all matters regarding arranging syndication.
- He leads negotiations with all parties, including on documentation aspects, which can be complex.
- He prepares the information memorandum.
- When all aspects have been finalized, the lead manage arranges the signing ceremony, press release and publication of the 'tombstone'.

In very large deals, there may be more than one lead manager. It is quite common for a number of major relationship banks to assume the role of co-managers, which assist the lead manager in his responsibilities. The lead manager(s) and co-managers will underwrite a portion of the required loan with the balance being provided by other syndicate members (also known as 'participants'). Once the loan has been established, day-to-day matters will be coordinated through a nominated agent bank.

2.6 Sequence of events

Although deals can take varying forms, the following is a typical outline of events leading to draw-down.

- The borrower identifies its needs and advises its relationship banks and, possibly, others, with a view to them bidding for lead manager status.
- Offers are submitted to the borrower, who then selects lead and co-managers.
- The information memorandum is prepared and circulated to nominated prospective syndicate members, ie with a view to their taking a slice of the finance required.
- Involvement of legal advisers in drawing up the loan agreement.
- Receipt of offers from invited syndicate members and selection by the lead manager; formation of the entire syndicate.
- Completion of formalities; execution of the loan agreement at the signing ceremony.
- Publicity and publication of 'tombstone' announcement.
- Draw-down, in accordance with terms stated in the loan agreement.

3 The information memorandum

- ♦ An information memorandum is prepared by the lead manager(s), outlining details of the borrower and the required loan. This is a 'marketing' document to enable the lead manager to attract interest from prospective syndicate members. Typical contents of the information memorandum include:
  - amount, term, purpose of the borrowing
  - borrower's financial statements (balance sheet and profit and loss account)
  - the borrower's current financial position and plans (cash-flow forecast)
  - significant and relevant contracts
  - capital and expenditure forecasts
  - internal management details
  - analysis of competitors
  - country risk exposure analysis

3.1 Prospectus legislation

Prospectus legislation may require the published material to provide information on specified matters and to be registered with a supervisory body such as the UK Listing Authority, which is part of the Financial Services Authority – breach of either gives rise to criminal-type sanctions and it may provide automatic civil liability to investors for any breach. All securities that are listed on the London Stock Exchange are governed by The Listing Rules under Part VI of the Financial Services and Markets Act 2000. The body responsible for The Listing Rules is the UK Listing Authority.

It may be that the legislation will not apply in the case of invitations to 'sophisticated investors'. In England, the Companies Act 1985 applies prospectus rules only when there is an offer 'to the public', defined to include any 'section of the public' but to exclude any offer that is not calculated to reach persons other than the initial recipients (sections 56–60). The rules do not apply if the information is distributed abroad to foreign companies nor if distributed to certain professional dealers in securities. A private company is prohibited under section 81 of the Companies Act 1985 form issuing a prospectus to the public subject to certain exceptions.

In the USA, the strict provisions of Securities Act 1933 and the Securities Exchange Act 1934 have been restrictively interpreted to exempt invitations to banks for commercial loans (as opposed to investments).

4 Lead manager problems

The lead manager has problems of:

(1) confidential information from borrower which it is privy to him;

(2) conflicts of interest re different parts of a bank possess different information on borrower;

(3) events arising after information memo is circulated and non-disclosure would amount to fraudulent misrepresentation.

If the information package contains a misrepresentation about the borrower or the loan this may give rise to criminal liability for breach of prospectus legislation and civil liability connected to that breach or on general principles. Civil liability is based on misrepresentation by a party to a contract and on negligent misrepresentation. Misrepresentation involves a wrong statement.

5 Legal liability of the lead manager

Potential liability under the prospectus is as follows:

(i) Fraudulent misrepresentation

(ii) Negligent misrepresentation.

5.1 Fraudulent misrepresentation

This is where liability is based on the common law of tort relating to fraudulent misrepresentation laid down in the case of *Derry v Peek* (1889) 14 APP Case 337. Misrepresentation may take the form of a false statement of intention, eg of what to use the proceeds of the loan for; unrealistic forecasts of results which are implicitly held out to be reliable, *Esso Petroleum Co v Mardon* (1976) CA. Assumptions should be stated but these too must be reasonable; statements of opinion dressed up as statements of fact and the opinion must not be contradicted by facts known to the maker; legal opinions on foreign law are statements of fact, *Andre et Cie SA v Ets Michel Blanc et Fils* (1977) CA – although domestic legal opinions are not. A statement about the existence of exchange controls would undoubtedly amount to one of fact; an inaccurate summation of the security of financial documents; omissions to correct misleading impressions created by other true statements or another's false statements, *Gluckstein v Barns* (1906) HL; failing to correct a true statement which becomes false before the contract is signed. Merely stating that lenders have access to documents or should rely on their own credit evaluation will not remove the borrower's liability, *Redgrave v Hurd* (1881). The lender does not have to prove he would not have lent if he had known the true facts but he has no claim if he would have lent in knowledge of them.

In *Smith New Court Securities Ltd v Scrimgeour Vickers (Asset Management) Ltd* (1996) involved a seller of shares who 'invented' two fictitious buyers in order to encourage the real buyer to purchase certain shares[1]. The facts of this case could be transposed into that of a syndicate loan if the lead manger made any fraudulent statements with a view to induce other banks to participate in a syndicated loan. Where a bank participates in a syndicated loan on the basis of any false information or omitted material information a lead manger can be held liable for fraudulent information.

5.2 Negligent misrepresentation

More likely than fraudulent misrepresentation is the liability for statements/representations made and whether such information was relied upon by syndicate members when they joined the syndicate.

Negligent misrepresentation is a tortious liability arising not from any contract but from a special relationship that may exist between the statement maker and the recipient, whereby the former has a special skill and should know the latter is relying on it. Thus a bank's answer to a status enquiry was in principle actionable in *Hedley Byrne v Heller* [1964] AC 465. This leads to a right of action for damages only – not for rescission.

If the lender establishes the borrower's liability for misrepresentation he has a right to rescind the contract and, probably, damages. The loan documentation itself will provide for the right to accelerate the loan in the event of default of financial covenants. If the borrower is insolvent any rights against him will have been exhausted without fully satisfying the lender and the question of the manager's liability will arise.

In order to be liable for misrepresentation, the manager must be a party to the loan contract that he may be as a lender or as manager/agent. Where the manager is merely the agent of the borrower, he can only be liable under a collateral contract with the lender. The Statue of Frauds Amendments Act 1828 exempts the maker of a credit reference from liability unless it is in writing and signed, in the case of a company by a duly authorized officer. This applies to fraudulent and to negligent misrepresentation under the Misrepresentation Act 1967 where damages are being claimed. Where liability for negligent misrepresentation in tort is claimed the manager will have no special defences. There is however no liability where a bank simply passes on information, as was held in the case of *Royal Bank of Trinidad v Pampalonne* (1987).

Potential liability for misrepresentation in respect of such documents would include liability under section 2(1) of the Misrepresentation Act 1967 that is fundamentally based in negligence. Secondly liability for inaccuracies could also be based in the common law of negligence on the principles laid down in *Hedley Byrne v Heller* [1964] AC 465 and restated by the House of Lords in *Caparo Industries plc v Dickman* [1990] 2 AC 605. The liability of the lead manager to negligent misrepresentation will be even greater in the event of one of the participants being inexperienced. *Hedley Byrne v Heller & Partners Ltd* (1963) provided that where a special relationship exists between the relevant parties the liability is significantly higher. The relationship envisaged by the case was one where one party is much more experienced than the other. A lead manager is therefore also under greater examination where syndicate members are inexperienced and greater reliance placed on the agent's skill. This of course will depend upon the complexity of the transaction and the availability of information to the syndicate. If a syndicate bank has actually relied on the misrepresentation the ultimate loss may actually be caused by the misstatements contained within the information memorandum.

Two relevant cases have arisen on each side of the Atlantic concerning the insolvent Colocotronis group. In the USA, *Re Colocotronis Tanker Sec Litigation* (1976) was settled after a claim by American regional bank participants against the manager alleging that untrue and incomplete representation induced them into joining the syndicate. In England, *UBAF Ltd v European Banking Corpn* (1984) CA concerned a claim by an English bank against the New York bank defendant who invited the plaintiff to participate in two loans to two Panamanian ship-owning corporations and who by letter enclosed 'term' sheets on the loans, a study of the Colocotronis group prepared by the defendants and a valuation of the ships. The defendants described the proposition as 'attractive financing of two companies in a sound and profitable group'. In reference to the issue of the defendant's liability for negligent misrepresentation, the court spoke of the defendant acting in a 'fiduciary capacity' for all the other participants because it received the loan advances and arranged for and held on their behalf the security (ship mortgages and assignments of charter contracts). This fiduciary duty included informing the participants if the security became inadequate and would seem to extend (backwards in time) to not misleading them in the information package.

In a recent case, *Sumitomo Bank Ltd v Banque Bruxelles Lambert SA* (1997), the lead bank was expected to ensure that the borrower who was a commercial buyer of security had given sufficient security in favour of the syndicate of lending banks. The lead bank Banque Bruxelles Lambert was held to be negligent to the syndicate of banks because inadequate security had been taken notwithstanding any provisions or statements contained in the information memorandum.

A case that illustrates the issue of negligence is *Nat West Australian Bank Ltd v Tricontinental Corpn Ltd* (1993). The managing bank, Tricontinental, had entered into separate guarantees with the borrower but had failed to tell the other syndicate banks about these. This was the position even though Tricontinental had been specifically asked particular questions by Nat West Australian Bank Ltd, which was a syndicate member, about the existence of such guarantees. Tricontinental was successfully sued for negligence by NatWest Australian Bank Ltd[2].

6 Exculpation clauses

A lead manager will typically wish not to be underwriting the borrower and therefore would not expect to be held liable except perhaps for fraud. The manager will therefore seek to exclude liability by inserting exculpation clauses into the information package. Exculpation clauses are escape or get-out clauses which a lead manager may seek to rely upon to exclude his potential liability. Such clauses are as follows:

(a) the manager has not verified the information and makes no warranty as to its accuracy. Summaries of documents are not to be relied upon;

(b) the manager does not undertake to review the borrower's position nor to pass on any information it receives;

(c) the manager is not providing a credit reference nor 'recommending' the borrower, each participant must make its own assessment;

(d) the information is confidential and should not be revealed to others.

In the actual loan documentation, each participant will warrant that it has made its own assessment and has not relied on information exclusively provided by the manager or agent bank. Further warranties may oblige each participant to monitor the borrower's financial position and may exempt the manager/agent from providing further information.

In any exculpation clause, in order for it to be valid and effective, the exclusion clause will have to comply with the Unfair Contract Terms Act 1977 and will have to be fair and reasonable. Any exclusion of liability for misrepresentation will be ineffective in the case of fraud and also in the case of negligence unless it can be shown to be 'reasonable', Misrepresentation Act 1967, section 3 and the Unfair Contract Terms Act 1977. The main criterion for reasonableness is the balance of bargaining power between the parties. The manager may also obtain an indemnity from the borrower to cover any liability to the participants; such a protection clearly has its limitations.

In addition, the exclusion clause is in wide form, excluding liability for all statements made, which is a standard type of clause that banks use. If clear language is used, the courts will give effect to it. In *Armitage v Nurse* (1997) CA, Millett LJ, as he then was, gave a ruling on a clause that excluded the liability of trustees save for deliberate acts. This exclusion clause had been taken from a book of precedents. In the judge's opinion, this showed that there was a clear intention to exclude liability and the court would give effect to it. However, the case involved trustees and is not a precedent on the scope of the Unfair Contract Terms Act 1977. The fundamental point is that having established the test of reasonableness, it must then be applied to the particular problem or facts given[3].

Much will depend on the facts of a given case as to whether an exclusion clause is held to valid and effective. Both the liability for negligence and liability for misrepresentation can be excluded only if such a clause satisfies the test of reasonableness under the Unfair Contract Terms Act 1977. In particular the following factors will be relevant in determining the issue as to whether the exclusion clause is both fair and reasonable.

- The length of the relationship between the managing bank and the borrower.
- The knowledge of the managing bank about the borrower.
- The knowledge and relative knowledge of the other syndicate banks about the borrower.
- The relative sophistication of the other syndicate banks, their bargaining strength, with damages being greater if the participants are inexperienced.
- The inquiries and investigations carried out by the managing bank about the business and the proposals by the borrower.
- The extent to which it is possible for the managing bank to effectively make inquiries and investigations about the business and proposals of the borrower.
- Whether the information contained in the information memorandum is supplied only by the borrower.
- Liability cannot be excluded for fraudulent misrepresentation[4].

7 Due diligence

Exculpatory clauses should not be relied on and a manager should exercise appropriate due diligence. Due diligence means that the manager will do his own analysis of the proposition and any projections or information that is supplied by the borrower. Of particular importance will be:

(1) the relative sophistication of the banks involved;

(2) access to independent information;

(3) standard of care expected of the lead manager.

Also distinction between corporate (particularly project finance) and sovereign borrowers where information is readily available.

The greatest danger will concern opinions or future projections. These should wherever possible be avoided or if included they should be substantiated. Project loans often have a large number of such projections, in which case they should be prepared by experts and the lead manager should state this.

Furthermore there will be a clause that all participants will have carried out their own investigations and due diligence and have not solely relied on the contents of the information memorandum. As banks are commercial organizations and are able to carry out their own researches, there is no need for reliance on their part upon any statement made in the information memorandum. This is the reason why such a clause could be held to be reasonable as in the case of *Smith v Eric S Bush* (1990).

8 The role and responsibilities of the agent bank

The principal role includes the following.

(i) Paying agency duties to receive centrally the proceeds of advances made by the banks and distribute them to the borrower and to receive payments of principal and interest from the borrower and distribute to the syndicate pro rata.

(ii) Satisfaction of conditions precedent in relation to the underlying loan documentation.

(iii) Receipt of notices and generally to act as a representative of the syndicate for the receipt of notices from the borrower, the selection of interest periods, prepayments and the like and to notify the syndicate banks accordingly.

(iv) General banking duties including, for example, determination of the interest rates on the basis of quotations of reference banks and to certify the rate to the borrower and the syndicate banks.

(v) Monitoring duties particularly with regard to financial and other information received from the borrower under the loan and the power to call for compliance certificates and other information in order to monitor progress pursuant to the covenants contained in the agreement.

(vi) General default duties which may be to generally inform the banks of actual or impending events of default of which the agent becomes aware.

(vii) Power to accelerate the loan on the occurrence of the event of default which may include a duty to do so either generally or if so instructed by a specified proportion of the banks.

9 The relationship between the agent bank and the members

The agent bank is usually paid by the borrower yet is the agent of the members. Payments in both directions will typically be routed through the agent and he will also perform administrative functions. The documentation will usually seek to limit the agent's liability to the borrower and members and to limit the agent's right to make important decisions for the syndicate. Many member banks were vexed by American and Japanese agent banks' decisions on events of default during the Iran hostage crisis.

Agent banks are subject to general principles of agency law but most of these principles will yield to express provisions in the contract, thus many matters are clearly set out in the documentation.

An agent would normally have as his principal he who pays him, thus the documentation will expressly make him the agent of the members. As such the agent will not be liable to the borrower if a member fails to advance his share, *Paquin Ltd v Beauclerk* (1906) HL. This may be expressed. An agent may be liable to the borrower for breach of warranty of authority, *Collen v Wright* (1857). To counteract this, the agent's powers and duties may be (exclusively) set out in the loan documentation and the borrower therefore has notice of them. This will equally reduce the possibility of the member being liable to the borrower on the basis of the agent's unauthorized acts under the ostensible authority rule.

The agent's duties will include channelling of payments, examination of documents provided to satisfy conditions precedent, perfecting securities, processing notice communications, determining interest rates in floating-rate loans, forwarding financial information to be used for monitoring the borrower's performance, informing members of events of default, serving notices to cure, granting waivers and consents, accelerating, suing. The latter duties will be subject to strict control by the members, perhaps under their majority vote. Legal action is often an individual right of each member.

If an ambiguity arises in the agent's powers it is his duty to seek clarification, *Woodhouse AC Israel Cocoa Ltd SA v Nigerian Produce Marketing Co Ltd* (1972) HL. Under general principles an agent may expand his powers to include matters incidental to his main duties – *Pole v Leask* (1860), matters usually included in that type of agent's powers – *Hely-Hutchinson v Brayhead Ltd* (1968) CA or even matters arising by necessity – *Springer v GR Co* (1921).

The members may be liable to the borrower if they have led him to believe the agent had authority but not if he should have raised enquiries, *AL Underwood v Bank of Liverpool* (1924) CA.

10 Duties of the agent bank

The distinction between lead manager and agent is often blurred. Obligations of agent come into operation after those of the lead manager have ceased. The agent's obligations should be clearly stated in the hope of limiting any potential liability. The legal duties of an agent under the law of agency are as follows, of which any breach of can give rise to the agent being found guilty of negligence.

10.1 Duty to exercise reasonable care and skill

Under general principles an agent must obey his principal's instructions. An agent may be instructed to perform an act that is illegal in his own country but valid under the contract's proper law. A double jeopardy clause would allow the agent not to perform in these circumstances.

Generally, an agent is bound to exercise a reasonable degree of skill, care and diligence, based on what is necessary for performing his duties. Effectively an agent bank must match the standards of the average agent bank. Reasonable care and skill is also a statutory criterion under the Supply of Goods and Services Act 1982.

The agent will seek protection from liability in performing its specific duties. Thus when receiving 'condition precedent documents', the agent is expressly allowed to rely on legal opinions. When monitoring the borrower, the agent is obliged only to furnish copies of accounts received from the borrower to members and is not bound to provide any additional information nor to check the accuracy of what it does provide. Failure to notify members of an event of default could lead to substantial liability so the agent is not bound to notify unless it receives notice marked as such. Without this protection, difficulties may arise as to the agent's general duty to pass on any material information and the 'split-knowledge' problem where one branch or employee of the agent bank has information which in fact amounts to an event of default but that branch has no knowledge of the details of the loan or even that it exists.

Whether knowledge can be 'imputed' depends on the seniority of the recipient and the capacity in which he acts. In *Powles v Page* (1846) the knowledge of the bank's directors was not imputed to the bank as a whole when they were not concerned with the relevant transaction. The agent may acquire information about the borrower that he knows amounts to an event of default but which is subject to the banker's duty of confidentiality – a specific clause permitting non-disclosure in these circumstances would assist.

10.2 Duty to act personally

Generally an agent is barred from delegating but this rule is subject to exceptions, eg where it is authorized – *Palliser v Ord* (1724). A clause may permit delegation and exclude the agent's liability for the sub-agent's negligence. Of course the members will have no contractual remedy against the sub-agent.

10.3 No conflict of interest

The agent may have a conflict of interest due to being a lender, to having other private loans to the borrower or to being the agent to another syndicate. It is permissible only if the principal has full knowledge and consents – *Boulting v ACTAT* (1963) CA. A clause may allow the agent the same rights as if he were not the agent and the right to act as a banker in any capacity to the borrower.

10.4 Duty to make no secret profit

The rules on secret profits are strict. Thus if the agent takes a commission from the borrower or uses information acquired as agent for his own profit even if it does not harm the syndicate and involves a risk for the agent, he is liable to the members – *Boardman v Phipps* (1967) HL.

If an agent fails to pass on funds received from the lenders, they remain liable to the borrower. However, if he fails to pass on funds received from the borrower, the borrower is discharged. The members' claim then may be as unsecured creditors or as beneficiaries; the latter position will permit tracing except from a bona fide purchaser for value without notice and will bypass creditors' claims in an insolvency.

10.5 Clawback clauses

The agent may transfer funds to the payee before the transfer to him is cleared. A 'claw-back' clause or right to delay payment clause may be included. Without the express right to claw-back, the agent could rely only on the principles in *Barclays Bank Ltd v WJ Simms Son and Cooke (Southern) Ltd* (1980) – payment under a mistake of fact is recoverable if the payer did not intend at the time to pay in any event and payment is not made for good consideration, eg discharging a debt, and the payee has not changed his position in good faith. In *Chase Manhattan Bank NA v Israel-British Bank (London) Ltd* (1981) a bank that mistakenly paid twice over could trace from an insolvent payee who knew of the mistake.

The members have contractual rights against the agent for any breaches of contract in damages and dismissal. They also have rights of tort under the 'fiduciary' duty described in *UBAF Ltd v European American Banking Corpn* (1983) CA.

11 Exculpatory clauses

The agent bank will ensure that appropriate exculpatory clauses are incorporated within agreements that seek to limit the scope of the duties and discretions of the agent bank so as to reduce the responsibilities that could give rise to liability.

(i) By providing that the agent bank should have only those powers and duties specified in the agreement and powers incidental thereto;

(ii) By providing general immunity to the agent and its officers it will not be responsible for any default: An agent generally has a right of indemnity against losses incurred in proper performance of his duties but an express clause is often included, making each member contribute pro rata to its commitment. The express indemnity may extend to losses caused by the agent's negligence.

(iii) By incorporating specific immunities which state that the agent bank will not be responsible for any inadequacy in the contractual documents which may have been negotiated and that the agent may rely without enquiry or notice on all communications and will not be deemed to have knowledge of an event of default unless specifically notified of that fact.

The statutory limitations and exclusion clauses as contained in section 2 of the Unfair Contract Terms Act 1977 and section 3 of the Misrepresentation Act provide that exclusion clauses must be reasonable. A specific clause may expressly exclude a fiduciary relationship. Exclusion of liability clauses will be effective against a claim for negligence, so long as that is clearly stated, but never against fraud. The Unfair Contract Terms Act 1977 requires such exclusion clauses to be 'reasonable' – related to equality of bargaining power – but section 27 removes this requirement in the case of contracts where English law has been chosen and were it not for that choice, a non-UK law would govern.

12 The relationship between syndicate members

If the members are regarded as a partnership under English law there will be joint liability for any individual partner's actions in the ordinary course of business, section 5 of the Partnership Act 1890, which is clearly not desirable in this situation. Because the members share gross, not net, returns they cannot be regarded as a partnership. There are separate, similar, contracts between each member and the borrower. The members will normally wish to be separately obliged to lend to and separately entitled to recover from the borrower. This is known as several rights and obligations and a clause will be inserted to ensure this to negate any implication of joint liability where, if one bank fails to lend, the others would be obliged to make this up or any one bank would be unable to take legal action against the borrower on its own. A US case where such a clause was not included was *Credit Francis International SA v Sociedad Financiez de Comerco* (1985) and the New York Supreme Court held the syndicate was a 'joint venture' which debarred the plaintiff member from taking an individual action against the defendant borrower because each member had implicitly surrendered its right to do so to the agent bank.

All syndicated loan agreements should state specifically that the obligations of each member of the syndicate to the borrower are several and not joint. This notion of several liability is normally clarified by clauses that state that the failure of any one bank to carry out its funding obligations shall not relieve any other bank of their obligations and that no bank shall be responsible for the obligations of any other bank is also very common.

The purpose of the above wording is to provide that in the event of one particular bank failing to make available its commitment under the syndicated loan no other bank shall be relieved of any of its obligations and in addition no other members of the syndicate will be required to make up the difference. In other words, the facility is not 'underwritten' by any of the other banks.

The 'several' nature of each bank's relationship with the borrower is not uniform throughout the agreement because there are certain clauses that seek to 'bind' the syndicate. The best example of such clauses are those that relate to the agent bank's authority to call an event of default on behalf of the syndicate at the agent bank's discretion.

'Syndicate democracy' is the term used to describe the process by which members may vote upon matters arising during the currency of the loan. Votes are proportionate to the degree of exposure. A majority may thereby impose a decision to waive a breach of covenant on a minority, for example, to accelerate after an event of default occurs or to extend a maturity. English law insists that any exercise of majority power must be based on express and unambiguous declarations in the documentation, *Mercantile Investment and General Trust Co v International Co of Mexico* (1891) CA. To the extent that a clause may provide for such majority rights, the syndicate ceases to be a series of purely several rights and a 'pro rata sharing clause' will go still further by stipulating that all members must be equally treated by the borrower and if any one should receive more than any other by voluntary preference of the borrower or the exercising of a right of set off over a credit balance in a current account in the borrower's name, the surplus must be shared out equally among all the members. A similar result will occur if one member holds direct security from the borrower or obtains judgment before his insolvency. Where one member has a sum available for set off or direct security that exceeds the value of the debt to him, the possibility of 'double-dipping' arises. The member concerned may purchase equal parts of the debts owing to other members up to the point where his security is exhausted. This may be done by assignment of part of the other members' loans or by redistribution of payments provided for in advance in the documentation. The main drawback of both 'double-dipping' schemes is they will probably fail under English law if the borrower's insolvency process begins before the assignments or redistribution's take place. Other legal systems may negate the schemes by formal requirements, for example by assignments in France. Other protective clauses may include a pro-rate sharing in reverse so that if a bank entitled to an extra payment by exercising set off later must return that payment (and after it has shared if among the syndicate), eg because under the *lex fori*'s set off rules it is not entitled or it has failed as a fraudulent preference, then that bank may claim back the sums distributed to the members with a contribution for interest due. It seems under English law a creditor is not obliged to exercise a right of set off but this could be expressed.

The agent bank may also be required to call default on the request of a majority of the syndicate banks. However, such binding clauses do not affect the right of each syndicate bank to enforce its right to interest and principal where this right is expressly preserved by a clause in the syndicated loan agreement.

13 The sharing and binding clause

A further clause to 'bind' participants is the sharing clause that requires that payments of interest and/or principal paid by a borrower should be shared rateably between all members of the syndicate. This is one of the more effective binding clauses in syndicate loans. The sharing clause relates to the sharing or redistribution of payments clause, which reinforces the fact that each lender should receive pro rata payments and the borrower should not be permitted to discriminate in making such payments.

The wording of this clause will be important in determining precisely what payments have to be shared. Some clauses include all payments, include those received by effecting set offs, whereas others are restricted to payments received directly from the borrower in repayment of the loan agreement.

Precise wording is very important to ensure it covers set off. This was aptly demonstrated in 1979 during the Iranian Hostage crisis whereby Chase Manhattan Bank had large deposits held on behalf of the Iranian government at the outbreak of the crisis and refused to apply such deposits under the sharing clause with other banks under the syndicated loan agreement. The sharing clause can be so drafted to prevent any lender elevating its position.

Again during the Falklands War in 1982 a number of French banks refused to pay monies received from Argentina on the grounds that the crisis was a force majeure thereby preventing the sharing clause from operating. This was rejected by British banks.

14 Problems in a default situation

There are difficulties that may be posed in the event of an emergency situation arising where it may be reasonable to expect the agent bank to act quickly without waiting to consult the syndicate banks in order to generally protect their position.

There is also the general obligation of an agent bank particularly in a default situation where information comes to its knowledge that may influence it in acting in a particular way. Banks also consider the desirability of establishing the agency function in a separate division of the bank outside of its general lending function and corporate finance departments, in order to ensure there is no conflict of interest. Notwithstanding the establishment of a separate department/division to fulfil the agency function there will nevertheless be potential liability in the event that the agent bank receives information or enters into other relationships that might be deemed to influence it or be taken into account in some way in the discharge of its obligations.

The conclusion is that the relationship between the syndicate members is an uneasy balance between independent and collective rights and obligations.

15 Loan Market Association (LMA)

The Loan Market Association was opened for membership in December 1996 with the objective of fostering liquidity in the euroloan markets. Specifically the LMA set out to facilitate the constructive development of a secondary market for loans. The Association was established as a response to market conditions and to a perceived willingness on the part of the banking community to bring greater clarity, efficiency and liquidity to the relatively underdeveloped secondary market that existed at the time and to enable more efficient loan portfolio management.

As the LMA has gained recognition in the market, it has expanded its activities to include all aspects of the primary and secondary syndicated loan markets. With membership currently standing at over 120 banks, law firms and other institutions, the mission of the Association is to act as the authoritative voice of the syndicated loan market in Europe vis-à-vis banks, borrowers, regulators and other affected parties.

London is the leading international centre for banking, and syndicated loans are a key product in that business. In order to make the market for lending more efficient, the key syndicated lending banks involved in the Loan Market Association began an initiative to provide more efficient lending documentation. While aspects of every deal may be different, for example with regard to financial covenants, more common documentation should reduce the operational costs of lending, with the benefits that brings.

Both the British Bankers' Association (BBA) and the Association of Corporate Treasurers (ACT) have been actively involved in providing comment and input to the LMA.

The recommended forms of syndicated facility agreements (the 'Primary Documents') have been developed by a working party consisting of representatives of the Loan Market Association, the British Bankers' Association, The Association of Corporate Treasurers and major city law firms. It is hoped that the existence of the Primary Documents will encourage a more harmonized approach to loan documentation, making for more efficient primary and secondary loan markets.

Through the involvement of the three associations in the working party, together with the law firms represented, the objective was to balance the interests of borrowers and lenders. In the Primary Documents, financial covenants and related definitions have been deliberately left blank.

When considering use of the Primary Documents it is recommended that borrowers and lenders should:

- consider the option of continuing to use existing documentation;
- carefully consider changes to the Primary Documents that may be required;
- always have the benefit of independent legal advice.

The three associations believe that the Primary Documents will provide a valuable aid to the development and efficiency of the syndicated loan market.'

Notes

1. Paragraphs reproduced from ***ifs*** Examiner's Report, October 1998 (Corporate Banking – Practice and Law).

2. Paragraphs reproduced from ***ifs*** Examiner's Report, April 2001 (Corporate Banking – Practice and Law).

3. Paragraphs reproduced from ***ifs*** Examiner's Report, October 1999 (Corporate Banking – Practice and Law).

4. Paragraphs reproduced from ***ifs*** Examiner's Report, April 2001 (Corporate Banking – Practice and Law).

Eight

Loan transfers and participations (secondary syndication)

1 Transferability

Transferability is the right, incorporated in the loan documentation, of a lender to transfer its rights and obligations to another lender. Banks or lenders may wish to sell their commitments in a loan agreement in whole or part to another bank. There are many reasons why a bank may wish to free up its balance sheet, which are discussed below. Normally transferability is achievable without the prior consent of the borrower but it is possible for the borrower's consent to be a pre-condition.

A borrower may not be happy about the bank selling the loan and may seek to restrict transferability in the loan documentation.

1.1 Reasons for banks selling loans

There are sound reasons and benefits to both the bank and the corporate for transferability, and these are as follows:

- impact of the capital adequacy ratios on banking, discussed in more detail above;
- to realise capital previously tied up in long-term loans;

- transferability is effectively a form or syndication. The originating bank uses its knowledge/expertise/relationship to originate the deal while delivering keen pricing to the customer;
- there should be no real effect on the relationship. Most transferee banks see this transaction as an investment and will not seek to establish a bilateral relationship;
- to control the risk if the portfolio has become imbalanced;
- there is absolutely no reflection on the borrower's credit standing. The prime bank (the original lender) will expect to retain a proportion of the deal on its book and therefore will maintain a commitment to the client;
- the prime bank will generally consult on the acceptability and suitability of a transferee bank;
- there is a likelihood of the development of a two-tier pricing structure. If the customer insists on having exclusive access to the bank's balance sheet, then he may have to pay a premium compared with the more competitive pricing a transferable loan will command.

1.2 Advantages to the borrower

Thus a clear argument can be made to the borrower for accepting the transferability clause such as:

- it enables the bank to undertake larger transactions if it has the right to sell down a proportion of its exposure;
- indeed it will be possible to underwrite the smaller transactions in total;
- because of the wider distribution base, pricing will be more competitive;
- selling down existing or new exposure allows space for further deals in the future;
- transferability exposes the borrower's name to a wider range of banks.

2 Methods of transferability

2.1 Novation

Novation is the arrangement pursuant to which mutual rights and obligations of the selling bank are relinquished and discharged, in consideration of the establishment of new rights and obligations, on identical terms, between the buying bank and the other parties to the underlying loan agreement. Also, novation gives rise to an entirely new contract and is essentially a contract of substitution for the old loan. Novation can thus be described as a transfer of rights benefits and obligations, and as such, no stamp duty is payable.

Since the novation operates as a contract of substitution there is the effect that a novation has on existing security interests namely that they will be discharged unless an appropriate transfer mechanism has been built into the original facility, other possible consequences may be loss of priority and recommencement of limitation time periods such as preferences and transactions at an undervalue.

When applying such principles to loan agreements it is possible for the loan agreement to be expressed in such a way that delivery to the agent bank of some form of certificate (a transfer certificate) together with the payment by the novatee of an appropriate sum to the selling bank could give rise to a novation. If the certificates are for less than the total value of the loan (say 10%) this can lead to syndication 'through the back door'.

There is also, possibly, the need for the borrower's consent to be obtained, as discussed in section 1 above, to any such transfer mechanism and also the need, in the case of a syndicated facility, to enjoin all the original parties to the syndicated loan in the transfer agreement.

Insofar as the actual techniques are concerned, as has already been indicated, the cleanest form of transfer would be the novation and it is of course possible to incorporate a transfer mechanism within the body of the original facility pursuant to which all of the parties agree that portions of the facility can be 'sold' after the date of execution to new banks. This particular technique borrows heavily from the principles of *Carhill v Carbolic Smoke Ball Co* which held that it was possible for an offer to be made to the whole wide world on day one, which offer could be accepted by the performance/payment of a certain price.

Since a novation operates as a new contract, the obligations imposed in the loan agreement (for example the revolving nature of the facility and the multi draw-down option) would be passed to the novating bank.

This has particular consequences in the event that a novation is adopted because a novation under English law has the effect of discharging the underlying obligations of the 'novated' contract. The new contract is substituted for the old and for a scintilla of time all underlying obligations are discharged. Consequently, any security (unless it is expressed to be a continuing security) will be automatically discharged in the event that a novation is entered into.

Summary of novation

Novation can therefore be summarized as follows.

(a) Novation involves a completely new contractual relationship between the various parties and such an agreement will relieve the selling banks entirely of both rights and obligations.

(b) The buying bank obtains all rights and obligations of the selling bank and can sue the borrower.

(c) Novation is a cumbersome procedure because all parties need to be involved in the transaction (*Tolhurst v Associated Portland Cement Manufacturers* (1900)), although this has been reduced by use of Transferable Loan Certificates (TLCs), which permit the borrower to make an open invitation when the agreement is originally executed.

2.2 Assignment

The assignment, completed by notice to the borrower, is the basic way of implementing a sale where rights and not obligations are to be transferred, and gives the new participant a direct claim on the borrower. The assignment is usually in writing, and notice is given to the borrower, and is usually of the whole debt. These are the requirements of a legal assignment section 136 of the Law of Property Act 1925. If any of the above is absent, it may constitute an equitable assignment.

The legal assignee will have the ability to enforce its claim against the underlying debtor without the need to enjoin the assignor whereas, purely as a matter of procedure, the equitable assignee will have to enjoin the assignor as either co-plaintiff or co-defendant. An equitable assignee cannot sue in its own name – it must join with the assignor as co-plaintiff and if notice has not been given to the borrower, an assignee will have no right to set-off and may be prejudiced by prior equities.

In addition, an assignee who purchases a loan which has not been notified to the underlying debtor will be subject to the rules in *Dearle v Hall* (1912) that the underlying debtor will get a good discharge, until it receives notice by making payments to the assignor thereby giving rise to a potential double credit risk. Intervening equities will continue to arise until notice has been given to the underlying debtor.

Also, an assignment cannot increase the obligations of the borrower (under increased costs clauses for instance) unless the borrower expressly agrees in the loan documents that a buyer can take full benefit of those provisions, *Tolhurst v APCM* (1900) HL. In England an assignment contravening a prohibition is void as in the case of *Linden Gardens Trust Ltd v Lenesta Sludge Disposals Ltd* [1994] 3 All ER 417, HL. The onus would be upon the assignor to prove that consent is being unreasonably withheld or delayed as in the case of *Hendry v Chartsearch Ltd* (1998). An assignment may conflict with the banker's duty of confidentiality and as such this should be covered in the assignment agreement.

The loan agreement may law down procedures or limitations (eg the need for a borrowers' prior consent for formal assignments). Stamp duty is payable on legal assignments in the UK, 1% ad valorem. One also needs to consider the conflict of law principles as to whether the loan assignable and to look to the proper law of the loan contract.

It is important to note that if the loan is one of a revolving nature with multi-currency draw-downs the continuing obligations under English law are that it cannot be assigned because under English law only rights and not obligations can be assigned. Consequently, it will not be possible for the secondary syndication to take the form of an assignment for revolving loans.

2.3 Sub-participation

A sub-participation is an arrangement whereby the seller transfers part of a loan to a buyer without affecting existing rights and liabilities between the seller and the borrower. The sub-participation may take one of two forms – namely a fully-funded sub-participation or a risk participation. The actual choice will depend on the commercial needs of the parties.

The fully-funded sub-participation

In a funded sub-participation the buyer will put the seller in funds and will receive amounts by way of repayment of principal and payments of interest pro rata to his share.

The risk participation

A risk sub-participation is in essence a deposit agreement pursuant to which the buying bank places a deposit with the selling bank upon terms that the deposit will be repaid only to the extent that repayments are made on the underlying loan. Therefore in a risk sub-participation the buyer guarantees, in return for a fee, a proportion of any failure of the borrower to pay. Consequently the buyer funds only if a default occurs and is akin to a guarantee, in which case complex issues may arise in relation to such guarantees. You must focus on the fact that in a sub-participation the buying bank does not enjoy contractual relations with the underlying borrower and is therefore subject to a double credit risk, namely of default on the part of the underlying borrower and also default on the part of the selling bank.

In the case of *Lloyds TSB Bank plc v Clarke (liquidator of Socimer International Bank Ltd) and Chase Manhattan Bank Luxembourg SA* (2002) UKPC 27, the Judicial Committee of the Privy Council considered the status of a risk participation agreement. The Privy Council is the highest court of appeal for some commonwealth countries and is treated by the English courts as being a strongly persuasive authority. The Judicial Committee of the Privy Council confirmed that the effect of sub-participations that are properly documented as such provided that the grantee (Lloyds) will receive no proprietary rights in the facility. The risk participant was found to have no claim in the underlying facility and was just an unsecured creditor in the grantor's (Socimer's) insolvency. This approach was then followed in the case of *Adolfo Altman v Australia and New Zealand Banking Group Ltd* (2000) EWHC2488.

Problems of sub-participations

In either type of arrangement the failure of sub-participations to transfer any security interest in the underlying loan to the sub-participant is a serious disadvantage to the sub-participant. The problem (insofar as the sub-participant is concerned) with such agreements is that they provide for nothing more than contractual relations between the selling bank and the sub-participant. Consequently, the sub-participant will have no direct contractual relations with the underlying borrower (as would be the case in the event that a novation was exercised) nor would there be any direct rights against any underlying guarantor. There is also the problem, that because there is no contractual relationship with the borrower, a sub-participant will be unable to set off any deposit with the borrower in the event of default.

3 Loan transfers and capital adequacy

For banks incorporated in the UK that are regulated by the Financial Services Authority (FSA), there is a notice issued 26/6/98 by the FSA called Securitization and Loan Transfers. Where novation occurs it is regarded as a clean method of transfer and the FSA will no longer count the loan in calculating the capital ratio of the selling bank. Similarly assignment is also regarded by the FSA as a clean method of transfer of obligations, provided it has been properly notified to the borrower. In addition, the selling bank must agree that it will loose any rights of set-off. With assignment, the FSA will no longer count the loan in calculating the capital ratio of the selling bank.

Where sub-participation is used, the risk of default by the borrower under the loan is still that of the selling bank. The FSA will then continue to count the loan in calculating the capital ratio of the selling bank.

In all cases novations, assignments and sub-participations must satisfy the following conditions in order to qualify for FSA capital adequacy treatment of loan transfers:

(a) the transfer does not contravene the terms and conditions of the underlying loan agreement and all necessary consents have been obtained;

(b) the buyer has no formal recourse to the seller for losses and the seller is not obliged to repurchase the loan;

(c) there is also the need for the documentation evidencing such agreements to include a reference that any rescheduling obligations would be passed to the buying bank. Compare and contrast a sub-participation with a claim collateralized by cash (which may in certain circumstances be zero risk-weighted for capital adequacy purposes and therefore achieve the same effect as an off balance sheet item);

The off-balance sheet treatment of legal assignments and indeed equitable assignments is subject to the FSA caution that lending banks should monitor assignments that have not been notified to the underlying debtor because of the above problems which present themselves in such cases.

(d) the seller has no obligation to repurchase the loan.

4 Factors in choosing the method of transferability

Factors in the choice of granting participations are:

(a) whether participation is granted at the time the loan agreement is entered into or after that time,

(b) whether the original bank wishes not to disclose the participation but intends to appear as the sole lender,

(c) whether the original bank wishes to transfer its obligations as well as its rights after the loan agreement has been entered into,

(d) whether there are any stamp duty, taxation or assignability problems in the way of a particular mode of granting a participation.

5 Assignments and sub-participation's contrasted

5.1 Advantages of sub-participations

(a) Restrictions on assignment in loan documentation – common. Restraints on sub-participations – rare.

(b) Sub-participation – no notice need be given to the borrower.

(c) For the buyer – management time and cost left to seller.

(d) Usually no stamp duty.

5.2 Disadvantages of sub-participations

(a) The buyer has no direct claim against the borrower, merely a contractual right against the seller – the buyer has double credit risk, both that of the borrower and of the seller.

(b) The buyer has no interest in any security.

(c) The seller may have a double risk – of the borrower failing to pay and in a risk. Sub-participation the bank buying the risk – Sub-participation going into insolvency.

(d) The buyer cannot take advantage of any grossing-up provisions.

(e) Usually the buyer will have no say in syndicate management.

As we have seen, in 1996 a number of banks formed the Loan Market Association (LMA) whose objective is to enhance trading in primary performing loans. The LMA, which has a substantial membership, has produced standardized documentation, settlement procedures, and has a code of practice for market activity, all of which has helped to create a more active and efficient secondary market.

6 Summary of problems and issues with transferability generally

(a) In the case of assignments, if they are not legally assigned there is the problem of default by the assignor bank to the assignee bank in addition to that of default by the borrower. This is known as the double credit risk and is also the principal danger in sub-participations as to the double credit risk of the borrower and original bank.

(b) In terms of consultation and representation, a sub-participant and an equitable assignment may have little or no say in any restructuring or rescheduling unless it is provided for in the respective agreements.

(c) There is the problem of weak banks in having novations to the extent that the borrower may wish to control any transferability. The borrower may insist on a blanket ban but it is more usual for there to be a clause having a compromise position whereby the consent of the borrower is not to be unreasonably withheld. There is also the problem of withholding taxes resulting in extra costs to the borrower because of an obligation to gross up, which is not so with sub-participations.

(d) Sub-participants not having a contractual relationship will hardly if ever hold any interest in any underlying security. Obligations flow only between the buying and selling bank and the sub-participant has no real rights in securing only in that it may enforce it through the selling bank subject to sub-participation agreement. In the case of novation this extinguishes the original contract therefore any security relating to it will fall away. A buying bank therefore could take fresh security but may loose priority. This is not a problem though if security is held by an agent bank or third party and is held on trust. In the case of an assignment it can be so structured that security is also assigned or the security is held in trust by an agent. Any new security taken for new banks may need a ranking agreement.

(e) It is usually a condition of any assignment or sub-participation agreement that buyers must undertake their own independent investigation of the financial condition of the borrower and cannot rely on the selling bank to have done any due diligence, as in the case of *National Westminster Bank v Utrecht America Finance Co* (2001).

Nine

Events of default

1 Reasons for default

The most common default is failure to pay interest or failure to repay a tranche of the loan on the due date. This can happen through carelessness or as a result of a failure in the banking system as well as for the reason that constitutes the true default, wilful withholding of payment or just inability to pay. Carelessness would be an unusual situation because agent banks, responsible for receiving payment, are usually punctilious in reminding borrowers of their obligations, often doing so indirectly with a polite enquiry about which bank the funds are coming from, or some such similar technique. Even so, borrowers should not rely on such reminders and the treasurer should regard the operation of a foolproof diary system as one of the most important responsibilities within his department. The implications of a default are much too severe to be casual in this area. Further, even though the bank may overlook the error, the lack of professionalism on the part of the corporate will not go unnoticed.

2 Period of grace – uses and abuses

Failure of the banking system could be a more serious problem. With the huge volume of transactions passing through the banking system, it is not surprising that funds are occasionally misdirected. Over the life of a term loan there will be a substantial number of payments to be made, thus increasing the chances of a mistake occurring. It is accordingly prudent to ensure that such an incident cannot be legally construed as a default – while a bank would not normally treat it as such, it could have technical grounds to do so if a transmission error were to occur at a time when the bank was already concerned about the company's credit standing. The normal requirement of a borrower to avoid this risk is a period of grace varying from three to ten working days. These 'days of grace', as they are called, are intended to provide the borrower with an opportunity to not be penalized for what is, in effect, a technical default. There are three points to be made.

- First, it is not enough to have a period of grace – such a line of defence would be quite useless to a corporate that was unaware that, for whatever reason, payment had not been made. The borrower should seek to ensure that the period of grace does not begin to run until such time as it has been notified that payment has not been received. However, it is not normal practice for banks to have to give notice; the onus rests with the borrower to ensure that payments are made.
- Second, the existence of a period of grace should not tempt the corporate into thinking that he is free to use it as a device for obtaining a few extra days' credit. Technically it might well be legitimate to do so but the effect on the overall relationship would be devastating, as it would also be on the individuals concerned. The company would rightly find the bank taking a much harder line on subsequent loan agreements, not just in this area but also on all the terms. Such wilful exploitation of a loophole which all recognize to exist would very quickly prove to be self-defeating.
- The third point concerns the way in which the relevant clauses are drafted. There is a tendency for failure to pay on the due date to be classed as a default even though the corporate is then allowed a period of grace in which to rectify it. This is not satisfactory from the standpoint of the company because it leaves it exposed to the risk that the existence of a default, albeit a technical one, may bring the cross-default clause in another agreement into operation. Although this should not occur if the various cross-default clauses by which the company is bound have been written with adequate care, many companies have long-standing agreements, made when corporate treasury work was less professional, and are accordingly vulnerable. The payment clauses should be worded in a way that make it clear that no default shall arise until the period of grace, after notice, has expired.

3 Enforcement and waivers

The wording of loan agreements is usually such as to place the obligation on the company to inform the bank that an event of default has occurred. The bank will then review the situation to establish the circumstances of that default and whether or not it can be remedied. If not, it will have the right to demand immediate repayment of monies lent (with interest) under the terms of the agreement. This will impact on any cross-default that the company has in other agreements. If , however, the bank decides that the default can be remedied, it may agree to waive the default in writing to the company. By this means the default is technically negated and cross-default (discussed below) provisions will not apply.

Such waivers can be more readily negotiated with close relationship banks, who will know the company and understand the reasons for default. However it is more difficult in syndicated loan situations, because all the banks would have to agree. The most difficult situation is likely to occur in the eurobond markets because the securities are bearer instruments. In this instance the bond holders are unknown and the company has to deal with the trustees to the bond issue. The natural remedy is for the trustee to call a bondholders' meeting where the chances of getting a quorum to agree a waiver are slim. Such a meeting could prove detrimental to the company's position, particularly if the bond is trading at a discount, and any enforced prepayment by the bondholders, seeking repayment at par, would in turn trigger the company's other cross-default clauses. Careful negotiation is therefore required, if appropriate, to ensure that the trustee is won round to the situation and grants a waiver. The trustees will, in all instances, be guided by their lawyers.

Where a lender knows of an event of default but declines to accelerate the loan there is a risk that this may amount to a waiver by conduct not only of that event but permanently of the entire proviso, eg allowing a breach of the negative pledge covenant may have the effect of striking the covenant from the agreement, *Birmingham and District Land Co v London and North Western Rail Co* (1888). Delays in acting (except long ones) will not constitute a waiver and nor will receipt of payments. Making fresh advances, however, probably will amount to a waiver by conduct. A lender should ideally express his waivers in writing, obviously limiting the waiver to the occasion in question, to preserve the event of default and remove any suggestion of a waiver by conduct.

4 Events of default in a loan agreement

The following paragraphs illustrate events of default that are likely to be typical in a loan document. They will provide the bank with a contractual right to terminate the loan, cancel any commitment and to demand repayment for all outstanding principal and interest (known as 'acceleration').

4.1 Failure to repay

The clause will identify the distinction between failure to pay principal and failure to pay interest. The event of default will include breach of the obligation to make payments (making the borrower pay interest on accelerated payments will be ineffective, *United Dominions Trust v Thomas* (1976)). In relation to failure to pay one needs to consider the desirability of appropriate grace periods (discussed above) and the need for the grace period to be long enough to enable the borrower to remedy a technical default but not too long as to prejudice the position of the lending banks.

4.2 Breach of representations and warranties

Breach of representations and warranties might include 'evergreen' ones; insolvency of the borrower (so the lender does not have to wait for failure to make the next due payment before proving); threatened cessation of business by disposal of a significant part of the assets; material adverse change in the borrower's financial condition; and the cross-default. This latter event allows the lender to accelerate if the borrower is in default in any other loan to him. It seeks to allow the lender, whose loan is not in default, to join in the action or negotiation with the borrower at an early stage and obtain *pari passu* treatment. Unless expressed, the clause will not extend to breaches of obligations under title financing schemes, such as sale and leaseback or even to default on acceptance credits.

Events of default that are triggered as a consequence of breach of underlying representations and warranties can be mitigated by the incorporation of a 'materiality' test. This will provide that the various representations and warranties will give rise to acceleration pursuant to an event of default only if they prove to have been incorrect or misleading in a material respect. Further prejudicial language could incorporate not only materiality, but also the fact that breach of the representations and warranties must be material and prejudicial.

The problem with materiality tests is that they beg the question. They seek to overcome this difficulty by specifying a financial limit whereby materiality is to be gauged, although such an approach may be difficult to apply in relation to the majority of representations and warranties.

4.3 Breach of covenants

It is usual to incorporate appropriate grace periods in order to seek a remedy in respect of any breach of covenants. Alternatively, materiality tests could be sought in respect of those covenants that a borrower considers fundamental to the nature of its business.

4.4 Cross-default

This is a clause in the events of default whereby if a borrower defaults under someone else's agreement then it is a default in their agreement. Therefore, banks gain comfort and protection from other banks or lenders events of defaults and covenants. In this way it means the bank can demand repayment if another lender declares an event of default. The borrower must however be aware of what is known as the 'domino effect', whereby one default means all loans in default with all lenders.

The cross-default clause is one of the most fundamental anticipatory events of default, which can be incorporated into a term loan agreement. It is intended to give the lending bank equality in the race to the courthouse door and also the ability to be present at the table in debt restructuring negotiations (because it should include the sanction of acceleration to bring the borrower down).

It is common to incorporate appropriate limitations to the clause, of a type similar to those in the specimen provided, namely that the default will have to continue for more than the original grace period incorporated in the loan documentation and the further proviso that claims being contested in good faith should not give rise to a cross-default acceleration.

An important feature of the specimen clause is that the third-party acceleration need not actually be triggered by the borrower. This clause is a 'capable of' cross-default clause that is significantly more powerful than the clause that can be triggered only in the event that the third party credit is also accelerated.

The most effective way of mitigating the harsh effects of the cross-default clause is to provide that the clause will not give rise to a right of acceleration unless third party facilities, in respect of which the cross-default clause is sought to be triggered, are actually accelerated. A borrower should seek to avoid, in particular, the 'capable of' cross-default clause which will permit lenders under the syndicated loan to accelerate their facility, notwithstanding the fact that the borrower may have successfully avoided acceleration under a third-party facility. Also corporates may wish to incorporate both grace periods and materiality tests in respect of the cross-default clause.

Borrowers often seek to limit the cross-default remedy to specific types of third-party indebtedness, for example, loans made available to a borrower over a certain figure (say, US$ 50 million). This will avoid the possibility of the cross-default clause being capable of being accelerated in circumstances where a relatively small debt is not repaid on its due date. Another important consideration for a borrower is that the cross-default clause should not cover facilities made available to its subsidiaries.

4.5 Liquidation or moratorium

The event of default in relation to liquidation should be mitigated in order to protect a borrower against frivolous or vexatious claims/orders that are bought against it. A borrower may also argue that the clause should not be capable of acceleration in circumstances where a borrower is defending any liquidation/ bankruptcy order in good faith.

4.6 Changes in control/ownership/merger

This clause can also be drafted as a covenant and has been discussed above. The changes in control of events of default can also be mitigated by the incorporation of a materiality test. This particular event of default is one that particularly lends itself to the materially prejudicial test. In other words, if any change in control is not materially prejudicial to the interests of the lenders, then it should not be capable of being accelerated.

4.7 Major disposal of assets

Again this clause could also be drafted as a covenant or as an event of default and insofar as disposal of assets are concerned, the clause can be mitigated to exclude disposals in the ordinary course of business. This is particularly important for a borrower, so that its core business is not hampered by the strict application of the clause.

4.8 Material adverse change clause

This has already been discussed in detail above and, as well as being a covenant, this clause can also be an event of default. The material adverse change clause should be avoided by a borrower altogether, if possible. A borrower should argue that provided appropriate covenants are incorporated within the terms of the syndicated loan, there should be no need for a material adverse change event of default. In the event that a borrower is unable to avoid the inclusion of the clause, strict materiality wording should be sought in order to limit its use.

5 Acceleration and termination

An express event of default clause in the contract will normally permit the lender to accelerate payment of loans already advanced and cancel further loans on the occurrence of any of the specified events. The lender thereby normally has the right to repudiate/rescind for breach any of the representations or covenants.

Inserting the right to accelerate in simple triggering of an event of default in another loan (whether or not it is waived) may discourage another lender from inserting over-powered events of default into his agreement. Where it is expressed that the opinion of the lender determines whether or not a breach has occurred, this is always subject to a reasonableness test, unless that is expressly excluded and even then it must be made in good faith. Where the borrower has already cured the event of default, the lender is nevertheless entitled under English law to assert his rights for the breach, *Mardorf Peach & Co Ltd v Attica Sea Carriers Corpn of Liberia, The Laconia* (1977) HL.

In the absence of any express provision, general principles would permit the bank an action for non-payment of a debt due, damages (although this will often add nothing more), an injunction (eg to prevent breach of a negative pledge or *pari passu* covenant if action is taken swiftly), specific performance (eg of an agreement to grant security) or petitioning the liquidation of the company borrower. Remedies not requiring court action include exercising a right of set-off, repudiating the contract for breach of condition or liquidation or rescission for misrepresentation. These remedies will be discussed in more detail in the next unit.

One should also consider the control of the acceleration device if the facility in question is of a syndicated nature. Obviously the higher the percentage of banks that are required in order to approve acceleration the better for a borrower. Although 'majority bank control' is the norm it is not wholly unusual for the definition of majority to be calculated at figures over 60% of the outstanding liabilities under a facility. If possible, of course, a borrower should seek to negotiate a much higher figure.

6 Default interest clause

A default interest clause seeks to give a lender additional interest should there be a default on the part of the borrower. Such extra interest must be sought by the lender on the basis of extra risk, or additional administrative burdens on the part of the lender. If this is not the position then such a clause will be invalid as constituting a penalty clause, designed to intimidate the borrower.

On the other hand if it is a genuine pre-assessment of loss then the clause will be upheld as a valid and enforceable liquidated damages clause as in the case of *Lordsvale Finance plc v Bank of Zambia* (1996). The court took into account the evidence of the widespread use of this clause and their use in many syndicated loan agreements.

Ten

Remedies, enforcement of remedies and rescheduling

1 Outline of default

The lender's right to accelerate the loan, ie to declare all sums owing due and payable immediately and to cancel the commitment to advance further loans, is normally provided for in the loan agreement as the express remedy for an event of default. In the absence of express provision, the common law remedies of rescission for misrepresentation and repudiation for breach of condition will have the same effect, if available to the lender, as acceleration. Insolvency or liquidation of the borrower will constitute an implied repudiation by the borrower that the lender is free to accept. A borrower's failure to make one or more payments when due would only entitle the lender to sue for these payments. In this type of action, or in one following an acceleration, the lender is suing for a debt due which would include capital and interest due. It has a right to sue for damages for breach of representation or covenant, but will only receive compensation for actual loss incurred, and only then if that loss was reasonably foreseeable when the contract was entered into.

2 Internal remedies

2.1 Acceleration

As stated in above the bank can demand the outstanding amount and cancel further commitments to lend.

2.2 Set-off

Set-off is potentially one of the most useful remedies available. There is no need for court action. Terms of set-off may be incorporated within the terms of an international loan agreement. They also exist at common law subject to certain conditions being fulfilled.

In insolvency, rights of set-off become automatic. Thus set-off would be available to any particular syndicate bank despite any contractual provision to the contrary as in the case of *MS Fashions Ltd v Bank of Credit and Commerce International SA (No 2)* [1993] 3 All ER 769.

Additionally, under section 426(4) and (5) of the Insolvency Act 1986, it is possible for a foreign court to request that the English courts apply foreign set-off rules (but this could apply only if English law and jurisdiction did not apply).

Deposit funds cannot be set off against a loan unless the loan is due and payable.

Set-off is a useful remedy when available because it requires no court action by the lender, rather it is up to the borrower to take action to recover the seized funds. The classic scenario is the setting-off of a credit account against an overdrawn account in the same bank under the same name, but there are further variations.

The right to set-off depends upon the debt in question being due and payable; if it is not the borrower should be free to withdraw his funds. The loan agreement may make the disposal of assets, or the commencement of liquidation, an event of default, so rendering the debt due and payable. In the event of an individual insolvency, s 164 of the Insolvency Act 1986 allows set-off against unmatured debts, except those incurred after the lender knew of the presentation of a bankruptcy petition; similar rules are extended to corporate insolvencies, Companies Act 1985, s 612.

Mutuality of the debit and credit balances is a requirement for the right to set-off, yet this is not a rigid rule. The courts may be willing to decide that the entity with the deposit (eg a Central Bank or subsidiary company) is not truly separate from the entity owing the loan (eg a state department or parent company), *Trendtex v Central Bank of Nigeria* (1977) CA. We have seen how the pro rata sharing clause may allow the setting off of disproportionate parts of a syndicated loan.

Set-off is available across different domestic branches, *Garnett v McKewan* (1872), and probably this extends to foreign branches and to accounts in different currencies.

The main block to set-off is an express or implied agreement not to set-off. *National Westminster Bank v Halesowen Presswork and Assemblies Ltd* (1972) HL establishes that such an implied agreement normally applied in the case of a current account in credit because otherwise the customer may never feel safe in drawing cheques if his loan account balance was greater. It is advisable to give notice when setting off and some jurisdictions insist on it. A borrower is always free to assign his deposit before his loan matures and providing the assignee gives notice to the bank in time, he acquires the deposit free of the set-off. A bank therefore should take no comfort in holding deposits against an unmatured loan. Any specific agreement not to set-off is overruled in insolvency.

The availability or otherwise of a set-off is generally considered to be a matter for the *lex fori* because it is a procedural matter. Consequently, a different law will govern the issue according to where the lender or borrower brings the action.

3 External remedies

3.1 Freezing orders (formerly known as Mareva injunctions)

Freezing orders or Mareva injunctions are more generally known as pre-judgment attachments. They are sought by a plaintiff A freezing order is an injunction given by a court using a summary procedure to prevent assets fleeing the jurisdiction. It is taken from the case of *Mareva Compania SA v International Bulk Carriers* (1975) and is, in effect, a freezing order over all assets. Its importance was reinforced in *Hill Samuel & Company v Littaur* (1985).

Borrowers' assets can be secured against removal to another jurisdiction as per section 37(3) of the Supreme Court Act 1981. Courts, before granting an injunction, will be satisfied that:

(a) the person seeking the injunction has a good arguable case;

(b) the defendant appears to have assets within the jurisdiction;

(c) the claimant issue must be one over which the court has jurisdiction;

(d) there is a real risk the defendant will be unable to satisfy the claim;

(e) the balance of convenience is in favour of granting the injunction.

The court may require to be satisfied that it has jurisdiction to hear the claim for damages and the plaintiff will invariably be required to undertake to compensate the defendant should he lose his claim at trial (the undertaking in damages). The injunction is available against assets held by third parties if there is evidence that they are mere nominees, *X Bank Ltd v G* (1985). As well as its importance to a bank as plaintiff, the injunction is also relevant where the bank holds assets belonging to the defendant. Any international breach of the order will amount to a contempt of court; there is no rule of imputed knowledge. Where the court orders the freezing of only part of the defendant's assets the bank may be in a difficult position when the defendant argues sufficient assets have been frozen in another account.

Where the order is limited, therefore, a bank would prefer it to specify a sum to be frozen in each account. The injunction does not apply to items held in safe custody unless it specifically includes these and the same rule applies to accounts in joint names. Letters of credit, bonds and bills of exchange are entirely unaffected by an injunction because they involve commitments of the bank directly to third parties. The injunction also does not affect sums coming into the account after the date of the court order, unless specified in the order. Any accounts held in a different currency from that expressed in the order must be converted and then frozen in the expressed currency. Where the bank is itself a creditor of the defendant it should seek specific provision in the order allowing it to exercise its right of set-off in respect of facilities granted to the defendant before the date of the injunction. Where this has not been done, the bank is entitled to have the injunction varied to free assets for the purpose of such set-off, *The Theotokos* (1983).

In the case of *Bank of China v NBM LLC* [2002] All ER 717, the Court of Appeal considered the protections that should be given to third parties with a presence outside England, particularly banks, upon whom a worldwide assets freezing order of an English court is to be served. Such orders are often obtained in cases involving fraud or where there is a concern that assets may be dissipated. There are now three protections:

1. Where the third party is not subject to the jurisdiction of the court within England, the order would affect only the third party outside England to the extent that it was declared enforceable in the relevant jurisdiction where the third party was located.
2. Where the order would be enforceable against a third party within England (for example, by its presence in England, by submission or otherwise), the order would be enforceable against the third party if it has been given notice of the order and is able to prevent a breach of the order outside England.
3. In respect of assets located outside England, nothing in the order should prevent the third party from complying with what it reasonably believes to be its obligations, under the civil or criminal law of the state in which those assets are located, nor from complying with the orders of the court of that state, provided that reasonable notice of any application by the third party to such courts is given to the person who had obtained the freezing order.

3.2 Specific performance

Specific performance and injunctions are discretionary remedies, at the option of the court. The general rule is that they are available only if damages would be inadequate. Further, they are not available if their effect has to be supervised or it would be futile to award them. Specific performance of an agreement to create a charge should be available and an interim injunction to prohibit a threatened act by the borrower such as granting a charge contrary to a negative pledge covenant or the selling of valuable assets.

English courts will therefore not normally grant an order for specific performance where damages would be an adequate remedy, or where the loan agreement makes provision for a more suitable remedy, ie termination and acceleration. The general rule is that they are available only if damages would be inadequate.

3.3 Prohibitory injunction

English courts would look more favourable on this, particularly those that would restrain the borrower from performing acts that are in breach of its obligations, such as breaching the negative pledge or by selling assets.

3.4 Other external remedies

These other remedies can be summed up as having (1) the right to sue for damages; (2) the right to rescind a loan agreement and (3) the right to sue for unpaid amounts.

A court has power to award interest on a money claim but this is at the standard court rate and only from the date of the writ. A lender would normally insert a default interest clause into the agreement whereby a premium rate is charge for sums paid late and whereby the default interest may be compounded at intervals. Some jurisdictions, eg Germany and Switzerland, treat an obligation to pay interest on interest as unenforceable.

A 'remedies cumulative' clause in the agreement removes a possible argument that the express remedies are exclusive of common law and court-awarded remedies.

4 Restructuring corporate debt

It should go without saying that a corporate should always plan ahead to avoid a default at all costs by ensuring that it has:

- the right levels of gearing;
- the right financial structure; and
- the right mix between short- and long-term debt.

There must also be the right mix of floating and fixed-rate debt. Adequate reliable back-up facilities are also very important. However, this is often not the case and default follows. Sadly (for both corporation and lender), even when a corporation has done everything 'properly', external factors can lead to default.

The restructuring of a corporate debt takes place in private between the lender(s) and is geared towards enabling the defaulting business to survive and ensuring the lenders get repaid.

Restructuring corporate debt is an entirely different matter from rescheduling sovereign debt. The creditor has more options in a corporate debt, ie he can use court procedures to enforce liquidation or to appoint an administrator. The bank's first consideration must therefore be whether it is possible and appropriate to save the company by the restructuring, taking into account profit forecasts, the willingness of the directors to continue, the possible liability of the directors for wrongful trading (section 214 of the Insolvency Act 1986) and even of the bank as a 'shadow director' on the basis that it is giving instructions on the running of the company, eg to sell assets.

Restructuring may take a number of different forms:

(1) if the object is to *preserve cash flow*, the current debt may be deferred, converted into long-term *debt* or into *equity*. Altering the nature of the debt may jeopardize the bank's existing security, taking equity for debt may be prohibited and taking preference shares may make the bank an 'associated person'.

(2) A *divestment* and contraction of business may involve exchanging debt for assets, a take-over of the business, a hiving-down into a new company or a straightforward termination of new business and sale of assets. Acquisition of assets at less than cash market value may amount to a fraudulent preference or fraudulent conveyance. Restructuring into a new company may avoid these problems because the new company pays cash for the assets then transfers the assets to the bank. Some other creditors may have to be paid off to permit this process. Termination of existing contracts may lead to an action by the third party for inducing breach of contract.

(3) *Joint action* with other creditors may be taken involving perhaps a sharing of security, providing new finance, an agreement to share future losses and profits and a sharing of equity. Where some creditors are bondholders this hinders action because they cannot be found in order to be brought into the negotiations.

Many restructured credits themselves face restructuring a little later in time. This need not indicate a failure, rather the first restructuring may serve as a softening-up process.

The court process may be used to bring a reluctant creditor into line or to administer the entire restructuring, although this will restrict freedom of negotiation. The role of the corporation's government may be relevant in making foreign exchange available, nationalizing the company, limiting rates of interest payable, providing subsidies and even to legislate to permit a desired restructuring that would otherwise offend local law.

4.1 Corporate restructuring – the process

The corporate should always plan ahead to avoid a default at all costs by ensuring that it has the right levels of gearing, the right financial structure, the right mix between short- and long-term debt. Also is there the right mix of floating and fixed-rate debt and – very important – are back-up facilities adequate and are they reliable?

If the corporate then faces a severe crises the corporate should compile a worst case scenario of cash-flow analysis to assess the situation and also for discussion with its bankers. The treasurer should have kept his few selected or core banks informed of the worsening situation. Most good banks will bear with a corporate with whom they have a good relationship if there is bad news providing they are adequately and honestly informed in time.

If banks are not informed adequately and honestly of the position the corporate may face a siege situation of disgruntled bankers clamouring for their money back. At worst the interest of different groups of banks may diverge to the extent that one group of banks may decide to push for receivership, as nearly happened to Laura Ashley in 1990. From this the lesson for corporates is to carefully select the banks with which they wish to do business with. Corporates who have borrowed from a large number of banks have found that non-relationship banks are more reluctant to cooperate, for example, in amending covenants in times of crisis. Recent examples also include Marconi and Meridien Hotels Group, where there has been fractious behaviour by banks in syndicates. This underlines the fact that the corporates should develop close relationships with selected banks at an early stage and not wait until there is a need to refinance or restructure.

4.2 The standstill agreement

If, however, banks are genuinely and honestly informed of the situation of the company's finances they are likely on the whole to be supportive. This process is the informal remedy of a consensual support operation as outlined by the Bank of England and known as 'The London Rules'.

If the corporate does get together with its banks then the first object may be to put in place a standstill agreement. This would give the corporate time to formulate a strategy to deal with the crisis situation. A standstill agreement is where the banks agree to a standstill of all of their borrowings at the date of default and also agree to take no action in taking any acceleration or enforcement against the borrower until the outcome of negotiations has taken place. The negotiating phase usually takes up to three months to complete. A solution will require the involvement of all the banks and the corporate will want to know that it is negotiating with banks who have the confidence in the corporate. Equally the banks must have the confidence that they are receiving honest information from the corporate and regular updates.

An all-bank meeting is likely to be called which will have the object of setting up a steering committee to handle the restructuring negotiations with the corporate. There are however problems of syndicate democracy and the question as to what decisions are made by steering committee. The steering committee will also handle the negotiation of the standstill agreement. The steering committee should insist on the borrower disclosing such information to all banks, especially as English law takes a stern view towards secret deals (*Re Milner* (1885)).

Despite this there may be conflicts among the banks and between the corporate management, who will be attempting to represent the interest of the shareholders, employees and creditors as a whole, whereas the banks have their sights on getting their money back. The corporate will need to present a refinancing plan to its bankers who will need to provide an incentive to them for continued support. What is crucial is to avoid giving a plan that initiates conflict between the various groups of banks, who may feel they are being treated inequitably.

The corporate will need to use its own resources in helping with the refinancing together with their merchant bank advisors and also with the help of their lead bank. There may be the necessity of having investigative accountants and the corporate may be required to give security, especially if the refinancing plan requires new or additional financing. The corporate will probably have an increased burden in providing regular information to its bankers concerning the cash position and compliance with its covenants. It must be stressed that such information must be accurate.

4.3 The facilities agreement

Following the refinancing plan, negotiated between the borrower and the banks, there will be new documentation for the restructured facilities, which is likely to take the following form:

(1) New provisions – particularly new money.

  (a) Comparable indebtedness covenants.

  (b) Mandatory repayment covenants as discussed above.

  (c) Priority of treatment as discussed as above.

(2) Security – is security equal and shared among all banks? Hardening periods (section 245 of the Insolvency Act 1986).

(3) New money – this is the most contentious issue in corporate restructuring and often one in which corporates may fail, because banks are unwilling to put up extra money. If a rescue does require new money, it is usual for those banks that provide new money to have preferential treatment and priority in terms of both repayment of the new money and security.

(4) Loss sharing agreement among the banks.

(5) Ranking agreements of security between the banks.

(6) The need for continued information and how often the steering committee will continue to meet.

Despite all this the corporate must retain its right to manage itself albeit in conjunction with its bankers. The scenario outlined is how both the corporate and its bankers should react to a crises situation. If this does not happen and corporates do not provide accurate information and contact with its bankers, banks may panic and take precipative action leading to receivership. Equally, if banks do not react rationally to the crisis situation, or if they are non-relationship banks, they may overreact and again push the corporate towards receivership. Once again, this only underlines the need for the corporate having selected the right banks in avoiding such a situation.

5 Rescheduling sovereign debt

In rescheduling a sovereign debt, the availability of sovereign immunity (and consequently the onerous commercial nature of the act) must be considered, as must the possibility that local courts would strike down terms under public policy considerations and that a moratorium of repayments may be declared, or exchange controls introduced. There are, of course, no alternatives of a court-imposed rescheduling or a forced liquidation.

The guidelines appropriate to these problems are:

(a) not all debt will be rescheduled; sufficient should be within the package so as to assist the debtors, but not so much as to prejudice the cooperation of creditor banks;

(b) only external debt will be rescheduled;

(c) debts with longer maturities are less likely to be rescheduled, twelve months is often used as a watershed;

(d) a steering committee may be formed with a member from each major creditor, and sub-committees may be set up to draft documentation etc.

No liability will attach to any party except inasmuch as authority is given to an agent bank to conduct negotiation, either given in advance on the loan documentation or by express approval at the time. Any action taken by an agent on behalf of members presumably exposes him to liability for breach of fiduciary duty as stated in *UBAF Ltd v European American Banking Corpn* (1983) CA.

Rescheduling negotiations often take place in tandem with discussions with the IMF for a sponsored recovery programme, acceptance of which is vital to the rescheduling and may be a condition precedent to it. Failure to adhere to the programme may be an express event of default in the rescheduling documentation. The World Bank is active in the international debt crisis but refuses to reschedule its own loans. The Bank of International Settlements often provides bridging finance while discussions take place.

The aim of the documentation is to prevent outside creditors being preferred by the debtor. A negative pledge covenant is therefore included and a comparable indebtedness covenant aims to prevent the debtor preferring other similarly placed creditors. A mandatory prepayment clause provides that if the debtor does prefer an outside creditor, the members must receive a pro rata payment – if they so demand. The usual sharing clause will be included to ensure equal treatment of the members as will the *pari passu* clause. An attempt should be made to bind the sovereign party to making the necessary foreign exchange available and an undertaking may be sought from the central bank.

5.1 Process of rescheduling

A sovereign borrower declares a moratorium and suspends payments of its obligations and such a declaration may mean individual creditors taking precipitative action, thus making major creditors unwilling to restructure. Consequently negotiations are conducted privately. A steering committee is set up with appointees from several banks, but principally the lead managers.

Rescheduling involves a discharge of existing debts and their replacement by new debts, new terms and a new repayment schedule.

The components of the restructuring process may involve the following.

(1) Rescheduling of the borrower's existing debt.

(2) Provision of new money.

(3) Need to conclude formal arrangements for maintenance of inter-bank lines of credit.

5.2 Argentina – an example of sovereign debt rescheduling

For background information of the relevance and immediacy of this students will find below a summary web article from Yahoo from 9 January 2002.

> BUENOS AIRES, Argentina (Reuters) – Argentina, which has shed the currency straitjacket it wore for a decade to ward off inflation, is trying to stop its devaluation from bringing a return of price rises that could re-ignite unrest.
>
> Populist new President Eduardo Duhalde untied the peso from its one-toone peg to the dollar on Sunday in a bid to cheapen exports and kick-start an economy that has not grown since 1998. Argentina has already stopped foreign debt payments. With people fearing a return to the hyperinflation of the 1980s and a rapid decline in the peso after the 239% devaluation, Economy Minister Jorge Remes Lenicov pleaded with shop owners and consumer groups to guard against mark-ups.
>
> 'This has a lot to do with consumer groups and people's conscience,' he said. 'We spoke with supermarkets yesterday and they promised to only mark up imported goods.'
>
> Some businesses heeded his warning that with such a steep recession likely to dominate 2002 as well, 'anyone who raises prices won't sell anything.' Bus companies vowed not to raise fares and the receptionist of a seedy motel said: 'We're not putting up prices and we'll keep charging in pesos, not dollars.' She had seen no drop in the number of furtive couples taking rooms by the hour. But Ana Laura, a 28-year-old woman shopping for shoes, complained: 'Everyone's putting up prices but wages will stay the same, so what kind of recovery will there be? It's worst in the supermarkets, they're really taking advantage.'
>
> With foreign exchange markets closed until Wednesday to allow time to adapt to the new official and free-floating peso rates, the city was calm after unrest that saw five presidents in two weeks, 27 people killed and supermarkets looted.
>
> The middle class, reassured by Duhalde shifting the cost of devaluation to banks and companies, refrained from bashing pots and pans in the kind of protest that ousted President Fernando de la Rua and his short-lived successor Adolfo Rodriguez Saa. There were also two interim presidents lasting a few hours.
>
> 'TIME MACHINE'
>
> 'This conversion of debts into pesos is the first time they have done something good for the people,' said 42-year-old Pedro Garay. But he

will not stay to see how it pans out: he is leaving for New York to escape the recession and cash crunch. 'I remember the devaluation of 1989 and it was terrible. Argentine is like a time machine,' said a flower seller.

In another move likely to win popular support, an economy ministry official said unpopular bank curbs limiting Argentines to 1,000 pesos per month in cash withdrawals – put in place last month to stop a run on banks – may be raised to 1,500 pesos for some accounts as soon as Tuesday.

Despite Remes Lenicov urging 'the rich's collaboration' and vowing the poor would not suffer, people used what cash they can access because of limits on withdrawals to hoard goods.

Inflation has been zero or less for five years. Just before the 'convertibility' currency peg was introduced by then economy minister Domingo Cavallo in 1991, inflation hit 5,000 percent. However, critics of the dollar peg say it has kept exports expensive and prolonged the recession.

The window of one clothing store had a huge sign reading 'One dollar = 1.40 pesos' – but foreign exchange traders in London said the official rate might not last the four to five months it should be pegged before being floated freely.

'A foreign exchange regime is only as strong as fundamentals underpinning it and if they aren't in balance then it doesn't bode well for the system,' said Mike Noone, an emerging markets analyst at WestLB.

Argentina's inherent inability to balance its budget has been the main factor behind fears it would default on its $141 billion (98 billion pound) public debt and be forced to devalue. Such worries have preyed on Argentina for a year and routed its bond prices.

The subsequent drying up of credit forced it to issue phoney currency, in the form of bonds, to pay wages. The government announced the issue of $2.8 billion of federal paper to replace the chaotic scrip issues and honour its debts to the provinces. Economist Jose Luis Espert, whose gloomy devaluation and default forecasts have all come true, said Argentina still had a fiscal deficit of up to $11 billion. 'If it doesn't balance that by spending cuts, inflation will be over 10 percent.'

The International Monetary Fund, which sent $22 billion in aid in a year, has withheld $1.3 billion due to overspending. Its technicians were in Buenos Aires on Monday and managing director Horst Koehler said any solution would be 'painful' – something Argentina's 36 million people know too well.

> The IMF team was likely to return to Washington on Tuesday, a spokesman for the lender said.
>
> With unemployment at 18 percent, 2,000 people a day join the third of the population living in poverty who cannot afford basic goods and services priced at $1,500 a month.
>
> Such poverty is shocking in a country with Latin America's highest incomes and most solid middle class, which in the early 20th century was one of the world's seven richest nations.
>
> OLD-TIME PERONIST
>
> Duhalde is a 60-year-old Peronist Party leader who lost to De la Rua, from the centrist Radicals, in 1999's elections but will now complete his mandate until 2003. Duhalde was Carlos Menem's vice-president early in Menem's 1989-99 government.
>
> Living up to a reputation as a throwback to the nationalist and working-class values of party founders Juan and Eva Peron in the 1940s, he wants banks and oil companies, not savers and debtors, to pay for the devaluation.
>
> In a country with wages in pesos but 80 percent of debts in dollars, banks expect $15 billion losses from converting debts under $100,000 to pesos and returning dollar savings in full.
>
> But Remes Lenicov estimated their losses at just $6 billion and said this would be compensated by a tax on oil exports.
>
> One US investor spoke of a return to 'interventionist policies that have failed in the past.' Others called them a 'necessary, temporary evil' to stop the haemorrhage of cash. Remes Lenicov plans to travel to Washington at the end of the month and is looking for $15-20 billion in multilateral aid.
>
> Worries about Argentina's impact on Spanish banks, oil and phone firms caused Madrid shares' biggest loss in three months. Spain is Argentina's second investor after the United States.

Although this article highlights the danger for US and Spanish Banks the major UK players will undoubtedly be exposed to some extent.

5.3 Duties in restructuring

There is a view (according to Horn) that both the lead managers and agent banks who formed the original syndicate will be obliged to take a leading role in any restructuring on behalf of the syndicate. It is in their interests and the view must be correct given the contractual relationship within the loan agreement.

The agent bank is under a duty to inform banks of a need for a restructuring operation. There could be a problem of the agent bank having a significant stake. An agent bank will not generally have power to conclude a restructuring.

It is most important for members of the steering committee to ensure they do not become agents of the banks on whose behalf they are acting otherwise they will have significant duties.

The steering committee should insist on the borrower disclosing such information to all banks, especially as English law takes a stern view towards secret deals (*Re Milner* (1885)).

5.4 Documentation – main provisions

The documentation is drafted heavily in favour of lenders. For example, comparable indebtedness, ie the treatment vis-à-vis those creditors who have not been included in restructuring. The main provisions are outlined below.

New money agreement

Fresh money is usually expressed a percentage of lending banks' existing commitment. A considerable degree of control is exercised over a borrower's ability to draw-down fresh money. This is the most contentious issue in any rescheduling and one in which banks may well resist.

Comparable indebtedness covenants

The borrower agrees not to pay comparable indebtedness without the consent of the lenders whose debts are rescheduled. The problem is that it is difficult to monitor – possibly also of a debtor being unable to comply because it may disrupt its trading activities and be counterproductive. The clause may impose a tortuous liability on third parties, inducing the debtor to breach contractual obligations to third-party creditors.

Mandatory pre-payment provisions

This is similar to sharing and binding clauses which require that a reduction in the exposure of third-party creditors must be accompanied by a pro rata reduction in the exposure of those lenders whose debts have been rescheduled.

Parity of treatment

Negative pledge, *pari passu* sharing, cross-default loss sharing, security sharing – all have the purpose of preventing discrimination and preserve equality as between creditors of the debtor.

Other considerations

(1) Problem of how rescheduling achieves parity of treatment between all rescheduled debt, eg various sharing clauses.

(2) Remedies in the event of more favourable repayment of other debt subject to rescheduling.

(3) Difficulty in linking non-rescheduled debt with rescheduled debt to achieve parity of treatment.

(4) Also of linking default to performance under any IMF scheme.

(5) Underlying security, particularly by certain creditors and even to which such creditors could have relevant priority, ie deposits held in central banks.

(6) Any exchange control regulations.

(7) Also consider debt for equity swaps, and pure debt swaps.

Eleven

Project finance

1 What is limited recourse project finance?

'A financing of a particular economic unit in which a lender is satisfied to look initially to the cash flows and earnings of that economic unit as the source of funds, from which a loan will be repaid and to the assets of the economic unit as the collateral for the loan.'

Peter Nevitt, Chairman BankAmeriLease Group of Companies

Under normal circumstances a bank will lend to a company on the strength of the credit of that company. In project financing, the project, its assets, its contracts and its cash flows are separated out from its sponsors. This permits a credit appraisal and loan to the project independent of the credit of the sponsors. This distinguishes project finance from corporate finance.

At the same time it enables borrowing for a project that will benefit the sponsor, while being without recourse to the sponsor. That is the sponsor does not take full responsibility for repaying the finance in the event the project fails and therefore in no way affects the sponsor's credit standing or balance sheet. Such financing is also known as off-balance sheet financing.

Lenders are not in the business of taking equity risks, however, and project finance is more commonly by way of limited recourse rather than wholly non-recourse. This involves the sponsor and/or interested third parties providing undertakings or guarantees so that lenders will be satisfied with the credit risk.

The key to a successful project financing is risk-sharing whereby those parties to a Project take the risks they are in the business to take, so that the finance becomes secured by a series of contractual commitments.

Project financing is especially attractive in capital intensive industries such as:

- mining, eg a gold or copper mine development;
- petroleum, eg an oil and gas development;
- petrochemical, eg refining;
- utilities, eg power stations;
- steel production, eg seamless steel facility;
- infrastructure, eg roads, rail, bridges.

Project finance is predominantly about finance against the future cash flows of a project and not asset values. Consequently we can distinguish project finance from other types of structured finance such as property finance, aerospace finance and shipping finance.

Project finance is normally associated with highly leveraged transactions with a limited amount of equity from the sponsors.

1.1 The concept of project financing

Private companies use project finance to:

- finance a project beyond the means of an investor's corporate resources. An example here would be smaller, independent oil companies who often use project finance to fund their share of an oil and gas field development. Some projects are so large that they are beyond the means of virtually any corporate investor, for example Eurotunnel;
- preserve corporate banking lines. By financing off balance sheet the existing financial arrangements of the company are unaffected;
- bring forward capital investments. A company may have many competing investment opportunities that consume capital. By using project finance, capital is restricted to equity contributions and can therefore gear up the company's overall level of activity;
- improve the return on capital in a project by leveraging the investment to a greater extent than would be possible in a straight commercial financing of the project;
- limit the risks of a project to a company. By using limited recourse project finance part of the risk is laid off either to financial institutions or other commercial companies;
- insure against political risks. Major oil companies in particular fund oil and gas developments in politically secure areas of the world on their own balance sheet, which is cheaper, but look to use project finance in politically less stable areas, eg Africa to limit their exposure;

- develop joint-venture projects. These projects bring together a number of disciplines and interested parties. Thus a company may be a contractor wishing to build a plant, a supplier seeking a plant to provide an outlet for its materials, or a company hoping to secure long-term supply from the plant's output. In this instance no one company would want to take the project on its own balance sheet and a special-purpose company is created with the risks being shared among the participants;
- improve tax efficiency. A common structure used is leasing whereby the project exchanges tax benefits in return for a lower cost of funds. Many tax-driven project finance facilities have recently been put in place for subsidiaries of oil companies operating in Norway, following a change in the taxation rules whereby interest was tax deductible only on finance not supported by the parent company.

1.2 Government's uses of project finance

- Improving the infrastructure. Increasingly a number of countries, including the UK, look to the private sector to develop and finance infrastructure development, eg Channel Tunnel, Dartford River Crossing, Second Severn River Crossing. The reasoning is a mix of political, ideological and financial reasons. In order to preserve the public interest in infrastructure projects governments will grant a private company a concession to build and operate a facility for a fixed term whereupon it reverts back to the government. These financings are commonly known as Build, Own, Operate, Transfer or BOOT. The Eurotunnel concession expires in 2055 when it reverts back to the UK/French governments.
- Expanding their economies and as a surrogate way of financing their balance of payments. Developing countries in particular encourage project finance to raise their level of industrialization, introduce new technology, finance investment etc.

2 The characteristics and structure of project finance

Generally the players in a project finance structure are:

- developer or sponsor
- equity investor(s)
- debt provider(s)
- government
- construction contractor(s)
- operator
- input supplier(s)
- output or offtake purchaser(s)

Figure 11.1

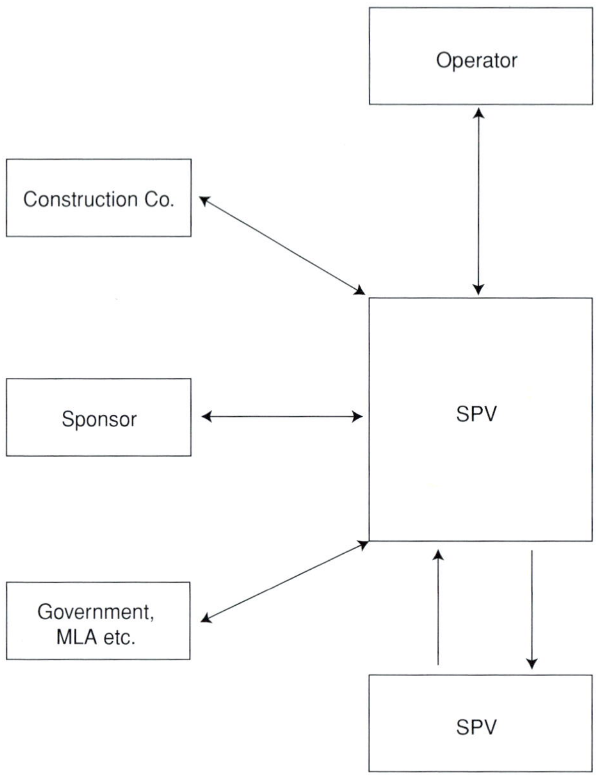

A typical project financing involves three distinct phases when the risk characteristics change:

- the first phase is the construction phase. Projects generally begin with a long period of planning and engineering, contracts are let and construction begins. It is here that the debt starts to be drawn down and interest builds up. Note the company is not trading yet and consequently interest needs to be capitalized;
- the next phase is the commissioning phase. Once construction (or mechanical completion) is finished the facility or plant needs to be tested in order that it fulfils the design specifications on which the work contracts were let and the basis on which the lenders made available funds. This will usually involve fully operating the plant for a period of time; and finally

- the operating phase. Once the plant has passed the commissioning phase successfully, it is passed over by the contractor to the operator and the project begins to function like a normal trading company. During this phase revenues are earned, enough hopefully to pay operating costs, repay the lenders and provide a return to the equity providers.

3 Essential prerequisites of project finance

Under normal circumstances a bank will lend to a company, and in assessing risk will look to the strength of that company. With limited recourse project finance a bank is normally lending against a particular project, and as such will require detailed examination of the project. There are some basic criteria that must be met before lenders will consider limited recourse finance:

- it must be possible to identify a project that can operate on a reasonably stand-alone basis (for some such reason limited recourse finance is often called 'project finance'), and either
- the project must have a clearly defined output that is capable of generating the cash-flows necessary to service the debt, or
- the assets of the project must be sufficient to act as collateral for the debt.

These requirements tend to be most easily met by projects in the area of mineral extraction and processing, for example the exploitation of a metal deposit, the operation of an oil-field or the construction of an oil pipeline. They have also long been used in the world of commercial property development, while in recent years interest in project finance techniques has been stimulated by the determination of governments in certain countries, including the UK, that infrastructure projects should be financed in the private sector.

Often a government grants a concession to the project company to build and operate the concession, eg an oil or gas production licence, a mining concession, or a permit to build and operate a power plant or pipeline. These concessions vary from one-off mining concessions to routine permits, eg planning and environmental permissions from local authorities. These projects may be described as BOOT (build, own, operate, transfer) or BOO (build, own, operate), according to their individual characteristics. They may be found (or discussed) in the developed world (eg Channel Tunnel, Second Dartford Crossing) or in countries such as Turkey, Pakistan, Thailand and Indonesia. In the case of BOOT or BOO projects the government transfers the land to the project company on terms that it is to be re-transferred after a period sufficiently long to repay the finance and to give the project sponsors a reasonable profit margin. The concession by the government will be given to the project company by way of a Concession Agreement.

4 Inherent risks of project finance

Invariably a lender on a limited recourse basis is incurring a higher risk level than if it were lending on a conventional basis to a major corporate borrower. This is because in loans to a company the risk will be spread across a number of operations or projects – by definition in limited recourse single project finance there is no risk-spreading.

Project risks are related to the operations and economics of the project itself within the environment of the industry, as well as all the normal financial factors. Lenders to projects will want to be fully aware of all aspects of the project in order to analyse its overall credit worthiness. Borrowers need to be aware of this, and of the ways in which lenders may seek to limit their risk. Factors that will be considered by lenders include the following.

4.1 Completion risk

This is the risk that, for whatever reason, a project will not be completed in line with the project timetable or within the financial resources established for the project. Because the lenders will have advanced funds to finance progress, non-completion will leave them in an impossible position, there being no revenue with which the outstanding borrowing can be serviced.

A major concern to lenders will be that the project can be completed to budget and on time. Cost overrun causes serious problems because unless the remaining construction costs are paid the facility will not be completed and the Project will not generate funds to repay the debt. This was the single most important feature for lenders in the Eurotunnel financing. Costs to complete the project have risen from around £5 billion forecast in 1987 to over £7 billion forecast in 1992. In October 1990 the existing syndicate agreed to put up a further £1.8bn to meet the increased costs.

A delay in completion also has a serious affect both in delaying the revenue stream and raising capitalized interest, resulting in a cost overrun. Delay in completion may also adversely affect other contracts such as an offtake agreement.

Lenders normally look to obtain fixed price construction contracts from the contractor to cover the risk of cost overrun and for completion guarantees. Clearly the credibility of the contractor is key in its ability to perform the contract at the fixed price and by a certain date. Lenders will look for a contractor with a good reputation, the necessary technical competence and resources and one this is financially strong. A contractor may be asked to provide a performance bond from its bankers to guarantee its performance.

Where a contractor cannot deliver it can lead to disastrous consequences for the contractor and project alike. Davy Corporation essentially lost its independence and was taken over by Trafalgar House in trying to complete an oil production facility for the Emerald Oil Field. Eventually the contract was finished at a cost to Davy massively over the fixed price and was delivered two years late on an 18-month contract. The field was being developed by a small company on a project finance basis and had to survive two years without oil revenues.

4.2 Technical risk

This will clearly depend on the type of the project under consideration. As an example, for a mineral resource project the technical risks would include the following:

- Estimation of reserves. How much is available and how much can be recovered economically?
  Determining answers to these questions is difficult and often can be done with some degree of confidence only after the project has already been in operation for some time. For example, an accurate determination of the reserves of an oil field can be made only after oil has been produced for a period of time sufficient to allow the characteristics of the reservoir to be assessed
- Speed of development. How quickly the reserves can be developed will be a major factor in determining the amortization (capital repayment) schedule of the loan.

4.3 Market risk

The marketability of the project is clearly crucial; both price and volume considerations are important, and are a key element in determining the amortization schedule of the loan.

The success of many project finance structures depends on how the market risk for the product or service produced by the project is handled. Structures vary considerably.

At one extreme a major customer may be required to sign a contract for up to all of the output, based on an agreed pricing regime for a term to produce a revenue stream to at least repay the debt. Known as 'take-or-pay' contracts, the purchaser has to pay for the output whether he takes it or not. These are more common where there is a monopoly or virtual monopoly purchasers as in most power station financings. In the case of the UK Independent Gas Fired Power Financings an element of the pricing mechanism under the take-or-pay contract will be a charge for the gas used which under efficient operating conditions exactly matches the gas price under the supply contract. In this way the gas price input risk is passed through to the electricity purchaser.

At the other extreme, banks are willing to take full market risk on oil-field developments in the knowledge that there is a well-developed spot market for oil and banks can take their own view on oil prices. The danger of this approach was highlighted in the mid-1980s when oil prices collapsed and a number of oil companies went with it. Some banks exited from oil-field finance because of this.

Infrastructure projects represent a challenge to project financiers in dealing with the market (eg traffic) risk. To date in the UK only projects where there has been a local monopoly on traffic have they succeeded in attracting project finance, the bridge over the Thames at Dartford has an effective monopoly linking the M25, and the second crossing over the Severn Bridge on traffic between England and South Wales. In the case of both the Dartford and Second Severn crossing transactions the project company was able to take over the existing crossing so that they did not compete. The UK government is currently encouraging project finance for proposed toll roads of which the Birmingham Northern Relief Road, expected to open in Summer 2003. It remains to be seen whether there is a future for project finance for such projects where toll roads complete with free roads.

4.4 Political and country risk

As indicated above an attempt to protect the project against political risk can be one of the major reasons for considering project finance. Political risk can manifest itself in a variety of ways, from a change in tax regime to outright expropriation.

The ultimate political risk, and closely allied to it country risk, is expropriation (confiscation of assets). This risk of direct expropriation in certain areas of the world, notably developing countries, is obvious. Problems occur when a country is not in an economic position to permit transfer of foreign currencies to overseas lenders, or changes in government lead to a new political regime with a different ideological creed. Political and country risk also covers such things as war, trade embargos, etc.

Lenders also need to consider creeping expropriation. For example, this can take the form of increasing taxes, failure to renew licences or import/export permits. Creeping expropriation is not restricted to developing countries. An example might be that UK tax on revenues from North Sea Oil production has doubled from the original rate of 31% in the early 1970s.

Unless covered by insurance the risk of expropriation can never be fully mitigated where the assets are located in the particular country. Offshore escrow accounts are a feature of project finance structures whereby moneys from sales of say oil are deposited outside the country in question. This reduces the temptation of a hard-pressed foreign government to acquire it.

Project finance facilities in countries where political risk is a concern are often linked with a World Bank loan, so that seizure of the asset results in cross-default under international loans. The assumption by lenders is that a country is less likely to default under World Bank loans and threaten their international credit standing.

4.5 Assured input supplies

Supply sources and contracts for feed stocks to be used by a project must be assured at a cost consistent with the financial projections. Where the input is critical lenders will require a Long-Term Supply Contract for a term sufficient that the debt will have been repaid. Lenders will need to be comfortable with the reliability of the supplier, its ability to perform and the enforceability of the supply contract. In the case of many of the UK Independent Gas Fired Power Station Financings the station purchases gas under a 15-year supply contract from British Gas at a base price with agreed escalation clauses. In waste-to-energy deals the waste company delivers waste under a 'put-or-pay' contract, ie fail to deliver and the company pays the lost revenues of the power station. There may also be equipment supply contracts whereby manufacturers agree to supply the equipment for the project. These contracts may also be bonded.

4.6 All necessary licences and permits in place

Bankers will not disperse any funds until regulatory approvals are in place. This is something that will be specifically drafted into the conditions precedent of any project finance legal agreements. This ranges from such things as local planning consent to the UK government giving consent to an oil-field development plan. A particularly key area is environmental consents in relation to, say, a coal-fired power station or a waste-to-energy facility. All permits relating to emissions and discharges need to be obtained and regularly monitored to ensure that they are complied with. The issue of lender liability, especially in the United States, is a sensitive one.

Where licences are not available until after the facility is built a lender needs to be assured that they will be granted in a fair manner based on the standards at the time of the start of the project. Where there has been a change in law from the start of the project the lenders and the project need to be protected.

4.7 Experienced operator

The operator must have the financial and technical expertise to operate the project in accordance with the specifications and budgets that form the basis of the financial feasibility. Normally one of the sponsors has the expertise to operate the facility; alternatively professional operating companies may be employed under long-term contracts. An operator enters into an operating and maintenance agreement with the project company to operate the project in return for a fee.

4.8 Other aspects

Foreign exchange risk

Where revenues and expenditures are in different currencies potential losses to the project from currency fluctuations arise. Hedging instruments can mitigate this risk as well as a well-structured loan, eg a multi-currency facility.

Adequate insurance cover

This needs to be in place during both construction and operation of the project. Business interruption insurance will provide protection against the possibility the project cannot be operated. Insurance proceeds should be assigned to lenders.

Force majeure

Force majeure events are those that arise beyond the control of the parties to the financing. Events include fire, flood and earthquake that are generally insurable and events such as war, strikes, nuclear explosion, civil disturbances etc. which may or may not be insurable. Key parties such as the supplier or offtaker are also of course subject to force majeure risk. Where possible lenders will need to lay off these risks either by insurance or through contractual obligations of the sponsors, suppliers etc.

Inflation and interest rates

Both of these macroeconomic variables need to be considered although it is often real interest rates (the difference between nominal interest and nominal inflation rates) that lenders are most concerned with. A variety of hedging contracts can be used for interest rates: swaps, collars, caps, floors etc.

5 Limiting the risk

Although the aim of the sponsor of a project will be to raise finance that is essentially non-recourse, the lenders will be seeking to minimize their risks. As a first step, they will aim to familiarize themselves completely with the project, to take technical advice, make independent assessments of the marketability of the output, and so on. The project sponsor must be prepared for detailed analysis of the project by potential lenders and be prepared to allow complete access to all relevant information, as the financial package is put together.

Thereafter, there are a number of common ways in which the lenders can limit their risk, most of which involve the giving of some form of undertaking and, therefore, the participation in the risk by the individual parties interested in the project. Examples are:

5.1 Completion guarantees

This may take the form of guarantees from one or more project sponsors that the project will be completed on time and/or on budget and that, if it is not, the sponsor will service the lenders' debt or, as appropriate, provide subordinated funds to allow completion.

It will be realized that the lenders can achieve similar protection in a different form if contracts are signed for the building of the project on a fixed-price turnkey basis with liquidated damages sufficient to cover the debt service.

5.2 Offtake agreements

A major customer may be required to sign contracts requiring him to purchase a set amount (or even all) of the output of the project or to pay for it even if he does not (a 'take or pay' contract). This is an important safeguard to the lenders, ensuring them of revenue from which their debts can be serviced. Where such agreements exist much discussion is likely to centre on the price to be set for the purchases. The following have all been known:

- purchase at ruling market price (or even at a discount thereto);
- purchase at market price but with guaranteed minimum price;
- purchase at price that, after payment of operating costs and taxes, will allow payment of debt service. (This is an extreme case but it is encountered in oil pipeline financing.)

5.3 Fixing of interest rates

Lenders may wish to ensure that hedges are in place at least during the construction period to limit the impact of rising interest rates on the project's financial plan.

5.4 Insurance

Lenders may require that certain residual risks are covered by insurance. Political risk and force majeure are common examples but the insurance markets can be surprisingly flexible in their willingness to cover elements of project risk. For instance it is a little remarked element of the Channel Tunnel financing that there was limited insurance against late opening of the tunnel. Conditions precedent in the loan agreement will require lenders to see sight of relevant insurance policies. Also the representations and warranties will require the borrower to have valid insurance cover in force prior to any draw-down.

5.5 Government guarantees

There may be opportunities for obtaining some (probably limited) guarantees from the government of the host country to the project. These may be of many varied types. Provision of tax-free periods, exemption from withholding tax on interest remitted overseas, and provision of standby equity are all examples. One should remember that issues relating to sovereign immunity may attach to such guarantees in that they may be unenforceable against a state unless it has consented to waive any immunity form both jurisdiction and enforcement.

5.6 The provision of equity or quasi-equity

Any normal project, even one that is primarily financed by limited recourse borrowing, will require some element of equity or quasi-equity (sponsor's guarantees or subordinated loans) before it is acceptable to lenders. This provides the risk capital for the project. The exact mix of equity and limited recourse borrowing will be the subject of negotiation between the project's sponsors and the lenders. In general, a higher debt/equity ratio will be found in project finance than in the financing structure of most major companies.

From the examples quoted, it is hoped that it will be appreciated that there are no hard and fast rules in this area. The lenders will wish to reduce their risks to a minimum acceptable level. They do not mind how this is done. Plainly it is simplest if a risk is covered by one clear guarantee from as creditworthy entity, but the same risk in another project may be split up and taken in portions by different parties, with a residual element even being left with the lenders.

Clearly there are no precise criteria that can be applied for a successful project financing. However, a viable project finance proposition is all about identifying, understanding and sharing risk and will need to consider the financial viability of the project. The feasibility study will be separate from the sponsor's business plan and supported by independent studies from outside consultants. Independent consultants can be used to confirm such things as the project, and the size and extent of the market for the output.

An appraisal of reserves needs to be made if an oil or mining company is involved. The obvious risk here is whether there are insufficient recoverable resources to pay operating costs and repay the debt. Independent consultants can determine to a high degree of confidence the quality of such reserves, the technical feasibility of recovery and the proportion of reserves that are economic to recover. Some banks employ their own in-house engineers to conduct such approvals.

In order that the economics can be understood a computer-based model is developed to reflect the cash-flows (cash-flow modelling and sensitivity analysis is discussed in greater detail later). The independent studies form the basis of the assumptions used in the cash-flow model, the result of which will show whether the project is prima facie a viable financing proposition. As the project develops the cash-flow model assumes increasing importance for lenders in optimizing the finance structure and demonstrating the strength of the project to downside assumptions or 'What If' scenarios.

6 Legal documentation

6.1 Syndication of the project finance facility

The sponsors also prepare an information memorandum with the help of the banks in order to solicit banks interested in participating in the credit. This contains a description of the project, the terms of the financing, and cash-flow forecasts showing the financial feasibility of the project.

A project finance agreement will be like a conventional syndicated credit agreement on usual (but modified) syndication principles, eg severalty of lender commitments and rights, syndicate democracy, pro rata sharing between banks, and the appointment of an agent bank. There will also be the appointment of independent experts to advise the banks, such as engineers and insurance brokers.

Where a project finance agreement varies form a an ordinary loan or a conventional syndicated loan is in that the purpose clause will be very specific, in that the loan can be drawn down only to pay specific project costs for approved capital expenditure and construction costs. The purposes for which funds can be drawn down will be specifically stated in the Purpose clause or cross-referenced to another document.

6.2 Other project finance documentation

The project company grants the financiers the maximum security available locally over the assets. There may be an inter-creditor agreement between the lenders or banks. The other agreements have already been mentioned in the text but may include the following:

(a) fixed-price construction contract;

(b) performance bond;

(c) long-term supply contracts;

(d) operating and maintenance agreement;

(e) offtake agreements;

(f) concession agreements;

(g) the project sponsors may guarantee the loans under full or limited guarantees during the high-risk or pre-completion period.

6.3 General terms of the inter-creditor agreement

Draw-downs are usually in tranches and the interest rate that is applied is usually floating. The repayment of the project finance loan is always tied to the projected cash-flows of the project, and often in the early years of the loan or in the pre-completion phase there are no repayments at all only interest, and that too could be deferred.

6.4 Conditions precedent

The conditions precedent to the loan include the usual legal documentation, accuracy of warranties, and no default, but also the obtaining of all necessary permits for the project. Each loan is usually subject to an additional condition precedent that there is sufficient finance to meet projected costs (including overruns). In order to be bankable, projects require an initial feasibility study prepared by experts, eg engineering, construction, and technical consultants instructed by the sponsors. These reports are also stipulated as being part of the conditions precedent.

Often there is no individual bank veto on draw-downs if the conditions precedent are not satisfied – contrary to normal syndication practice. This is subject to majority bank control to ensure finance availability: the banks stand or fall together.

Typical conditions precedent

The obligation of each bank to make any loan is subject to the prior receipt by the agent bank of:

- the borrower's constitutional documents;
- the borrower's authorizing resolutions for this agreement and all the documents specified below to which the borrower is a party;
- the information memorandum for the project;
- that all ancillary financial documents (security agreements, equity agreements, completion guarantees, hedging agreements etc) have been duly executed;
- acceptance by the agent for service of process under the jurisdiction clause;
- that all notices and acknowledgements of assignment (such as project contacts, government concessions and insurances) are in force;

- that all project-related agreements have been executed such as the joint-venture agreements, construction contract, operating and maintenance agreements, off-take agreements;
- all licences and permits in place;
- all insurances are in force;
- certificate that the conditions precedent in other project financing agreements are satisfied and the other lenders are committed;
- legal opinions.

6.5 Representations and warranties

The borrower represents and warrants:

- its due incorporation and valid existence;
- its powers and authority for the financial and security agreements, the concession and the project contracts (for these documents, see clause 3.1);
- the legal validity of those agreements, the concession and contracts;
- that the carrying out of those documents does not conflict with any law or regulation or the borrower's constitution or any borrower contract;
- that all authorizations and permits have been obtained for those documents and the project;
- that there is no event of default or pending default;
- that there is no material litigation or other proceedings involving the borrower or relating to the project;
- that the information memorandum is materially correct and there are no material omissions; there has been no adverse change since the date of the information memorandum; the forecasts are reasonably based;
- that the security is first priority, is not subject to *pari passu* security interests and is not liable to be set aside on insolvency;
- that the borrower owns the project site free from encumbrances and restrictions;
- that the prescribed insurances are in force and not liable to be set aside for non-disclosure or otherwise;
- that the borrower owns all necessary intellectual property rights for the project;
- environmental compliance and no environmental liability.

6.6 Evergreen repetition clause

The representations and warranties will remain true (subject to agreed exemptions for commercial warranties) so long as the loans are outstanding or any bank commitment is in force.

6.7 Covenants

The key covenants are:

(i) No changes to the project plan without consent. 'Not to be unreasonably withheld' is usually rejected as too vague and restrictive of the banking discretion.

(ii) Absolute control of the project contracts, eg the construction, supply, purchase, and operation and maintenance contracts. These controls tend to be tight and limit waivers, consents, relaxations and the variations without consent. If one thread in the contract web is to be cut, the banks often wish to be involved, even at the risk of administrative constipation.

(iii) Controls on capital expenditure, partly because of the risk of underfunding and of a change in the project (disturbing the agreed economics) and the need to control technology and to prevent odd bolt-ons.

(iv) Controls on other debt because other creditors may have harassment potential. The covenant limits hire purchase, leasing, borrowings and guarantees, and inhibits future funding without bank consent to finance additional works or variations. Frequently other debt is permitted if subordinated in a way that strips the other creditor of all his rights so that the senior creditors may act as if there were no junior creditor at all, ie the junior debt is in substance equity, not debt.

6.8 Financial cover ratios

The key financial ratios that may be incorporated into a project finance agreement are Project and Loan Life Cover Ratios to control an appropriate level of debt.

The tool of the trade for project financiers is Discounted Cash Flow or Net Present Value (NPV) analysis. This is the value of the future cash-flows of a project in today's money (or at the date of calculation). In the base case cash-flow and sensitivity runs the discounted value of the future cash-flows should always exceed the amount of debt outstanding. This ratio is known either as a Loan Life Cover Ratio (LLCR) based on discounted cash-flows to the end of the loan period or Projected Life Cover Ratio (PLCR) to the end of the economic life of the project, ie:

$$\text{LLCR} = \frac{\text{NPV of future cash-flow to end of loan}}{\text{Debt Outstanding}}$$

$$\text{PLCR} = \frac{\text{NPV of future cash-flow to end of project}}{\text{Debt Outstanding}}$$

This calculation is done for every year (or half-year) to determine the minimum ratio and when this occurs, although normally the minimum ratio occurs in the early years.

The question of what discount ratio to use is really outside the scope of this discussion.

For projects most susceptible to market risks (eg Eurotunnel) minimum base case cover ratios ought to be around 1.75 – that is there is forecast to be 75% more cash in the project than required to repay the debt.

For 'less' risk projects, for example oil financings for well-understood oil-field developments, minimum ratios more in the range of 1.25–1.5 are commonly used. A feature of some oil-field financings is the concept of a Borrowing Base Facility where the discounted cash-flows are divided by a number (say 1.25) to give an amount available to be drawn down under a loan agreement. This is recomputed every six months and if the discounted cash-flow increases or falls the Borrowing Base Amount rises or falls, and the company can either borrow more money or must repay some.

To the extent that LLCR falls below 1 the lenders are looking at a loan that will not be repaid on time. To the extent that PLCR falls below 1 there is insufficient cash in the project to repay the lenders.

6.9 Debt Service Cover Ratios (DSCRs)

DSCRs are more commonly used in Power Station Financings where an 'operating test' is required. This is simply the available cash-flow in a particular period to meet debt service divided by debt service in the period (interest and principal). Typical minimum values that lenders would accept would be 1.3/1.4:1.

6.10 Reserve tails

Generally lenders wish to see that the project is economically viable after the scheduled end of the loan. In the case of a power station this may be that the contractual structure stays in place for a number of years after repayment of debt. For an oil and gas field development this would be that a percentage of economically recoverable reserves remain to be produced from the oil-field.

These are known as reserve tails and provide further comfort to the banks.

6.11 Events of default

The view of banks is that events of default are not to be regarded as an opportunity to get one's money back or as an opportunity to pounce, but rather as an early warning device that will give the banks the ability to be heard in the management of the project if things should go wrong. If things continue to deteriorate the banks must have the ability to seize control and appoint, for example, a new operator to manage the project. Seizing control though is very much a last resort with the argument that banks do not call a halt to a project once their money is already in place unless the position is totally irredeemable.

Typical events of default are:

(i) There will be the usual defaults such as non-payment, non-compliance, breach of warranty, cross-default, insolvency, creditor's processes and a sweep-up material adverse change.

(ii) There will usually be events of default relating to non-completion of the project by a long-stop date, any abandonment of the project or insolvency of the sponsors, breaches of the financial cover ratios or debt service cover ratios; a variation of more than 10% of the financial projections because a 10% variation can be crucial.

(iii) Any revocation or variation of the government concession.

(iv) Any nationalization, expropriation or destruction of the project.

(v) Any legal or regulatory changes.

(vi) Insurance cover not available at commercial rates.

7 The project as security

Lenders will seek to take first fixed and floating charges over all the assets of the project including assignment of project contracts, insurance proceeds etc to protect their position in the event that security needs to be enforced. Ideally the security should cover all the project assets, but this may not be possible in all jurisdictions. These assets mainly comprise: the project land and fixtures; project plant, equipment and other moveable goods; project product in course of production; the project construction contract; contracts for the supply of raw materials, fuel or the like to the project; project sale contracts; the proceeds account and authorized investments; the project company's claims against third parties; the host government concession; the operating agreement; insurances; requisition and nationalization proceeds; and industrial proprietary rights.

The key element of the security package for lenders to an infrastructure project will be an assignment of the borrowers rights under the Concession Agreement.

The main objects of project security are to prime unsecured creditors, to act as a defence against unsecured creditors, and to confer control of the project on a default.

Project security is often defensive, a shield not a sword, because normal enforcement realization may be unrealistic. Thus project assets (pipelines, mines cables) are often non-marketable.

Another motive of project security is to confer control of the project on the banks if there is a default. Complete control is available only if the comprehensive floating charge is possible in the jurisdiction concerned.

Twelve

Raising capital – equity finance

1 Introduction

We shall now turn our attention specifically to equity finance – the various types and how it can be raised. The unit concentrates on the commercial and financial aspects of the acquisition process. Regulatory aspects and areas specific to listed company offers are covered in subsequent units.

2 Types of equity

In this section we shall focus our attention specifically on UK equities, taking a look at the various forms that shares can take. Remember that an equity investor is actually purchasing a share of the company and as such the holder is entitled to certain rights that tend to vary depending on the type of share in question. We shall look at the most common forms below.

2.1 Ordinary shares

Ordinary shares usually form the core of a company's share capital and the holders are commonly given the following rights:

- to appoint/remove directors;
- to receive dividends, provided such have been declared and any higher-ranking holders have received theirs;
- to exercise one vote per share at company general meetings;

- a holder's liability is restricted to the fully-paid value of shares held, therefore in the case of partly-paid shares the holder's liability is the payment outstanding; and
- in the event of the company being wound-up, once all other prior claims have been settled, any assets remaining are distributed to ordinary shareholders on a pro rata basis in line with respective shareholdings.

You must appreciate that the ordinary shareholders carry most of the financial risk because there is no guaranteed return, and in the event of financial disaster they may be unlikely to receive anything by way of distribution. However, the main attraction to the investor is the possibility of potentially very high rewards indeed, subject to the financial prosperity of the company, and that a degree of control, at least, is available through voting rights.

It is typical of the various classes of shares available that the rights and obligations of holders may vary to some degree depending on the requirements of the company. Such rights and obligations will be stipulated in the company's Memorandum and Articles of Association. A common practice, in this respect, is conferring different voting rights on different holders, for example by issuing 'classes' of ordinary shares ('A' Ordinary, 'B' Ordinary). The existing shareholders may thus be able to retain a greater level of control over the company's affairs. By issuing shares with either low, or even no voting rights, we must remember that this type of share is unlikely to attract the equity investor.

2.2 Preference shares

As the name implies, a preference share affords at least some differential treatment on its holder, compared to the ordinary shareholders. The 'preference' refers to the priority such holders have over others in connection with the right to dividends and to obtain distribution of any assets to the value of the amount paid up, if the company is wound-up. Normal voting rights are not usually associated with preference shares, although such holders will be entitled to vote in certain specified instances, for example, where dividend arrears occur or where the company is being wound up.

Preference share dividends are at a fixed rate and may be cumulative, ie any arrears have to be settled in full before dividends are paid to ordinary shareholders. In the case of non-cumulative preference shares no such right is available to holders and therefore unpaid previous dividends need not be met in future years.

Another variation is the participating preference share that provides the holder with a fixed dividend element plus the opportunity to benefit further from sharing any additional surplus profit remaining, in excess of the preferential amount agreed, with the ordinary shareholders.

Ordinary shares are almost always issued as permanent equity. However, it is possible, although not very common, for preference shares to be redeemable. In this instance the nominal value will be repaid by the company either on a predetermined future date or within a specified future period.

2.3 Convertibles

Convertibles are regularly examined, so more detailed information is contained in section 5 below.

There are essentially two types of 'convertible'. First, and least common, are convertible preference shares that may be converted to ordinary shares in certain circumstances. More often, though the term 'convertible' relates to a debt instrument that gives the lender/investor the right to convert to ordinary shares (or possibly preference shares) in the future, for example convertible bonds. Conversion will be at the holder's option, with the option period running between specified future dates. During the period leading up to conversion the holder will be entitled to interest (dividend) at a specified fixed rate.

2.4 Warrants

Warrants are usually associated with debt issues and are 'attached' in a similar way to the conversion option, as outlined above. The warrant is effectively the right for the holder to purchase a specified number of shares at a predetermined price, either on a stipulated future date or between two future dates. The warrants themselves clearly have value and hence may be traded as separate instruments to the underlying loan stock.

2.5 What type to choose?

Think about the various characteristics of all the above and identify the main benefits/ disadvantages of each to the issuer.

Ordinary shares

(i) Benefit

- Readily acceptable to investors as the most common form of equity.
- No commitment to pay dividends.
- May retain voting control by restricting holders' rights (although this may prove unattractive to investors).

(ii) Disadvantages

- Loss of control follows when voting rights are given (which is most common).
- Investors regard such as a high risk and will expect return to reflect this, particularly if the company is making good profits.

Preference shares

(i) Benefits

- No loss of control, given the usual absence of voting rights, except in certain circumstances.
- May be more attractive to the investor because there is a known level of return, assuming profits are sufficient.
- May be redeemable/cumulative/non-cumulative to suit the company's needs.
- The rate fixed may prove exceptionally good value in the future, if market rates rise and profits are high.

(ii) Disadvantages

- Commitment to pay dividends at a predetermined level.
- Cumulative preference shares give the right to holders to have arrears met in full from future profits.
- It may prove expensive to set the rate of return at an acceptable level to attract investors.

Convertibles

(i) Benefits

- By giving an option to convert, the investor may be more likely to accept a lower initial return on the loan stock, in anticipation of making a gain on conversion.
- May prove attractive to overseas investors, being an alternative source of financing for the issuer.

(ii) Disadvantages

- May be expensive if the investor is able to convert at a price well below the market rate (ie it may well be more beneficial to obtain straight debt finance, but at a higher cost, and raise equity to repay, also at the higher market price prevailing – assuming the market moves that way).

- Some investors may have a preference for either straight debt or straight equity.
- Uncertainty as to timing of conversion, if the 'between two dates' exercise period is allowed.

Warrants

(i) Benefits

- May be useful in keeping down the cost of the underlying stock.
- A means of combining debt and equity, ie the debt remains and new equity is raised (whereas with convertibles actual conversion from debt to equity takes place).
- The warrants themselves have trade value.

(ii) Disadvantages

- Uncertainty as to take up and timing.
- Overall true cost may prove more expensive, in the same way as for convertibles.

These various forms of equity are available from two broad sources. First, there is the 'private' injection either from the proprietors or a third party such as a bank. The second source of equity are the 'public' markets, and these feature in the next section.

3 Public markets

3.1 The reasons why companies would wish to become 'quoted'

There can be a variety of reasons but the main reasons are likely to be some, or all, of the following:

(a) long-term capital finance is required and is not readily available from more private sources;

(b) to achieve the ambition of the directors;

(c) to release existing shareholders' stakes;

(d) to improve company image;

(e) to provide access to other funds in the future, for example Sterling Commercial Paper or simply a Rights Issue;

(f) to provide the opportunity to raise substantial amounts that would otherwise be unavailable.

At present, the Stock Exchange operates two levels of entry into the market – the Full List and the Alternative Investment Market (AIM). Of the two, the full list is the senior market, and membership demands the most onerous responsibilities.

3.2 The UK Listing Authority

Before a company can be admitted to the Stock Exchange it must comply with the rules for admission contained in the Listing Rules, which is known as the 'Purple Book'. This details the requirements a company must meet prior to being admitted to the full list.

Under section 72 of the Financial Services and Markets Act 2000 the competent authority for listing is the Financial Services Authority ('FSA') though a department of the FSA known as the UK Listing Authority ('UKLA').

The general functions of UKLA are:

- to make rules relating to listing and related matters;
- to give general guidance relating to listing;
- to determine general policy and principles by reference to which it performs its functions.

All applicants must have a sponsor to guide them through the process of applying for a hearing and submitting documentation to the UKLA. Documentation in its final form must be submitted 48 hours prior to the hearing. This is known as the '48-hour rule'.

Companies are obliged to produce and include in that documentation a statement by the directors confirming that the working capital of the business will be adequate. This letter must be submitted and approved by the sponsor.

Fully-listed companies are generally required to produce a prospectus under the Listing Rules. This contains detailed information and a report given by the company's accountants on the information produced. The level of detail and the requirement for verification makes a prospectus under the listing rules much more expensive to produce than an ordinary prospectus produced by an unlisted company issuing shares.

Regardless of the type of issue the advertising requirement is one small box in a national newspaper, known as a formal notice.

3.3 Full Stock Exchange listing

Admission requirements

The basic conditions detailed in the Listing Rules are contained in Chapter 3 of the Purple Book and are summarized as follows.

(a) The expected market value of shares issued by the company must be at least £700,000. If the company is to issue debt, the expected market value of any such debt must be at least £200,000.

(b) All securities issued must be freely transferable.

(c) The company must have a trading record of at least three years.

(d) The shares of a company must be marketable. This will be assumed to be the case if 25% of the company's share capital is in public hands.

(e) The issue of warrants or options onto the stock of a company is limited to 20% of the existing capital base.

(f) The UKLA will not normally admit to the full list to a company that has a substantial shareholder holding 30% or more of the shares.

Any issue of shares for cash must contain a pre-emption right granted to the existing shareholders, eg offer to existing shareholders before taking it to the Stock Exchange. This protection is contained in the Companies Act 1985 that states that shareholders may give permission to waive pre-emption rights for a period of up to five years.

Fees are substantially higher for a full listing, largely due to the provision of full financial information and the need to print the prospectus in the national press.

3.4 Continuing obligations

All applicants for membership agree to be bound by the continuing obligations of the UKLA. UKLA therefore supplements the legal framework for disclosure by public companies (whether listed or unlisted) contained in company law through the Companies Acts. These obligations require the company to:

- notify the Stock Exchange of any price-sensitive information;
- publish information about important transactions undertaken by the company under the Class Tests Rule;
- inform the Stock Exchange of any changes in the important registers of ownership of the shares, such as notifiable interests and directors' share holdings;
- notify the Stock Exchange of dividends;
- issue reports. Annual financial statements must be available within six months of the year-end and, in addition, Stock Exchange companies are

obliged to produce half-yearly results within four months of the half year. This is an improvement on the rules contained within the Companies Act that require plcs to produce accounts within seven months (private companies have ten months).

These disclosures are made through the Company Announcements Office of the Stock Exchange, which is the information dissemination provider that is approved by the UKLA. The Stock Exchange Regulatory News Service then sells this information to public quote vendors and information systems such as Telerate and Reuters.

When an announcement is lengthy, Stock Exchange guidance is that prominence should be given to current and future trading prospects. These are the basic entry conditions that must be met prior to admission to the full list. However, even if all these conditions are met, the Stock Exchange may still refuse admittance on the following grounds:

- the applicant has previously broken the listing requirements of another member state of the European Community;
- the applicant is not fit and proper.

3.5 Underwriting

When the issue involves placing, offer or tender it is general practice for the company to take the precaution of having the issue underwritten, usually by major financial institutions. The latter undertake to take up the shares in the event that they are not taken up by the public, thus assuring the company that it will receive the amount it is seeking. The company will pay a fee to the underwriters for this 'insurance'.

This is not required for an introduction because this method of listing is used where the required number of shares are already held publicly.

3.6 The Alternative Investment Market

This market was introduced in 1995 and provides a forum for trading company shares within a very light regulatory regime. The aim is to thus provide easier access to the market for younger companies. There are no regulations governing minimum market value, percentage in public hands or trading record. Companies must produce a prospectus, although the level of information required is lower than that for a prospectus in connection with a listing. In such a case the contents of the prospectus are governed by the Public Offer of Securities Regulations. AIM companies must also appoint a nominated broker and nominated adviser while their shares trade through this market.

The key elements of the market are as follows:

- companies must publish a prospectus or equivalent document meeting the EU public offers Directives;
- accuracy of documents will be the responsibility of the company's directors;
- companies must publish price-sensitive information promptly;
- companies must meet certain ongoing obligations;
- sponsorship will be optional;
- companies must have a member firm supporting trading;
- there will be no minimum/maximum limits on capitalization for entry;
- there will be no minimum limit on the amount of shares in public hands;
- there will be no minimum trading record requirement;
- the market will be accessible to both institutional and private investors.

3.7 Summary

	Full list	**Aim**
Trading record	3 years	None
Percent in public hands	25%	None
Minimum market value	£700,000 for equity £200,000 for debt	None
Free transferability	✓	✓
Requirement to produce prospectus	✓	Obliged only to produce a less onerous prospectus
Advertising	One small box	One small box

4 Requirements of the Financial Services and Markets Act 2000

4.1 Restrictions on financial promotion

Section 21 of the Financial Services and Markets Act 2000 ('FSMA') imposes a restriction on engaging in financial promotion in the course of a business unless:

- the firm is authorized;
- the communication is approved by an authorized firm; or
- an exemption applies such as is the case with listing particulars and prospectuses.

Breach of this provision is a criminal offence for which the maximum penalty is a prison sentence of up to two years and an unlimited fine. This is intended to ensure that only those who are subject to regulation in the way they conduct investment business may advertise or otherwise promote (such as by cold calling), financial products such as shares.

4.2 Contents of listing particulars and prospectuses

All listing particulars must contain the information required by the Listing Rules under section 79 of FSMA. In addition there is a statutory duty of disclosure in section 80. This requires listing particulars to contain all such information as investors and professional advisers would reasonably require, and reasonably expect to find there, for the purpose of making an informed assessment of a company's assets and liabilities, financial position, profits and losses and prospects.

The content for requirements of listing particulars are fully contained in Chapters 5 and 6 of the UKLA Purple book. All advisers and investment bankers and lawyers must check these. They are summarized as follows:

- completeness of liabilities in the accounts;
- responsibility – who is responsible, and for what and evidence of this;
- contents – easily understandable and verifiable;
- approval – required before publication;
- exemption – for some AIM securities or where listed on another EU exchange;
- securities – nature, legal rights and administration of the issue;
- issuer and its capital – inspection of certain documents permitted;
- group activities – detailed information about the business;
- financial information about the issuer, accountant statements, profit and losses, financial position;
- management – who, how much do they get paid, their contacts and their interest in the securities;
- recent developments and prospects – general information on the business and its future prospects.

4.3 Public offers of unlisted securities

The detailed contents of a prospectus for unlisted securities are similar to those for listed securities as already discussed. There is also an overriding duty of disclosure, as for listed companies, which requires the disclosure of all information investors would reasonably require for the purpose of making an informed assessment of the assets and liabilities, financial position, profits and losses, and prospects of the issuer.

As with listed companies under section 81 of the FSMA 2000 the offeror may need to produce a supplementary prospectus which must be delivered to the Registrar of Companies and published where there is any material change in any of the contents of the original prospectus at any time between the opening and closing of the offer.

5 Methods of issue

5.1 Issue by public subscription

The first method that a company can employ is to make a direct offer to the public by publishing a prospectus inviting subscriptions for the securities.

This method used to be the normal procedure, but in recent years it has become less common in the case of companies, although it is still used by public authorities, the best example being when the steel companies were denationalized and their shares resold to the public in the late 1950s.

The reason why this method has declined stems from the fact that it was always necessary to arrange for the issue to be underwritten to ensure its success, which in turn meant that an issuing house was introduced to make the underwriting arrangements – and in these circumstances it was easier for the company to leave the issuing house to organize the whole issue.

5.2 Offer for sale

This method is the one that is now used by most new companies and involves the company or its existing shareholders selling securities to the issuing house, which in turn publishes listing particulars inviting the public to purchase the securities from it.

The detailed procedures by which the public subscription and offer for sale methods are carried out are almost identical, and the main difference is that the issuing house accepts primary responsibility for the sale of the securities.

In certain cases part of the amount offered for sale is underwritten by a firm, which means that the firm underwriter (such as an institutional investor) has agreed to subscribe for shares and will automatically be allotted them. However, prior approval must be obtained from the UKLA to do this, and the amount will be strictly limited, so as to ensure that the public will still have a fair chance of obtaining shares.

5.3 Offer for sale by tender

A variation on these methods of issue, which safeguards the vendors against a very large premium on the price developing immediately after the issue, is the offer for sale by tender.

The shares are offered for sale at a minimum issue price, and in the form of application the subscriber states not only the number of shares required but also the price, above the mini-mum, which he is prepared to pay. Allotments are then made from the highest price downwards until the issue is fully subscribed.

The UKLA would not allow a method that resulted in different subscribers paying different prices to be used. Thus, in offers for sale by tender, allotment is made at a single striking price with all applications above the striking price being accepted at that price and all those below being rejected.

5.4 Placing

In this method, the securities are not offered to the general public through a prospectus but are placed at a fixed price among institutions, such as insurance companies, pension funds, unit trusts and investment companies, by the sponsor, which has usually purchased the securities from the company or its existing shareholders in the same way as in an offer for sale.

This method is cheaper than an offer for sale because there are no underwriting costs, the advertising requirements are less onerous, and there will be lower receiving bank charges. Nevertheless, exactly the same information on the company must be made available to the places in the placing document, which constitutes a prospectus.

Because of the limited publicity and the restricted group of purchasers, this method is regarded by the UKLA as a concession that, in general, is allowed only when it is thought that there is not likely to be a significant public demand for the securities. In these circumstances there are only three instances where the Stock Exchange will allow placings:

(i) small issues – there are no distribution requirements for marketings of AIM securities where the value is less than £2m;

(ii) limited public interest – where it can be proved that the issue or the company itself is unlikely to attract public interest. In this category would fall the issue of fixed-interest debentures and loan stocks, and in the case of this type of issue the Stock Exchange will always give placings permission whatever the size of the issue. The Stock Exchange still insists on the public being able to obtain stock and in the case of debt issues it is necessary for sponsors to include at least two market makers in the marketing on the same terms as other places;

(iii) market conditions – if market conditions were poor or if there had been several recent unsuccessful issues, it could be argued that placing firm into institutional hands was the only feasible way of completing the issue successfully.

6 Rights issues

A rights issue is used where a company wants to raise more capital. Section 89 of the Companies Act 1985 provides that a company proposing to allot equity securities may not allot them for a cash consideration to any person unless it has previously offered them on the same or more favourable terms to the holders of relevant shares as nearly as practicable pro rata to their respective holdings. This is known as a pre-emption right but in certain cases a company can apply to have them disapplied.

The main points for rights issues are as follows:

(a) A rights issue is a means of raising additional equity finance by giving existing shareholders the opportunity to subscribe for new shares in proportion to their existing holdings.

(b) The price needs to be attractive enough to stimulate interest. The concern of the company is at what price to issue?

(c) Timing is vital and success may depend on market conditions prevailing at the time of issue.

(d) Depending on the discount to existing shares, underwriting may need to be considered. If a 'bargain' price is offered, underwriting may not be necessary and fees can therefore be saved in this respect.

(e) For very large issues, the consent of the government broker will be required; a queuing system operates.

(f) There may be a need to increase the authorized share capital to accommodate the proposed increase in issued capital.

(g) The rights of existing shareholders must be preserved and to achieve this they will have prior claim for any new equity being raised. This is called 'shareholder's pre-emption rights'. Such pre-emption rights are therefore the existing holder's protection and as a general rule will apply to new issues of equity where the amount exceeds 5% of the existing issued ordinary share capital.

6.1 Rights issue documentation

There are three documents for rights issue, being a Prospectus, Listing Particulars and a provisional Allotment Letter. Often though there are just Listing Particulars and a Provisional Allotment Letter.

The Prospectus together with the Listing Particulars will be shorter than that for a new issue but must include:

- a statement confirming the sufficiency of working capital and a schedule showing the indebtedness of the company at a date within one month of the issue;
- details of current trading, future prospects and dividends;
- reasons for the issue and the use which the funds will be put;
- if the company has sufficient authorized but unissued capital to cover the issue, a Provisional Allotment Letter (PAL) will be sent out simultaneously with the Prospectus and Listing Particulars;
- where it is necessary to hold a shareholders' meeting to increase the authorized capital, the PAL will be sent out afterwards;
- the PAL is a transferable document of value due to the rights issue being priced at a discount to the market value of the shares;
- dealings in the rights 'nil paid' commence on the first dealing day after the despatch of the PALs;
- UKLA regulations require that the offer must be open for three weeks to enable shareholders to consider what action to take;
- once taken up, ie the rights exercised by the shareholder making payment, the PAL is stamped 'fully paid' and will eventually be submitted for registration and replaced by a definitive share certificate.

7 Management buy-outs and buy-ins

7.1 Definition of a management buy-out (MBO)

An MBO occurs when the existing management team purchases the business from its owners. This should be contrasted with that of a management buy-in (MBI), in which a group of managers from outside the business join together and make an offer for the company to its owners. This approach may of course be rejected by the owners but it is likely that the buy-in team will have selected the target company carefully. MBIs are more risky than MBOs and a good example was Lowndes Queensway that collapsed in 1992. A leverage buy-out (LBO), is where very high gearing is employed in excess of a ratio of 5:1 and were popular inn the 1980s, but many such ventures collapsed under an unserviceable degree of debt. In general after an MBO the management's aim will be to reduce the gearing as rapidly as possible through operating cash-flow and disposal of underutilized assets.

7.2 Management buy-ins (MBI)

The emergence of the management buy-in has occurred more recently. In this situation, a group of managers within a sector identifies a business that they believe has growth potential in their hands. They persuade a venture capital fund of the merit of their strategy and the two parties then make an approach to the existing owners of the business to acquire it. Again a majority of debt is used in the financing structure to leverage (or increase) the potential equity returns when the growth is achieved.

Many small, medium-sized enterprises find themselves hampered by a lack of security to offer a lender – especially early in their existence, and this can often cause problems when they want to expand. The Department of Trade and Industry has addressed this problem (as growing SME's are a major economic driving force) and will provide security to the lender by the way of either the Small Firms Loan Guarantee Scheme (SFLGS). These loans (and the guarantees) are typically for between two and seven years and are made available only for new borrowing. The major restriction is in relation to buying into a company or partnership. As a further assistance the facilities can be made available via capital repayment holidays. The loan will be with a lender and interest needs to be negotiated as normal.

7.3 Principal features of a management buy-out

Usually an MBO is an acquisition involving existing management but recently there have been instances where the management team of a publicly quoted company buys the shares held by the public. Management will obtain a meaningful equity stake and there will generally be other investors such as venture capitalists. Funding involves a high degree of leverage and for the MBO to be successful the underlying business must be capable of generating sufficient cash-flow and profits to service the finance raised for the acquisition.

7.4 Key Criteria for an MBO

There are certain key criteria for the MBO to be successful and these criteria will also determine the price to be paid in an MBO. Firstly, there must be strong and highly motivated management team who are prepared to invest their own money. Secondly, there must be strong cash-flow and hence capable of supporting a high degree of leverage. This in turn must determine a realistic buy-out price to ensure a satisfactory investment return. Finally, there must be exit potential through flotation or trade sale within three to five years.

7.5 The MBO structure

Once a price has been established the structure of the MBO must be determined as to how much should be raised by way of equity capital and what amount by way of debt. Again what will be crucial is the ability of the underlying business to generate cash-flow to service and repay debt. There are certain legal restrictions to be overcome concerning the prohibition of a subsidiary giving financial assistance to a parent for the purchase of the subsidiary's shares. It is therefore usual that an MBO will involve the formation of a new company that is used as the vehicle to buy the shares and assets of the business that is being sold.

The Ideal MBO Target would have the following characteristics:

- proven and adequate management resource;
- stable, positive cash-flow;
- high asset backing;
- no major investment needs;
- low tech;
- high market share;
- mature market;
- little dependency on customers and suppliers;
- low level of vulnerability to other economic factors.

7.6 Exit routes

A key component of any MBO is in how the equity investors are going to realize their investment. This can arise as a result of any of the following three exit routes.

1. Redemption of the shares by the MBO company itself.
2. A trade sale or takeover of the MBO company by another company.
3. Going public by obtaining a quotation on the Stock Exchange or the Alternative Investment Market.

7.7 Documentation for management buy outs

Sale agreement

There will be a sale agreement between the acquiring company on the one hand and the selling shareholders on the other. This will generally cover the following points:

- the names of the vendor and acquirer;
- brief details of what is being bought;
- the price to be paid;
- the structure of the consideration, eg deferred consideration;
- any key warranties made by the vendor and any key conditions of the contract;
- additional work to be done prior to the final contract being signed, such as an accountant's investigation.

There will be a number of warranties and indemnities in the agreement whose purpose is to protect the acquirer. Notwithstanding the detailed investigation made by the acquirer's accountants, the vendor will often be obliged to give warranties that the company is as stated.

Typical examples of warranties are:

- completeness of liabilities in the accounts;
- good title to assets, particularly properties;
- tax warranties regarding the tax position of the company.

There will be a number of differences from the typical sale agreement, though:

- the acquiring company will not secure the standard warranties a purchaser would seek – after all, the management team will know the business better than the selling shareholders;
- the sellers often wish to be paid part of their consideration on a deferred basis related to future profits of the target; they are keen to ensure that they do not lose out completely if the company makes good in the future;
- another crucial area is the warranties regarding tax because an MBO will be a disposal for Capital Gains Tax. As a large tax bill can result and a considerable amount of time will be taken with the negotiation of any tax indemnity clause.

Subscription agreement

In addition there will be a subscription or shareholders' agreement between the directors/managers and their backers who are taking shares in the acquiring company. This will govern the management of the company and the board, future financing of the company and other issues such as the dividend policy. Accompanying the shareholders' agreement there will also be the need for articles of association for the acquiring company, which will reflect the shareholders' agreement.

Loan agreement

There will be a loan agreement between the lenders and the acquiring company. The clauses will be the familiar representations and warranties, covenants and events of default. In the case of an MBO the following clauses may be included or strengthened:

- restrictions on any change in the nature of the business;
- restrictions on disposals of the target's assets;
- security over all assets;
- dividend prohibition clause in that dividends cannot be paid before any scheduled loan repayments.

8 Private sources and venture capital

There may be cases where the company is unsuitable for such a listing but its proprietors have no available cash to inject and debt finance is inappropriate. For instance:

(a) where the criteria are not fulfilled;

(b) for very new companies;

(c) high-risk businesses;

(d) highly specialized concerns where widespread public interest is unlikely to be forthcoming;

(e) where events are such that the company may appear an unattractive investment, for example poor track record, high country risk;

(f) where the existing shareholders do not wish to dilute their ownership among a wide range of investors, ie where they want to minimize the physical number of new investors.

The usual source of such funds are the financial institutions and their requirements as to stake and level of control will vary. Many institutions will restrict their stake to between 10–25% of the share capital and some will wish to avoid taking a physical controlling interest, ie taking an active part in day-to-day management affairs, in the business. Typically, such assistance will be by way of:

(a) ordinary shares;

(b) preference shares;

(c) convertible loan, ie debt convertible to equity;

(d) debt with equity warrants.

This type of private equity injection is known by a number of different titles, most commonly 'Development/Growth capital', 'Equity participation' or 'Venture capital'.

There is perhaps an implied difference between venture capital and the others in that the former relates, more usually, to long-term funds provided to organizations at very early stages of development and in high-risk areas. In this way the investor carries a high level of risk countered by the hope of potentially very high rewards.

An example of venture capital might be to assume that a young computer expert has just formed his own company, with his wife, dealing exclusively in the manufacture and distribution of parts for highly specialized underwater equipment, used in the fishing industry. They have committed what they can, financially and in time, to the company and now urgently require additional capital to develop the products they have.

In these circumstances, at such an early stage of growth and given the very specialized area they are involved in, the more conventional routes are sold out, probably including a straight injection from an institution. This is a clear example of the need for venture capital, which is required to get the business up and running and to bring the product to the marketable stage.

Venture capital may take the form of straight equity (ordinary or preference shares) or, in some cases, a combination of debt and equity. Funds may be injected in the form of 'quasi capital' which is a type of half-way house, between debt and equity, possibly in the form of convertible debt or redeemable equity.

As far as the sources of venture capital are concerned, this is available from a wide range of institutions, both banks and specializt venture/development capital funds, including a number of local regional agencies. Probably the best known is 3i (Investors in Industry) that has been in existence for over 40 years, during which time they have invested well over £3 billion in businesses. 3i specializes in start-up and development capital, as well as finance for management buy-outs. The major benefit to the company is that an organization (investor) such as 3i will put up the necessary finance, usually as equity, to enable the business to grow. In taking on a new equity partner the existing shareholders are sharing the risks involved. The benefit of taking debt finance is that its cash-flow is free from the pressures of meeting loan repayments and interest. This is particularly important during the growth stage of development because cash-flows at that time are likely to be negative.

Most providers of such finance will look at propositions ranging from as little as £10,000 and up to several millions of pounds, obviously depending on the risk involved. The bulk of the activity is in the range of £50,000 to £250,000.

The legal documentation for venture capital is similar to that for management buy-outs in that there will be a subscription or shareholders agreement. A venture capitalist will often subscribe for cumulative convertible redeemable participating preference shares. Such preference shares have voting rights, share in all ordinary dividends as well as a fixed dividend, are cumulative and can be redeemed or converted into ordinary shares.

Thirteen

Acquisition finance

1 Introduction

The purpose of this chapter is to cover the key areas to consider when making an acquisition. It initially puts acquisitions in their strategic context. Having established the strategic justification, it considers how to identify and approach potential targets. It then focuses on key areas of the acquisition agreement. It finally looks at the legal and regulatory aspects of the acquisition process.

2 Rationale

The strategy of a group will generally call for growth in earnings that may be achieved organically (ie within the context of the existing business), or through external expansion (ie by acquisition of a new business). However, each strategy will also identify and define areas for expansion, and this will provide a framework for acquisitions to ensure that they fall within the group or business unit strategy.

There are several motives for looking for external expansion in addition to, or in place of, organic growth. These include the following.

- **Market position.** A strategic consideration may be the attainment of a position in a certain market. This may be difficult to achieve quickly through internal growth. Furthermore, the various business factors – marketing, production, distribution – may be enhanced through the economies of scale in the larger combined business.

- **Productive capacity.** The planning of substantially increased productive capacity may involve considerable delay until it comes on-stream. It may be quicker, and in inflation-adjusted terms considerably cheaper, to purchase additional capacity through the acquisition of an existing business.
- **Vertical integration.** There may be enhanced profit opportunities through adding business at the customer or supplier end of an existing business unit.
- **Complementary resources.** A business unit may have strengths in certain business factors, but weaknesses in others, eg strong distribution to major customers in the marketplace, but weak to smaller ones. Another business in the same market may be able to make up for those deficiencies, ie by strong distribution to smaller customers. Complementary managerial skills are often an important factor, especially in friendly acquisitions.
- **Eliminating inefficiencies.** A business unit may have strong management and capabilities in various aspects of its business, and may be in a position to acquire businesses with weaker management and capabilities. In this way the unrealized potential of the latter businesses will be achieved through better management. There are four further motives for acquisitions that require further examination, because they are not always valid, and may be advanced for dubious reasons.
- **Diversification.** This is justified where a group's management has shown the ability to make higher returns from businesses acquired than existing management (in effect an element of such a group's strategy would be to make better use of underproductive assets).The diversification motive is not justified normally for the sake of reducing shareholder risk, but because shareholders can diversify their own portfolios; however, shareholders cannot protect a company from insolvency, and on such grounds some degree of risk spreading within the corporate entity may be justified. The word diversification often refers to the shifting of corporate assets away from weak or declining markets; strictly speaking such moves are really strategic decisions that may have diversification of corporate risk as an incidental benefit.
- **Unbundling assets.** This is undertaken by groups that have a strategy and a successful track record of unlocking the potential of businesses with underutilized assets.These may be going concerns or, often, property assets. Unbundling may, in addition, be appropriate where a group wishes for strategic reasons to acquire a subsidiary of another business but has no use for the remainder of the latter. It might then seek to acquire the whole business and then sell the part it does not want.
- **High-rated shares for low-rated ones.** In the short term it is tempting for acquisitive groups with high price/earnings (P/E) ratios to buy businesses with a lower stock market rating. However, this should be undertaken only where the business acquired forms part of the group's acquisition strategy, and where the returns available on the new investment justify the price paid.

- **Tax advantages.** Groups are in business for commercial motives and not to avoid taxes. Having achieved profits, however, a major financial objective should be to minimize taxation. Accordingly, the tax advantages (tax loss carry forwards, using advance corporation tax surpluses, etc) should be examined only when the acquisition is justified for strategic reasons.

3 The legal and regulatory environment

In preparing the case for an acquisition or divestment, it is important to be aware of several potential legal restraints.

3.1 The Competition Commission

The Competition Commission, which was set up under the Competition Act 1998, has responsibility for the detailed investigation into merger, monopoly and regulatory issues referred to it by the Office of Fair Trading (OFT), sector regulators and government ministers, but with important new responsibilities.

First, it will become the decision-making authority in almost all merger and market cases referred to it. Ministers who currently have the responsibility for making the final decisions in respect of merger and monopoly cases will lose this determinative role except when matters of specific public interest, such as national security, arise. However, even when such public interest matters arise the ministers will be bound to accept the Commission's conclusion on the competition issues involved.

Second, the Commission will have the responsibility of deciding on, and implementing, remedies. In merger cases, these will be those judged appropriate, proportionate and practical to avoid any substantial lessening of competition and any resulting adverse effects; and in market cases those necessary to deal in a similar way with any adverse effects on competition and any resulting detrimental effect on customers. When doing so, the Commission may have regard to the effect of the remedial action upon customer benefits, which take the form of lower prices, higher quality, greater choice or greater innovation.

Third, in the light of its new determinative role, the Commission will adopt new procedures common to all merger and market inquiries and it will work within new statutory timetables.

The Competition Commission Appeal Tribunals, which came into being in March 2000 to hear appeals against decisions of the DGFT and sector regulators having concurrent powers under the Competition Act 1998, will become the Competition Appeal Tribunal and will be separated from the Competition Commission, so that it can hear appeals against the Commission in the new regime.

3.2 The Enterprise Act 2002

The main changes introduced by the Enterprise Act 2002 are:

- the Competition Commission (CC) will become an independent decision-maker in its own right;
- the CC will become responsible for deciding, on the basis of new competition-based tests, whether there is a substantial lessening of competition (in the case of a merger reference) or whether any feature of a market prevents, restricts or distorts competition (in the case of a market reference);
- the CC will also decide what action should be taken to remedy a substantial lessening of competition and any adverse effect arising from it (mergers) and any adverse effect on competition or any detrimental effect on customers (markets);
- the CC will become more transparent in its operations, eg by publishing guidance and by consulting parties about every decision that can be regarded as adverse to a party (mergers) or is likely to have a substantial impact on them (markets); and
- decisions of the CC will be open to scrutiny, on judicial review grounds, by the Competition Appeal Tribunal.

Under the Act the Competition Commission has the power to stop an acquisition, divestment or merger, or to require certain undertakings from the parties to the transaction if:

- the resulting UK market share exceeds 25% and/or the gross value of assets taken over exceeds £30 million, and
- the Secretary of State for Trade and Industry (SSTI) may decide on mergers, or any aspect of it, likely to operate against the public interest (presently only national security).

The process for applying the Act is as follows.

- The Office of Fair Trading carries out an initial investigation, following which its head advises the SSTI whether to refer the merger to the Competition Commission.
- The CC may then perform a detailed investigation and, once the Enterprise Act 2002 takes full effect, will take all decisions on mergers and markets against a new competition test. There will be a new right of appeal to the Competition Appeals Tribunal.

3.3 Industry Act 1975

The SSTI has the power to stop an acquisition by a foreign bidder for an important UK manufacturing concern. This power has never been used and is unlikely to be used unless there is a change in political climate

3.4 Transfer of Undertakings (Protection of Employment) Regulations 1981

These apply on the transfer of a business (as opposed to a company) and deem all employees of the business to be transferred together with the business. This can create a problem if the new owner does not need some or all of the employees. While the effects of this can often be mitigated by offering reasonable redundancy terms or attractive redeployment opportunities within the vendor company, it is important that this aspect is thoroughly thought through in advance.

3.5 Companies Act 1989

This requires notification to the target company of the acquisition of shareholdings over 3% within two days of any change. This gives the target's management warning of a possible bid.

3.6 Company Securities (Insider Dealing) Act 1985

This Act, inter alia, prohibits a person who has 'knowingly obtained' confidential price-sensitive information about an offer or contemplated offer from a person connected with the company from dealing on the Stock Exchange in shares in the target company. The penalties for breach include prison sentences of up to seven years.

3.7 Financial Services and Markets Act 2000

Much of the impact of the Financial Services and Markets Act 2000 was considered in the previous unit. The FSA is the sole regulator and the Stock Exchange is a recognized investment exchange for the purpose of the FSMA 2000. The Listing Rules pursuant to the power given to the FSA under Part VI of the FSMA 2000 are exercised by the UKLA, as seen in Unit 13. The requirements and contents of Listing Particulars have also been considered in Unit 13.

3.8 EU Merger Regulations

The impact of EU Merger regulations is considered below.

4 Companies Act 1985

The Companies Act 1985 (CA 1985) provides the framework for the regulation of companies in the UK.

Purpose	These rules are designed to allow companies to know who their owners are.
Summary	Under UK law all shares must be registered, thereby allowing the company to know who its owners are. Beyond this the law (CA 1985, section 212) allows the company to enquire of any named owner whether it is the ultimate beneficial owner. This rule exists to prevent share stakes from being disguised. Further to this the Act then requires disclosure from the shareholders once they exceed certain stakes (CA 1985, sections 198–211).

Notification of interests in a company's shares (sections 198–211 of the Companies Act 1985)

4.1 Material interests

The Companies Act 1985 requires that where a person knows that:

(a) he has acquired or ceased to have a beneficial interest in 3% of the issued share capital of a public limited company (plc), or

(b) if he has already has an interest in 3% or more of the plc's share capital and he increases or reduces his interest across one full percentage point, he must notify the plc within two business days.

Interests in shares

Interests in shares include the right or obligation to acquire an interest. For example, a person buying a call option or writing a put option would have to count these as interests. It does not, however, include shares held as collateral or shares held by UK market makers for the purpose of their business.

The holdings referred to above must include those held by:

(a) A spouse, infant, child or stepchild.

(b) Any company where the person controls more than one-third of the votes or which habitually acts in accordance with the person's directions.

(c) Any concert party with which the person is concerned (see below).

Interests to be disregarded

Under the provisions of Companies Act 1985, section 209 certain interests are to be disregarded from the above:

(a) an interest in shares held as collateral if held in the course of business;

(b) an interest held by a market maker if:

- the firm is a market maker (a person who holds themselves out at all normal times as willing to acquire and dispose of securities and derivatives) in the UK; and
- it holds the interests for the purposes of that business.

However, the LSE now requires that all market-maker stakes are declared to the Exchange within two business days. These stakes will be publicly disclosed via the Exchange's systems.

For FTSE 100 stocks that are traded via the SETS system, there are no longer market makers and consequently there is no exemption under the Act. For FTSE 250 stocks publication will take place only when the stake is 5%. This publication level is increased to 10% for stocks outside the FTSE 350.

Concert parties

A concert party, in this context, is a combination of people who have an agreement to acquire shares in the company in question.

A person becomes interested in shares as a result of a relationship with a concert party when the relationship is first formed or when another person in the concert party acquires an interest in the shares. He ceases to be interested in the shares when the concert party is disbanded or when the other member of the concert party disposes of his interest in the shares.

Penalties for non-compliance

Failure to comply with the above is a criminal offence with possible unlimited fines and imprisonment for up to two years.

For listed companies the Listing Rules require that whenever there is an update to the Material Interests Register the company must inform the Company Announcements Office of the exchange without delay (by the end of the following business day). These changes will then be communicated to the market.

4.2 Notifiable interests

An additional rule has been introduced whereby holders of non-beneficial interests in excess of 10% are obliged to disclose their interest in the share capital of the company. This will encompass fund managers and institutional investors who may hold a number of stakes for different funds which, taken together, exceed the 3% level. Under the previous rules they would have been obliged to disclose this holding; however, they are now released from this regulation.

This disclosure will be entered onto a second register which, as with the material interests register, is available for public inspection.

4.3 Company's power to request information on shareholders

Section 212 of the Companies Act 1985 states that where a company knows or has reasonable cause to believe that someone has at any time in the previous three years had an interest in the company's share capital, then it can send a notice to the person requiring him or her to confirm whether or not this is the case.

If the person has had an interest in the shares the notice can also require him or her to disclose details of their holding, whether it is part of a concert party holding and to whom he or she sold the interest. The person should reply within the time limit set by the notice, which should be reasonable. If he or she fails to do so then the company can suspend the shares' voting and other rights. Once the company has obtained information in this manner, it should enter the details on its share register.

Shareholders of the company holding at least 10% of the voting rights can require a company to use its powers under section 212 to identify another shareholder.

The section 212 notice is a valuable tool for a company in identifying potential predators who are gradually building up a stake in the company through nominee holdings. Otherwise, such a stake would not need to be notified until it reached 3%.

4.4 Investigation into a company's ownership

Under the Companies Act 1985, sections 442–445 the Secretary of State for Trade and Industry has the right to appoint inspectors to investigate the ownership of a company. Such an investigation may be instigated by the DTI of its own accord or may be prompted by a request of the shareholders.

In the course of the investigation all officers and agents of the firm must:

(a) produce to the inspectors all documents that are in their possession;

(b) when required appear before the inspectors; and

(c) offer all assistance that may be required by the inspectors in the fulfilment of their task.

In addition, the Secretary of State also has the power to request information from any person whom he believes has, or has access to, information concerning the ownership of the company.

If there is any difficulty in obtaining the required information then the Secretary of State has the power to apply to the courts to impose a restriction on the rights attached to the share. It is possible for the shareholder to apply to the court for a suspension of this restriction; however, this will be granted only where disclosure is made and the court is satisfied that no unfair advantage has accrued to the owner as a result of the original failure to disclose.

The order will also be lifted if there is to be a sale of the shares; however, all such sales will be subject to the approval of the Secretary of State. It is also possible under the provision of the Companies Act 1985 for the court to order the sale of the shares to take place if it deems this appropriate.

4.5 Financial assistance – section 151 of the Companies Act 1985

Section 151 of the Companies Act 1985 restricts the ability of a company to provide financial assistance for the acquisition of shares in it or its holding company. It prohibits two types of transaction. The first is giving financial assistance before or at the same time as an acquisition of shares where the assistance is for the purpose of that acquisition. The second is giving of financial assistance after the acquisition, where the assistance is for the purpose of reducing or discharging a liability incurred by anyone for the acquisition. There are some exceptions to these provisions although a breach of the section is a criminal offence.

Summary of the important share stakes

% stake	Consequence
Any	Ability of the company to enquire as to the ultimate ownership under section 212 of the Companies Act 1985.
	Once an offer is in the open all dealing by those connected to the offeror(ee) must be declared.
	May be a contravention of Rule 5 and may trigger mandatory offer under Rule 9.

1%	Must disclose dealings during the offer period. Disclosure will include the stake held. There is an exception here for market-makers, who are not required to disclose stakes taken in the normal course of market-making activity (subject to the LSE's own rules). Exempt market-makers are required to disclose aggregate trades but not the resultant stake that they hold.
3%	Beneficial interests will be disclosed to the company under sections 198–199 of the Companies Act 1985 (the material interests rules).
10%	Power to require an EGM and the service of section 212 notices on the part of shareholders controlling not less than 10% of the voting rights. Notifiable interests rules of the Companies Act 1985 become operative for non-beneficial stakes.
10% in a year	Requirement for a cash offer under the Takeover Code.
15%	SARs (Substantial Acquisition Rules) apply to acquisitions of 10% or more. Accelerated disclosure of stakes under the SARs. This requires that disclosure be made to the company and the Stock Exchange by noon of the following day and overrides the two business day limit in the Companies Act.
30%	Takeover Code definition of control. SARs cease to apply. Potential operation to bid for the entire capital of the company under Rule 9 (the mandatory bid rules). Note that Rule 9 applies only to actual holdings of shares whereas references to Rule 5 would also encompass rights over shares.
50%+	Companies Act 1985 definition of control because at this level the holder will have the ability to pass ordinary resolutions. First point at which a full offer could be declared unconditional with regard to acceptances.
75%	More formal control boundary because at this level the holder will be able to pass special resolutions.
90%	Minorities may be able to force the majority to buy out their stake. Equally, the majority may, subject to the way in which the stake has been acquired, require the minority to sell out their position.

5 Compulsory purchase provisions

5.1 Acquiring company's right to compulsorily purchase shares

Sections 429–430 of the Companies Act 1985 state that, where a bidder has acquired at least 90% of the shares in one class to which an offer relates, the bidder is entitled to acquire the remaining shares compulsorily.

5.2 Minority's right to sell shares to the acquirer

If the acquirer does not exercise this right, the relevant minority shareholders can force him to purchase their shares.

Given these legal rights for both the acquirer and the remaining minority interest, it is likely that, when an acquirer manages to acquire 90% of the shares bid for, he will automatically move to a 100% holding.

5.3 Legal requirements

The offeror must acquire the 90% holding within four months of making the initial offer and must notify the remaining shareholders within two months of reaching the 90% figure that he intends to use the compulsory purchase provisions.

He must pay the same consideration as that given to the other shareholders.

If the offeror does not wish to purchase the shares, he must within one month notify the remaining shareholders of their right to sell him their shares and give them at least three months to do so from the date when the original offer closed.

6 Protection of the minority

Majority rule is the basis of democracy. However, there must be provisions to ensure that minorities are protected from exploitation. The Companies Act seeks to protect minorities in a number of ways.

Firstly, it imposes restrictions on certain corporate actions requiring significant majorities, ie 75% and above in the case of special resolutions. In addition, there is the option given to a dissentient minority of complaining to the courts. With regard to the class rights of any shares, the protection is even stronger, requiring 100% of shareholders to agree to any alteration.

In addition to general restrictions and requirements for stricter majorities, there are also statutory remedies contained in the Act. In particular, section 459 of the

Companies Act 1985 allows individuals to bring an action for unfairly prejudicial conduct. This can be brought to enable the courts to decide whether the majority are abusing the minority and then either prevent the majority from taking action or require them to buy out any minority at a fair price.

This was demonstrated in *Scottish Cooperative Retail Society Ltd v Meyer.* In this case the Scottish Cooperative Retail Society Ltd formed a separate joint venture company to manufacture rayon. This company used the skills of Dr Meyer and Mr Lucas. Eventually the society wished to absorb the manufacturing plant into their own operations more fully and formally. They offered Dr Meyer a relatively unattractive price which he refused. They then set about effectively transferring the business by running the subsidiary down. It was held by the court that this was an oppressive course of action and they were then forced to pay a fair price for the company.

7 UK listing authority

The Admission of Securities to Listing (the 'Purple Book') places information requirements upon listed companies making acquisitions and divestments with the aim of ensuring the timely announcement of all price-sensitive information. It defines five categories of transactions, each of which involves disclosure requirements.

7.1 Class 1

Those transactions that are sufficiently material, either individually or in aggregate, to call not only for an announcement to be made to the Company Announcements Office and the press but also for either listing particulars to be published or a circular to be sent to shareholders.

A number of tests are used to help to assess the class of a transaction:

- effect on acquiror's net tangible assets;
- effect on acquiror's profit before tax;
- ratio of aggregate consideration to acquiror's assets;
- increase in acquiror's equity capital.

A transaction will normally be deemed to fall within Class 1 if it has an effect of 15% or more on any one of these tests.

A 'Major (or Super) Class 1' transaction is one that has an effect of 25% or more and should be made conditional on approval by shareholders in a general meeting.

7.2 Class 2

Those transactions that are of sufficient importance to require an announcement to be made to the Company Announcements Office and to the press.

A transaction will normally be deemed to fall within Class 2 if all the percentage tests are under 15% and any one is over 5%.

7.3 Class 3

Those transactions that do not require any announcement unless all or part of the consideration is satisfied by the issue of securities for which listing is being sought.

A transaction will normally be deemed to fall within Class 3 if all of the tests result in a percentage of less than 5%.

7.4 Class 4

Those transactions which, irrespective of size, require a Class 4 circular to be sent to shareholders and for which the Committee on Quotations deems to require prior consent of the shareholders in a general meeting.

A transaction will normally be deemed to fall within Class 4 if it involves a director, substantial (over 10%) shareholder, and/or an associate of either.

7.5 Very substantial acquisitions or reverse takeovers

Where a listed company proposes to acquire another business, company or companies, substantially all of which are not listed, and the transaction would be one where the relevant proportion would be 100% or more, or which would result in a change of control through the introduction of a majority holder or a group of holders, that transaction will be deemed a reverse takeover. For the purposes of determining a reverse takeover, separate acquisitions in any period of 12 months may be aggregated.

Such transactions are required to be subject to the approval of shareholders in general meeting. The acquiring company will normally be regarded as a new applicant for listing. Listing of the company's securities will be suspended until after the shareholders' approval has been obtained. Listing will then be cancelled prior to publication of listing particulars, following which the company's securities will normally be restored to listing.

8 Acquisition finance documentation

8.1 Private acquisition

The vast majority of takeovers are of private companies or parts of public companies. Within this category the majority of acquisitions are negotiated between a willing buyer and seller. In private companies the shares are often held by the managers and so a hostile bid would have no chance of success. The tactics will largely be associated with negotiating skills. There is no one best way to negotiate, but the following tips may prove helpful.

- Get to know your own position and that of your counterpart.
- Be prepared to compromise.
- Search for common ground.
- Be human – humour and respect help, acrimony hinders.
- Disclose key issues.
- Get the principals together – they can cut through weeks of argument between professional advisers.
- Avoid becoming emotionally involved.

The documentation will normally involve some or all of the following:

Confidentiality agreement

This legally binds the would-be acquiror not to disclose to third parties any confidential information received by it to evaluate the possible acquisition.

Contents of the confidentiality agreement

Typical points that would be covered in the confidentiality agreement include the following:

- the nature of information that will be disclosed by each party;
- to whom the information will be made available in each company and who will not be permitted to see it;
- a prohibition on photocopies being made of information passed over and an agreement to return all originals should negotiations fail;
- a prohibition on any information made available being used by the recipient for the benefit of its own business, unless it already knew the information from another source;
- agreement not to disclose the existence of negotiations to other parties and stressing the secrecy of the negotiations.

Enforceability of the confidentiality agreement

It is clear that it is difficult to enforce many of these points in practice. However, it does prevent blatant abuse of any information obtained and may make a more ethical company aware of its obligations.

Letter of intent/heads of agreement

This lays down the framework for subsequent detailed negotiations and shows a degree of interest on both sides. It may or may not be expressed to be legally binding. However, this stage can create extra work and hinder subsequent negotiations if any key matters were not fully understood at the time the letter of intent was prepared. It is, therefore, sensible to decide on a case-by-case basis whether to use this interim technique or whether to proceed directly to a legally binding contract.

The heads of terms will usually cover the following points:

- the names of the vendor and acquirer;
- brief details of what is being sought;
- the price to be paid;
- the structure of the consideration, eg deferred consideration;
- any key warranties made by the vendor and any key conditions of the contract;
- additional work to be done prior to the final contract being signed, such as an accountant's investigation.

Acquisition agreement

This is a legally binding contract between the two parties with the following elements.

- Recitals/preliminary information.
- Structure and consideration for the transaction.
- What is being acquired – where this is a business/assets the fluidity of working capital will often mean that it will be necessary to go to considerable lengths to define it carefully.
- Warranties and representations – eg accuracy of information supplied, no material adverse change, pending litigation, etc.
- Limitations on warranties – normally limited to the total level of consideration or less, and with a specified time limit (one to ten years) during which actions can be brought for breach of the warranties.
- Tax indemnity covering past, current and often future tax liabilities from trade up to the date of acquisition. The tax indemnity should cover all taxes, including corporation tax, income tax/PAYE and VAT. The tax indemnity may be contained in a Deed of Indemnity separate from the Acquisition

Agreement in order that entities other than buyer and seller (eg subsidiaries) may be party to it to simplify future payments, if required, under the indemnity.

- Disclosure letter – the contract will normally refer to a disclosure letter, in which exceptions to the warranties, representations and possibly indemnities given in the contract are tabled prior to contract and/or completion.
- Covenants – eg the seller will continue to run the business as normal between signing of the contract and completion.
- Conditions precedent (if any) – eg subject to no reference to the Competition Commission.
- Completion – when consideration passes in exchange for shares or legal title to the assets in the business.

Naturally, the agreement will include warranties and indemnities, the purpose of which is to protect the acquirer. Notwithstanding the detailed investigation made by the acquirer's accountants, the vendor will often be obliged to give warranties that the company is as stated. Typical examples of warranties are:

- completeness of liabilities in the accounts;
- good title to assets, particularly properties; and
- tax warranties regarding the tax position of the company.

The warranties will often be made in fairly general, wide-ranging terms and therefore the disclosure letter is needed to highlight specific exceptions to the warranties.

Where a warranty is found to be incorrect, the acquirer may sue the person giving the warranty for losses suffered as a result. It may be that an individual vendor giving a warranty has insufficient resources to cover the losses suffered, but giving the warranties will serve to focus the vendor's mind when making the agreement.

The indemnities given by the vendor provide for compensating the acquirer for any losses suffered due to specific liabilities mentioned in the sale agreement. This may include, for example, certain contingent liabilities.

The final contract

The final contract will typically be prepared by the acquirer's solicitor and will be a substantial document, aiming to cover all eventualities. The exact terms may be varied by a process of negotiation between the acquirer and the vendor and their respective legal representatives. The final contract will reflect the negotiating strength of each of the parties and will usually contain the following details.

- what is being sold;
- the identities of the vendor and acquirer;
- the price to be paid, how it is to be satisfied and the exact structure of the deal;
- any warranties and indemnities made by the vendor;

- any conditions of the contract;
- a disclosure letter which lists any exceptions to the list of general warranties in the contract; and
- the completion date of the contract.

The warranties indemnities will be as per the acquisition agreement, discussed above.

8.2 Public acquisitions

Bids for public companies represent a minority of all takeovers. Within this minority, some are friendly/agreed bids and some are hostile.

Accordingly the first tactical decision for a bidder is whether to seek the support of the target's board for the bid. The advantages of discussing/negotiating with the target's management are that it provides more information prior to the bid; it avoids the mud-slinging of a contested bid; and it increases the chances of shareholder approval. The problems are that it warns the target's management of the predator's intentions, thereby information on the bidder; it can restrict market purchases; and it generally reduces the options for post-acquisition management.

If it is decided to opt for a hostile bid, a number of further tactical options come into play. Because tactics can be of paramount importance, the advice of a merchant/investment bank will normally be sought because good tactics vary by country, by case and through time. Below are some common tactics.

- **Stake building** – through a slow quiet share purchase programme, a swift dawn raid, or the purchase of options.
- **Pre-emptive strike** – offering a high price initially to deter alternative bidders.
- **Low-ball offer** – offering low initially in the hope of getting a bargain and allowing scope for the target to barter upwards before recommending the offer.
- **Planned revision** – offer high enough to deter other bidders but low enough to allow revision.
- **Junk-paper offer and partial tenders** – restricted in the UK by the Takeover Code.
- **Underwriting** – having a non-cash offer underwritten can defuse some of the target's defence arguments, support the share price and avoid the 15% restriction on share purchases, but it is normally expensive, and sometimes impossible.
- **Proxy fights** – to displace the board – more common in the USA than the UK.
- **Press campaign** – constrained by the Takeover Code.
- **Lobby** – to persuade the Government not to use its monopolies or national interest legislation to block the bid.

- **Performance comparisons** – to demonstrate that the bidder is better managed than the target.
- **White knight attack** – ie being the second bidder into a dirty fight may enable a company to benefit from being seen as a 'white knight'.

8.3 Documentation for public acquisitions

The documentation for a public bid will depend upon whether it is friendly or hostile. If friendly, there may be a confidentiality letter (as discussed in section 8.2 above), covering the information given to the offeror; this information must be tracked in case a second bidder emerges and demands under the Takeover Code to receive the same information. When an 'agreement' has been reached there will normally be a press release followed by an offer document from the bidder and a letter detailing the management's recommendation from the target's board.

In a hostile bid, the target will not normally give the bidder any information it does not already have and therefore the main elements of documentation will be:

- a letter to the board of the target outlining the terms of the offer, followed immediately by a press release; and
- the formal offer document is then normally posted to the target's shareholders within 28 days of the announcement.

9 The UK Panel on Takeovers and Mergers

The regulation of takeovers and mergers is the last aspect of the UK regulatory environment that is left almost exclusively to practitioner self-regulation. However, it has not been immune to developments elsewhere in the regulatory structure and over the past 15 years it has become much more professional and much more complicated, with detailed rules being added to the general principles that were initially laid down as part of the City Code.

Purpose These rules are designed to create and maintain a level playing field in the context of takeovers. As such, most of the rules apply only once a bid has been announced or is likely.

Summary Rules 5 and 9 concern themselves with the overall stake held in the firm. Rule 5 prohibits a bidder from gaining control, defined as 30% stake. Rule 9 introduces the potential penalty of a mandatory bid if the 30% threshold has been breached.

Rule 4 places restrictions on whom among the parties to a bid can buy and sell shares either during the course of a bid or in the period prior to any formal announcement.

Rule 8 concerns itself with disclosure during an offer period. In general terms the parties to a bid must ensure that their transactions are made public. Within this rule there are detailed provisions designed to ensure that issues concerning who is or is not connected to the deal are resolved.

Overall the rules are interpreted flexibly in line with the overall spirit of the code.

9.1 The nature of takeover regulation in the UK

The Panel on Takeovers and Mergers (POTAM) is a grouping of all the important organizations in the City of London. Backing the panel is the Bank of England, which appoints the Chairman and Deputy Chairman. In addition, there are representatives of the following.

- Financial Services Authority.
- Association of British Insurers.
- London Investment Bank Association.
- British Bankers Association.
- Confederation of British Industry.
- Institute of Chartered Accountants in England and Wales.
- London Stock Exchange.
- LIFFE.
- National Association of Pension Funds.
- AUTIF.

Their duty is to monitor adherence to the general principles laid down in the City Code. Their only weapon (via the organizations that support the panel) is to withdraw the facilities of the market from anybody who breaks those rules. This is referred to within the City Code as 'reverse cold shouldering' and is such a powerful weapon that it seldom has to be used – the mere threat of it tends to bring people into line with the rules and regulations. As yet, no legal power is entrusted to the Panel on Takeovers and Mergers.

The Code has not and does not seek to have the force of law. It has, however, been acknowledged by both government and other regulatory authorities that those who seek to take advantage of the facilities of the securities markets in the United Kingdom should conduct themselves in matters relating to takeovers in accordance with best business standards, according to the Code. Therefore, those who do not so conduct themselves may find that by way of sanction the facilities of those markets are withheld.

9.2 The role of the panel

The basic idea behind the Panel and the City Code is to ensure that there is a level playing field in takeover activity in the UK.That is to say that each party has an even chance to state its case and make its point of view clear.The principles and rules contained in the Blue Book (the City Code) ensure that this takes place.The panel itself is staffed on a full-time basis by professionals seconded from the leading merchant banks, securities houses, accountants and legal firms.The Panel executive makes decisions promptly and has the power to waive or alter any rules should the circumstances indicate that this is desirable.The combination of experienced staff, flexibility, promptness and power makes the Panel an effective regulator of the UK takeover and mergers market.

9.3 Advantages and disadvantages of self-regulation

Advantages

There are a number of advantages of self-regulation, as follows.

(a) **Flexibility** – the Code can be quickly adapted to take account of changing circumstances.The law can be changed only very slowly.

(b) **Consultation in advance** – the Panel can be consulted in advance to ensure that the rules in the Blue Book are not going to be broken, albeit unintentionally.This facility is not possible with the law, which can only react to events.

(c) **Quick decisions** – unlike the law, which grinds slowly to a conclusion at much expense, the Panel can come up with speedy judgments.

(d) **Focus on principles** – whereas the law has to focus on the exact letter and must be precise, the Panel can apply general principles of fairness in making its decisions.

(e) **Practitioner involvement** – this makes the Blue Book and its application more realistic, acceptable and effective.

(f) **Links with other regulatory bodies** – organizations such as FSA require compliance with the Blue Book and may withdraw the authorization of persons who are severely censured by the Panel.

Disadvantages

The problems associated with running a self-regulatory system include the following:

(a) **The influx of new participants** – in the markets, especially from overseas, who are not acquainted with a self-regulatory system means that applying and enforcing the rules has become more difficult.

(b) **The development of a very competitive market** – in mergers and acquisitions advice, with great store set by victory, has led to firms being tempted to stretch the rules to the very limit. This means that they may break the spirit of the Code if not the exact letter.

Many of these criticisms, which came to light in the wake of the Guinness affair, were addressed in a report commissioned into the operation of the panel. As a result of the report the number of full-time staff was increased and further guidance given on certain key rules.

10 Companies, individuals and transactions to which the city code applies

10.1 Companies and individuals

Offers for public limited companies

The scope of the Code is covered in section A of the Blue Book. It applies to offers by companies or individuals for any listed or unlisted public limited company (plc) which is considered by the Panel to be resident in the United Kingdom, the Channel Islands or the Isle of Man.

Offers for private limited companies

The Code also applies to offers for any private limited company (ltd) resident in these areas if:

(a) the company's equity share capital has been listed on the UK Stock Exchange during the last ten years before the offer is announced,

(b) dealings in the company's shares have been advertised on a regular basis for at least six months in the last ten years,

(c) the company's shares have been dealt in on the Unlisted Securities Market, AIM or subject to any other marketing arrangement in the last ten years, and

(d) the company has filed a prospectus to issue equity shares in the last ten years.

The objective of these rules is to cover any company where the public may have had an opportunity to purchase shares in the recent past.

10.2 Transactions

Mergers and takeovers

The code applies to all takeover and merger transactions, including partial offers for less than 100% of a company's shares and situations where control of a company is to be obtained or consolidated. However, it does not usually relate to offers for non-voting, non-equity shares.

Control and consolidation of control

Control is defined in the definitions as where at least 30% of the company's voting rights are held. Although, strictly speaking, control becomes legally possible only when more than 50% of the voting rights are held, the Panel believes that effective control can be achieved at this much lower percentage.

Consolidation of control is defined in Rule 9 as where any voting rights are added to an existing stake of between 30% and 50%.

11 The general principles of the City Code

11.1 Introduction

Applying the spirit of the City Code

The general principles recognize that it is impossible to devise rules that cover every situation. The rules therefore introduce the general principles to assist companies and the Panel in interpreting and applying the spirit of the code.

Offeree shareholder protection

The purpose of the Code and the ten general principles is to protect the offeree shareholders from unfair treatment. The Code makes some references to employees but offeror shareholders, for example, are not protected at all.

Applicants in the detailed rules

Virtually all of the general principles are further developed in the detailed rules that follow. However, the principle will always override the detailed rule in any circumstance.

11.2 The ten general principles

1. **All shareholders of the same class of an offeree company must be treated similarly by an offeror.**

   The purpose of the Code is to ensure fair and equal treatment of all offeree shareholders. This general principle would prohibit two tier bids, for example, where one set of shareholders, such as the existing directors, are given preferential treatment at the expense of others.

2. **During the course of an offer, or when an offer is in contemplation, neither an offeror, nor the offeree company, nor any of their respective advisers may furnish information to some shareholders which is not made available to all shareholders. This principle does not apply to the furnishing of information in confidence by the offeree company to a bona fide potential offeror or vice versa.**

   Furnishing of additional information to some offeree shareholders but not to others will clearly not give fair and equal treatment, because some investors will be in a better position to decide on the merits of the bid.

   The exemption for a bona fide offeror, who may of course already own some shares in the offeree, is a practical point. The rationale is that a prohibition of information to the offeror in such circumstances may actively work against shareholder interests in general by frustrating a possible offer.

3. **An offeror should announce an offer only after the most careful and responsible consideration. Such an announcement should be made only when the offeror has every reason to believe that it can and will continue to be able to implement the offer; responsibility in this connection also rests on the financial adviser to the offeror.**

   If this principle were not in existence, it would be possible for frivolous bidders to constantly make meaningless and vexatious offers for a company, diverting the management and the shareholders from more important matters.

   The principle highlights the importance of the financial adviser and his responsibility to guide a client through the intricacies of an offer, a fact continually highlighted in the rules and in practice. While a financial adviser may not necessarily be held responsible for a breach of the Code by a client, it will be important for the adviser to show that, in the circumstances, he took all reasonable steps to advise the client of his own responsibilities.

4. **Shareholders must be given sufficient information and advice to enable them to reach a properly informed decision and must have sufficient time to do so. No relevant information should be withheld from them.**

Shareholders will be able to make a fully informed decision only if they have all the relevant information to do so. Note that section 397 of the FSMA 2000 makes it a criminal offence to withhold information dishonestly or recklessly when inducing another person to make an investment decision.

5. **Any document or advertisement addressed to shareholders containing information or advice from an offeror, or the board of the offeree company, or their respective advisers must, as is the case with a prospectus, be prepared with the highest standards of care and accuracy.**

As with Principle 4, this relates to the quality and nature of information that must be transmitted to shareholders. Note that the information contained in documents or advertisements should not only be true but also complete, fairly presented and not misleading. This means that care will need to be taken when presenting charts or diagrams, for example. Techniques acceptable in other sales documents will not be permitted in this context if they are ruled to constitute unfair presentation.

6. **All parties to an offer must use every endeavour to prevent the creation of a false market in the securities of an offeror or the offeree company. Parties involved in offers must take care that statements are not made which may mislead shareholders or the market.**

This principle is now also confirmed by section 397 of the FSMA, which makes it an offence to create a false market in shares. Manipulation of share prices can swing a bid one way or another. For example, it may give a false impression of the value of a paper offer.

Where the share price becomes volatile, defined as 10% fluctuations in price, the panel requires an announcement to be made. If no announcement is forthcoming they may take steps to force a potential bidder into the open. At the same time the directors of the target company may be obliged to seek a suspension from listing under the obligations of the Listing Rules.

7. **At no time after a bona fide offer has been communicated to the board of the offeree company, or after the board of the offeree company has reason to believe that a bona fide offer might be imminent, may any action be taken by the board of the offeree company in relation to the affairs of the company, without the approval of the shareholders in general meeting, which could effectively result in any bona fide offer being frustrated or in the shareholders being denied an opportunity to decide on its merits.**

This principle would prohibit many of the techniques used in the USA, for example, to protect a company from predators. Significant reorganizations of the company where divisions are sold off to make the offeree less attractive to the offer can be completed only with shareholders' permission.

However, this does not prevent a company from establishing effective defences in advance of the emergence of a bid. Some of the most obvious takeover targets have been able to avoid bids by ensuring that potential predators are aware of the defences that are already in place.

8. **Rights of control must be exercised in good faith and the oppression of a minority is wholly unacceptable.**

The concept of minority protection is also enclosed in UK company law. However, court action is often expensive, lengthy and uncertain. This principle ensures that minority investors have immediate protection from unfair treatment in an offer situation.

9. **Directors of an offeror and the offeree company must always, in advising their shareholders, act only in their capacity as directors and not have regard to their personal or family shareholdings or to their personal relationships with the companies. It is the shareholders' interests taken as a whole, together with those of employees and creditors, which should be considered when the directors are giving advice to shareholders. Directors of the offeree company should give careful consideration before they enter into any commitment with an offeror (or anyone else) that would restrict their freedom to advise their shareholders in the future. Such commitments may give rise to conflicts of interest or result in a breach of the directors' fiduciary duties.**

This principle will be of key importance in situations when offeree directors are going to continue their involvement in the company. This may occur with a recommended offer, where the offeree company's directors are to keep their seats on the board and receive an incentive scheme to make the company perform. It will also be very relevant for management buy-outs.

10. **Where control of a company is acquired by a person, or persons acting in concert, a general offer to all other shareholders is normally required: a similar obligation may arise if control is consolidated. Where an acquisition is contemplated as a result of which a person may incur such an obligation he must, before making the acquisition, ensure that he can and will continue to be able to implement such an offer.**

This principle relates to the mandatory offer covered in Rule 9 of the Code.

12 Making an offer

12.1 Introduction

The method by which a company should make an offer is covered in Section D of the Blue Book. This covers how approaches should be made, what announcements are required and what advice should be sought by the offeree board.

12.2 The approach (Rule 1)

Any approach must first be made to the board of the offeree company or to its advisers. The identity of the offeror must be disclosed and the offeree board is entitled to be satisfied that the offeror has the ability to implement the offer in full.

12.3 Announcements (Rule 2)

Secrecy

In order to prevent leakage of price-sensitive information, it is vital that absolute secrecy is maintained prior to an offer being announced (Rule 2.1). The advisers to the offeror or offeree should always warn their clients of the importance of this. They are required to draw their clients' attention to the Code and to highlight the rules restricting share dealings (these rules are dealt with below).

When an announcement is required

The purpose of announcements is to avoid the creation of a false market and to prevent some shareholders dealing with information that is still price-sensitive. An announcement is required in the following circumstances (Rule 2.2):

(a) A firm intention to make an offer has been notified to the offeree board from a serious source. The offeree board is obliged to make an announcement that it has received the offer regardless of its attitude to the offer.

(b) The offeror should make an announcement where an obligation to make an offer has arisen as a result of Rule 9 (dealt with below). The announcement should be made immediately after the obligation has been incurred.

(c) Where there is rumour and speculation or the offeree's share price moves untowardly (for example, by more than 5% in any one day or by more than 10% above the lowest price since an approach was made to the potential offeree), an announcement may be required in the following circumstances:

- if there has been an approach to the offeree company, in which case the offeree board should make an announcement;

- if no approach has yet been made but the potential offeror has reason to believe that its actions are causing the rumours or price changes, in which case the offeror should make an announcement.

Where there is any doubt in this respect, the panel should be consulted.

(a) Where negotiations or discussions are being extended to include more than a very restricted number of people outside of those in the company who need to know and their immediate advisers, then the offeree should make an announcement. If a company is unsure whether an announcement is required in particular circumstances, it should consult the Panel.

(b) Where a purchaser is being sought for a holding or aggregate of holdings that have 30% or more of the voting rights in the company or where a company is seeking potential offerors, the offeree company will be required to make an announcement in any of the following circumstances:

- the company is subject to rumour and speculation or there is untoward movement in its share price;
- the number of offerors being approached is increasing beyond a very restricted number.

Suspension of listing

Announcements should usually be made immediately in all the above circumstances. However, where a bid is to be recommended and the Stock Exchange is likely to grant a temporary suspension, it may be possible for the offeree to seek a suspension prior to making the announcement (note 1 to Rule 2.3).

Contents of the announcement of a firm offer

Where there is a firm intention to make an offer, the announcement should contain details of the terms and conditions of the offer, the identity of the offeror and any existing holdings in the offeree which the offeror (or people acting in concert with him) owns, controls or has options to buy (Rule 2.5).

Where a person proposes to make an announcement of a possible offer that is subject to a pre-condition, the Panel must be consulted in advance.

Offeror's obligations

An offeror should announce an offer only if he knows that he has the ability to see the offer through. After an announcement has been made, an offeror must proceed with the offer unless permitted to withdraw by the Panel (Rule 2.7). Once an offeror has stated that he does not intend to make an offer, he will normally be bound by that statement for at least six months or until there is a material change in circumstances (Rule 2.8).

The purpose of this rule is to avoid uncertainty and the possibility of vexatious offers that may create a false market in the offeree's shares.

12.4 Independent advice (Rule 3)

Competent and independent advice

After an offer has been received, the offeree board must obtain competent and independent advice on the offer (Rule 3.1). The substance of this advice must be made known to their shareholders. This is particularly important in the case of a management buy-out (MBO), where the MBO directors will have a conflict of interest and will be unable to give advice to their shareholders.

If an adviser receives a fee dependent on the failure of a hostile bid, this will give an impression of a conflict of interest. Such an adviser will normally be disqualified from acting as a Rule 3 adviser. In addition, the panel may require such arrangements to be disclosed in a defence document.

Reverse take-overs

A reverse take-over is typically a situation where a listed company makes a share offer for an unlisted counterpart. As a result of the offer, the original shareholders of the unlisted company end up owning more than 50% of the shares of the listed company. Effectively, the unlisted company becomes the acquirer and obtains a listing through being taken over in this way.

Where the offer is effectively a reverse take-over or the offeror directors have a conflict of interest, the offeror must also obtain competent independent advice (Rule 3.2). The basis of this is that the offeror is effectively the offeree.

13 The offer and defence documents

13.1 Introduction

General obligation as to information

Documents from the offeror and offeree boards are covered in section J of the Code. Rule 23 states that shareholders must be given sufficient information and advice to enable them to reach a properly informed decision as to the merits of an offer. This information must be made available early enough for them to make a decision in good time. Rule 23 is essentially a repetition of general principle 4 of the code, which has been covered above.

The offer and defence documents are both essentially sales documents. As such, much of the required information below, which is not necessarily exciting to shareholders, will be relegated to the small print at the back of the document.

The responsibility of the directors

Any document or advertisement issued in connection with an offer must state that the directors of the offeror or offeree company, as appropriate, accept responsibility for the information contained in the document and that, to the best of their knowledge, the information is in accordance with the facts and does not omit anything likely to affect the import of the information (Rule 19.2).

If the information relates to another company and has been taken from published sources, this responsibility is limited to ensuring that the information is correctly and fairly reproduced (note 3 to Rule 19.2).

13.2 The offer document

Principal contents

The offer document must be posted within 28 days of the announcement of a firm intention to make an offer (Rule 30.1). Its principal contents are as follows:

(a) The intentions of the offeror for the offeree company and its employees (Rule 24.1).

    This will include any major changes to be introduced and plans for continued employment of employees. The document should give the long-term commercial justification for the bid.

    Typically, offer documents will make rather bland statements concerning the offeror's plans for existing employees. For example, they may just state that the existing right of employees will be safeguarded. The commercial justification for the offer will be more fully developed, particularly in a share-for-share offer.

(b) Financial and other information on the offeror and offeree company (Rule 24.2).

This should include for both companies:

- profit and loss account details (such as turnover, profit before and after tax, dividends and earnings per share) for the last three years;
- the latest published and audited balance sheet; and
- profit and loss account details from any interim statement or preliminary announcement made after the last set of annual accounts have been published.

If the offer is share-for-share, these details will probably be included as part of the listing particulars for the new shares to be issued.

(a) How the offer is to be financed (Rule 24.2).

There must be details of how the offer is to be financed and the source of any finance.

Where the offer is for cash or includes an element of cash the offeror's bankers or another appropriate adviser should confirm that resources are available to satisfy full acceptance of the offer (Rule 24.7).

(b) Details of any relevant shareholdings and dealings (Rule 24.3).

These include shareholdings in the offeree by the offeror company and shareholdings in the offeror or the offeree company by the offeror's directors or people acting in concert with the offeror. It also includes dealings in derivatives referenced to the shares.

(c) Share price comparisons (Rule 24.2).

It is often the case that the value of the offer is compared to the share price of the offeree. If this is done, there must be a comparison with the offeree share price on the last business day before the offer was announced along with any other comparison that may be made. This is meant to prevent solely unfair comparisons being made. The problem is that the share price of the offeree will often have moved before the announcement in anticipation of the offer. This means that this share price will already contain an element of bid premium, reducing the validity of the comparison.

13.3 The defence document

Principal contents

The defence document should be posted to shareholders within 14 days of the publication of the offer document (Rule 30.2). Its main contents are as follows.

- **The views of the offeree board** on the comments and statements made by the offeror with regard to its plans for the offeree should be made known (Rule 25.1 and 25.2).
- **Relevant shareholdings and dealings** should be disclosed (Rule 25.3). These include shareholdings in the offeror held by the offeree or its subsidiaries and any shareholdings in the offeror or offeree company held by the offeree's directors or people acting in concert with the offeree. It also includes derivatives referenced to the shares.
- **Directors' service contracts with more than 12 months to run**, including the name of the relevant director and the remuneration payable under the contract (Rule 25.4).

14 Restrictions on share dealings (Rule 4)

14.1 General prohibitions

These rules apply in addition to the restrictions contained in the relevant insider dealing regulations.

Dealings by persons other than the offeror (Rule 4.1)

No person who is privy to information concerning the offer may either deal, or recommend a third party to deal, in the securities (including options) of the offeree company between the time when there is reason to suppose that an approach or offer may be made and the announcement of that approach or offer. Recommending to others that they deal is also prohibited.

No such dealing may take place in the offeror unless the offer is not price sensitive in relation to those securities, ie is a cash offer.

In essence this is simply reinvoking the law on insider dealing, in a perhaps more enforceable, self-regulatory environment.

Restrictions on the offeror and concert parties during the offer period (Rule 4.2)

During the offer period, the offeror or persons acting in concert with it may not sell securities in the offeree without prior permission from the Panel and then only after 24 hours' public notice has been given that the sales may take place. If the bid is a mandatory bid under Rule 9 (see below) no sales will be allowed at all.

If there is an announcement that sales may be made no further purchases of securities will be permitted and it is highly unlikely that the Panel will permit the offer to be revised. This means that the only way the offeror can acquire shares in the offeree after the announcement will be if shareholders accept the existing offer.

Acting in concert – definitions

The basic definition

The definition of acting in concert for the purpose of the Blue Book includes persons who, pursuant to an agreement or understanding, cooperate to acquire shares in a company to obtain or consolidate control. Note that this is not the same as the legal concept of acting in concert, which refers to an agreement between two or more people to acquire interests in shares (Companies Act 1985, section 204).

Specific examples

In certain cases, people will be deemed to be acting in concert unless it is shown to be otherwise. Specific examples include the following.

(a) A company together with its parent, subsidiaries and fellow subsidiaries, plus any company that is an associated company of any of the above or a company which itself owns 20% of any of the above. An associated company is defined as a company in which the investing company owns at least 20% of the voting rights.

The above relationships can be summarized as follows:

	Companies acting in concert with each other	
	XYZ's parent company	
Associates of the parent	XYZ plc	XYZ's fellow subsidiaries
Associates of XYZ	XYZ's subsidiaries	Associates of fellow subsidiaries
	Associates of subsidiaries	

In addition, any company that owns 20% of any of the above company's shares will also be presumed to be acting in concert.

(a) All the above companies will be presumed to be acting in concert with any other member of the total grouping.

(b) A company will be presumed to be acting in concert with its directors and their close relatives.

(c) The directors of a company subject to, or likely to be subject to, an offer are presumed to be acting in concert.

(d) A financial adviser will be presumed to be acting in concert with its client.

Exempt fund manager/market maker status

The normal assumption will be that any market maker or fund manager associated with a party to the bid will be acting in concert. It is possible through the application for exempt status to avoid this aggregation.

Exempt fund manager

An exempt fund manager is a person who manages investment accounts on a discretionary basis and is recognized by the Panel as an exempt fund manager for the purposes of the Code.

Exempt market maker

An exempt market maker is a person who is registered as a market-maker with the Stock Exchange in relation to the relevant securities, or is accepted by the Panel as a market maker in those securities and, in either case, is recognized by the Panel as an exempt market maker for the purposes of the Code. This definition also incorporates principal traders in SETS securities who are granted exempt status by the Panel. References to market makers should, therefore, be taken to encompass principal traders.

Notes on exempt fund manager and exempt market-maker

Persons who manage investment accounts on a discretionary basis and market-makers must apply to the Panel in order to seek the relevant exempt status and will have to comply with any requirements imposed by the Panel as a condition of its granting such status. It is in this context that the concept of Chinese walls becomes more relevant than in the conduct of business rules, where they are merely advisable.

When a market-maker or fund manager is connected with the offeror or offeree company, exempt status is relevant only where the sole reason for the connection is that the market-maker or fund manager is in the same group as a financial or other professional adviser to the offeror or offeree company. References in the Code to exempt market-makers or exempt fund managers should be construed accordingly.

Dealings by a connected exempt market-maker in a market making capacity will not normally be considered as coming within the acting in concert presumptions, although dealings in any other capacity will be. Exempt market-makers, while able to continue their business normally, are subject to a number of conditions.

Exempt market-makers – prohibited dealings

An exempt market-maker connected with an offeror or the offeree company must not carry out any dealings with the purpose of assisting the offeror or offeree company, as the case may be.

Suspension of exempt status

Any dealings by an exempt market-maker connected with an offeror or the offeree company with the purpose of assisting an offeror or the offeree company, as the case may be, will constitute a serious breach of the Code. Accordingly, if the Panel determines that a market-maker has carried out such dealings, it will be prepared to rule that the market-maker should cease to enjoy exempt status for such period of time as the Panel may consider appropriate to the circumstances.

Dealings Between Offerors and Connected Exempt Market Makers

An offeror and any person acting in concert with it must not deal as principal with an exempt market-maker connected with the offeror in relevant securities of the offeree company during the offer period. It will generally be for the advisers to the offeror to ensure compliance with this Rule rather than the market-maker.

Assenting Securities

Securities owned by an exempt market-maker connected with the offeror must not be assented to the offer until the offer is unconditional as to acceptances.

Voting

Securities owned by an exempt market-maker connected with an offeror or the offeree company must not be voted in the context of an offer.

Disclosure of Dealings (Rule 38)

Dealings in relevant securities by an exempt market-maker connected with an offeror or the offeree company, whether in or outside the United Kingdom, should be aggregated and disclosed to the Stock Exchange, the Panel and the press not later than 12 noon on the business day following the date of the transactions, stating the following details.

(a) Total purchases and sales.

(b) The highest and lowest prices paid and received.

(c) Whether the connection is with an offeror or the offeree company.

(d) In respect of dealings that take place outside of the United Kingdom, the relevant overseas location.

Guidance

Method of disclosure

Announcements of dealings by or on behalf of an exempt market-maker that are disclosed in writing (or by telex) to the Stock Exchange (Company Announcements Office) may be inspected there but are also published through the Regulatory News Service (RNS). Disclosure to the press is, therefore, unnecessary; separate disclosure to the Panel is, however, required.

Exception

If the offer is not a securities exchange offer (share-for-share exchange), there is no requirement to disclose dealings in securities of the offeror.

15 Dealings in offeree securities by financial advisers of the offeree (Rule 4.4)

Financial advisers to the offeree, apart from exempt market-makers and exempt fund managers, may not do the following during the offer period:

- purchase any securities of the offeree or deal in derivatives and options referenced to the securities during the offer period on their own account;
- lend money to others to enable them to deal in the shares other than on normal commercial terms;
- enter into any agreement to induce someone else to deal or refrain from dealing in the shares.

16 Restrictions on acquisitions (Rule 5)

16.1 Restrictions on obtaining control

The objective of Rule 5 is to prevent a person obtaining control or consolidating control over a company except in a number of acceptable circumstances.The basic rule states that when a person (including people acting in concert with him) holds shares or rights over shares that carry less than 30% of the voting rights in a company, he may not acquire any shares or rights over shares which would mean that he would hold 30% or more of the voting rights in the company.

16.2 Restrictions on consolidating control

If a person already holds shares or rights over shares with between 30% and 50% inclusive of the voting rights then he may not acquire shares or rights over any more shares other than in exceptions listed below. Even if the acquisition is allowed it is probably that a mandatory offer will be triggered (see Rule 9).

Exceptions to the restrictions

There are a number of exceptions where the above basic rule does not apply, as follows:

(a) where a person already holds shares with more than 50% of the voting rights, because they already have legal control;

(b) where there is a vote of independent shareholders (ie excluding the acquirer) that approves the acquisition (a 'whitewash');

(c) where the purchase of shares or rights over shares is from a single shareholder and it is the only purchase in a seven-day period. Where such a purchase is made, then no subsequent purchases will be permitted unless the situations given in (d) to (h) below apply;

(d) where the purchase is immediately before a firm announcement to make an offer or during an offer and either the offer itself or a competing offer will be/has been recommended by the offeree board;

(e) where an offer has been announced, the first closing date of the offer has passed and it is not to be referred to the Competition Commission (CC);

(f) where the first closing date of a competing offer has passed and that offer is not to be referred to the CC;

(g) during an offer that is unconditional in all respects;

(h) where the acquisition is by way of a shareholder accepting an offer, as opposed to selling in the market.

16.3 Rights over shares

It should be noted that Rule 5 refers to shares or rights over shares. This will include options over existing shares but will not include warrants to subscribe for new shares in the company or convertible debt (because the shares are not yet in existence in these cases). Exercise of such warrants or conversion rights would, however, be relevant for the purpose of Rule 5, when they would be treated as an acquisition from a single shareholder. The exercise of options over existing shares would not be relevant, because the options themselves have already been included as rights over shares.

16.4 Conduct during the offer

Dealings during the offer period

Dealings in the equity or other voting shares of the offeree or the equity shares of the offeror made during the offer period may have to be disclosed (Rule 8). Equally, contravention of the limits imposed by Rule 9 will result in a mandatory bid thereby removing all flexibility from the offeror.

17 The mandatory offer (Rule 9)

17.1 The purpose of the mandatory offer

The objective of Rule 9 is to codify in more detail the requirements of general principle 10, which states that where a person obtains control of a company then he must make an offer for the shares of all other shareholders. This means that other shareholders will not:

- be forced to keep a shareholding in a company where somebody else effectively controls the company's operations and financial policy; or
- have to sell shares subsequently at a lower price, which reflects the fact that there is a dominant investor who does not intend to make an offer for the other shares.

17.2 When the mandatory offer is required

Acquiring or consolidating control

Rule 9 covers two situations:

- when a person originally acquires effective control of a company (defined as holding more than 30% of the voting rights); and
- when a person consolidates control (defined as increasing a holding of between 30% and 50% inclusive of voting rights).

The rule specifically states that:

- where a person acquires shares which, when taken in aggregate with his existing holdings and those of people acting in concert, carry 30% or more of the voting rights of a company; or
- where a person or people acting in concert already hold shares with between 39% and 50% (inclusive) of the voting rights and the person or people acting in concert acquire shares with voting rights,

then that person must make an offer to all the holders of any class of equity share or voting non-equity share in which he or people acting in concert have a holding.

Contrast to Rule 5

This rule links in strongly with Rule 5. There are, however, some important distinctions between the two. Rule 5 basically prohibits purchases which take a holding to 30% or over except in certain circumstances. If a person takes advantage of one of the exceptions, he or she can purchase the shares. However, they will still be subject to Rule 9 and will be required to make a mandatory offer for the company in question.

A second difference is that Rule 5 refers to shares or rights over shares (such as options) but Rule 9 refers to shares. Thus a purchase of options taking a person over 30% would be relevant for Rule 5 purposes but would not be covered in Rule 9. If the options were exercised, however, then the acquisition of shares could trigger a Rule 9 bid.

Illustration

Table 1

	Before %	**Buy options %**	**Exercise options %**
Shares owned (= Rule 9 total)	25	25	31
Options over existing shares	–	6	–
Total for Rule 5 purposes	25	31	31

The purchase of the options has no effect on the total for Rule 9 purposes and hence no mandatory offer is required. It will nevertheless be relevant for Rule 5 purposes. If the options are purchased from more than one shareholder the purchase would probably not be permitted. If the purchase was from only one person it would be permitted but subsequent acquisitions would not usually be possible, in accordance with Rule 5.

The later exercise of the options is irrelevant for Rule 5 purposes but increases the total of shares to 30% or over. Hence a mandatory offer will probably be required under Rule 9.

17.3 Moving from a voluntary offer to a mandatory offer

Note that a person may be making an offer on a voluntary basis and then purchase shares in the market bringing his holding in the company to 30% or more. This will trigger Rule 9 and mean that the offer will become mandatory, can have only a limited number of conditions attached and must have a cash alternative.

Should an offeror plan to incur such an obligation, it should consult the Panel in advance.

17.4 Acquisitions of shares by people acting in concert

The prime responsibility for making a mandatory offer rests with the person who made the purchase that took the total concert party holding to 30% or over and triggered the offer. The obligation may, however, be extended to include any other member of the concert party, especially where the person with prime responsibility is a relatively minor member of the group.

17.5 Dispensations from making a mandatory offer

The dispensations from Rule 9 give a number of situations when acquiring 30% or more of the voting rights in a company or increasing a holding with 30% or more of voting rights will not necessarily trigger a mandatory offer. In all cases, the dispensation is not an automatic right but is granted by the Panel.

17.6 Whitewash

Where there is a vote of independent shareholders (ie not including the person making the acquisition or people acting in concert with him) that approves the acquisition.

17.7 Foreclosure on security for a loan

Where a lender forecloses on security for a loan and takes control of 30% or more of the company. This exception will not apply if the lender had reason to believe that foreclosure was likely when the loan was made.

17.8 Rescue operations

Where a person acquires 30% or more of a company as a result of a rescue operation when the company is in financial difficulty. There were a number of examples of this in the early 1990s.

17.9 Inadvertent mistake

Where the person made a genuine mistake in incurring an obligation to make an offer. However, the shares must be sold in a limited period of time to people unconnected to the original purchaser.

17.10 50% will not accept

Where holders of shares carrying 50% or more of the voting rights in the company have confirmed that they will not accept any offer. This would mean that a mandatory offer would be bound to fail because it must be a condition of the offer that the offeror and people acting in concert end up with more than 50% of the voting rights (see below).

17.11 Enfranchisement of non-voting shares

Where shares that were previously non-voting are enfranchised, giving a person 30% or more of the voting rights. However, the person should not have acquired the shares with reason to believe that they would be enfranchised.

18 Required conditions for a mandatory offer

18.1 Referral to the Competition Commission or the European Commission

The mandatory offer must be made subject to a referral to the Competition Commission or the European Commission, in which case it may lapse.

18.2 Acceptance condition

It must also be conditional on the offeror and people acting in concert holding shares with more than 50% of the voting rights after the offer.

No other conditions are permitted for a mandatory offer.

19 Required consideration to be offered

19.1 Cash or cash alternative

The offer must be for cash or with a cash alternative. The cash offer must be at a price not less than the highest price paid for shares in the offeree in the last 12 months by the offeror or persons acting in concert with him.

20 Similar treatment for all shareholders

20.1 General principle 1

General principle 1 (similar treatment for all offeree shareholders) must be adhered to for all offers, mandatory and voluntary. Particular points to note with respect to this are as follows.

Different classes of share capital and convertibles

All classes of share capital must be given comparable (but not necessarily identical) treatment. In addition, the interests of convertible debt and warrants investors should be safeguarded.

Special deals with favourable conditions

Favourable conditions should not generally be extended to any particular group of shareholders. However, in certain situations, the offeror may wish to retain the services of director shareholders of the offeree and to motivate them by means of an 'earn out' deal where they receive a higher price for their shares if the company's profits hit specific targets.

Such special deals may be permitted only if the following criteria are satisfied.

- The directors suffer extra risk as well as having the potential for higher gains. It will be important that the price received by the directors can fall below the price offered to other shareholders as well as rise above it. For example, an offer to general shareholders of 200p together with an offer of between 100p and 350p for director shareholders, dependent on future profit performance, may be acceptable.
- An independent adviser states that, in his opinion, the terms are fair and reasonable.
- The deal is approved by a vote of independent shareholders.

21 Timetable of an offer

21.1 Summary bid timetable

The following summary highlights the main dates in an offer. These and other important dates are dealt with in more detail below.

Summary Bid	**Timetable**
Announcement	of Offer
28 days	?
'D' day	Posting of offer document
	?
D + 14	Posting of defence document
	?
D + 21	First closing date
	?
D + 39	Last date for announcements by offeree
	?
D + 46	Last date for revision of the offer
	?
D + 60	Last day an offer can be declared unconditional as to acceptances

Posting the offer document ('D-day')

The offer document should normally be posted within 28 days of the announcement of a firm intention to make an offer (Rule 30.1). The Panel must be consulted if the offer document is not to be posted within this period. However, the document will usually be posted well before this date, particularly in a hostile situation.

Offeree board circular (D + 14)

The board of the offeree company should advise its shareholders of its views on the offer as soon as practicable after publication of the offer document, and normally within 14 days (Rule 30.2).

First closing date (D + 21)

The offer must initially be open for at least 21 days following the date on which the offer document is posted (Rule 31.1). If there is any announcement of an extension to the offer then the next closing date must be stated (Rule 31.2). If the offer has been declared unconditional as to acceptances a statement may be made that the offer will remain open until further notice. In this case, at least 14 days' notice must be given in writing to shareholders who have not yet accepted before the offer is closed.

Purchase of shares in the market

After the first closing date has passed and provided that the bid has not been referred to the Competition Commission, the restrictions on purchasing shares carrying more than 30% of the votes in Rule 5 is lifted (Rule 5.2). However, such purchases could trigger a mandatory offer.

Unconditional acceptance period

After an offer has become or is declared unconditional as to acceptances, the offer must remain open for acceptance for at least 14 days after the date it would otherwise have expired, unless it has been unconditional from the outset (Rule 31.4).

Fulfilment of conditions

All conditions must be fulfilled or the offer must lapse within 21 days of the later of the first closing date and the date the offer becomes or is declared unconditional as to acceptances (Rule 31.7).

Withdrawal of acceptances

If an offer has not become unconditional by 21 days after the first closing dates, then an acceptor must be entitled to withdraw his acceptance from this date (Rule 34).

Offeree board announcement (D + 39)

The offeree board should not, without the Panel's consent, announce trading results, profit or dividend forecasts, assets valuations or proposals for dividend payments after the 39th day following the posting of the initial offer document (Rule 31.9).

Revision of offers and final revision date (D + 46)

There is no requirement for an offer to be revised or extended (Rule 31.3). However, if an offer is revised, it must remain open for at least 14 days following the date the revised offer document is posted (Rule 32.1). This means that the latest possible date that an offer can be revised is 46 days after the initial offer, because the time limit for the bid is 60 days after that date (see below).

On revision of an offer, all shareholders who accepted the original offer must be entitled to the revised consideration (Rule 32.3).

Where it has been stated that an offer will not be extended or increased, only in exceptional circumstances will the Panel permit the offer to be extended or increased (Rules 31.5 and 32.2). It is usual for a 'no extension' or 'no revision' statement to be accompanied by a rider stating that the offeror specifically reserves the right to extend or revise the offer should a competing offer emerge. The Panel will normally accept this (notes 2 and 4 to Rule 31.5).

When an offer includes shares, the offeror will have to ensure that it does not release information after D + 46 which will affect the value of the share consideration. For example, the issue of interim results which are better than expected might increase the share price and effectively revise the offer. Release of such sensitive information will be possible only if it fits in with the offeror's normal results timetable, every effort was made to ensure that the release date was not after day 46 and it is not likely to affect materially the outcome of the offer.

Final time limit (D + 60)

An offer may not become or be declared unconditional as to acceptances after midnight on the 60th day after the day the initial offer document was posted, without the Panel's consent (Rule 31.6). The Panel will normally consent to an extension beyond this if:

- there is a competing offer, in which case both offerors will normally have to follow the timetable of the competing offer;
- the board of the offeree company consents to the extension;
- the board of the offeree company has made an announcement on profits, etc more than 39 days after the initial offer document was posted.

In establishing whether acceptance conditions have been satisfied, the offeror can only take into account acceptances or share purchases where the relevant documents are received by its receiving agent by 1.00 pm on the 60th day.

Settlement of consideration

The consideration must be posted within 14 days of the later of:

- the first closing date;

- the date the offer becomes or is declared unconditional;
- the date an acceptance is received (Rule 31.8).

Impact of OFT investigation on timings

It is often the case that there is a significant delay before a decision is made subsequence to an OFT investigation. In such a case, the Panel will typically rule that, should the offer be cleared, day 39 will be two days after the clearance and subsequent dates will be adjusted accordingly to maintain the usual relationship thereafter (note 3 to Rule 31.6).

22 Restrictions following offers

22.1 Delay of 12 months before making new offer

Where an offer is unsuccessful or an announcement is made that raises the possibility of an offer but no offer is forthcoming within a reasonable period, the offeror or any person acting in concert with it should not within 12 months (Rule 35.1):

- make an offer for the company;
- acquire shares in the company if this would result in an obligation to make an offer under Rule 9.

22.2 Partial offers

The above restrictions also apply where a partial offer has been made which could have resulted in a holding of between 30% and 50% inclusive of the voting rights of the offeree, regardless of whether the offer has been successful or not (Rule 35.2).

22.3 Dispensations

The 12-month waiting period may be dispensed with if the Panel consents. Circumstances when consent is likely to be forthcoming include where (notes a and b to Rules 35.1 and 35.2):

- a new offer is to be recommended;
- a competing offer has been announced;
- the original offer lapsed due to a Competition Commission referral and has now been cleared;

- a 'whitewash' proposal, whereby another shareholder will acquire 30% or more of the company without the requirement to make a mandatory offer, is announced;
- a reverse take-over of the original offeree is announced.

22.4 Delay of six months before buying shares above the offer value

If a person or people acting in concert hold shares carrying more than 50% of the voting rights of a company, they may not acquire shares in the company or make an offer for it on better terms than those available under a previous offer within six months of the closure of the previous offer which became unconditional (Rule 35.3). Should they do so then the Panel may require that the better terms are offered to the shareholders who accepted the previous offer.

As with the rules concerning purchases above the offer price during the offer period (Rules 6.2 and 32.3), the purpose of this is to ensure equality of treatment for all offeree shareholders.

23 The rules governing substantial acquisitions of shares

These rules were initially introduced by the Stock Exchange but are now the responsibility of the Panel.

Purpose These rules are designed to restrict the speed at which stakes are accumulated. The idea behind this is that without these restrictions large purchases (dawn raids) might be used to build up a position and thereby circumvent the disclosure rules. These raids have in the past caused disturbance in the market, temporarily distorting the price of the securities in question.

Summary The basic rules place limits on how fast a stake can be built up, beyond a limit of 14.9%.

In addition, there are accelerations to the disclosure requirements of the Companies Act.

Prior to the introduction of the SARs (Substantial Acquisition Rules), the only restraint on a company mounting a 'dawn raid' on a target was the Rule 5 restriction. This means that it was possible to acquire up to 29.9% of the target prior to launching a public offer. This provided an excellent base from which to achieve success. With the SARs, the maximum holding that is usually possible is 14.9%, giving the target more of an opportunity to mount a defence and ensuring that offeree shareholders are treated fairly.

The SARs apply to transactions in the shares of companies resident in the United Kingdom, the Channel Islands or the Isle of Man if their shares are listed on the Stock Exchange or are dealt on the AIM.

23.1 Restrictions on acquisitions

The basic rule

The SARs effectively state in Rules 1 and 2 that purchases of shares will not be permitted if:

(a) The purchases comprise shares or rights over shares with 10% or more of the voting rights in the company; and

(b) The purchases are all in the same seven-day period; and

(c) The purchases are from more than one shareholder; and

(d) The person's total holding of shares and rights over shares after the purchases comes to 15% or more but less than 30% of the voting rights of the company in question (at 30% Rules 5 and 9 of the Code come into play).

The purchases need to fail all four criteria before they are prohibited.

24 EU merger regulation

In the late 1980s as part of the drive to harmonize European Regulations the European Commission introduced a proposed directive with regard to take-overs. This was always going to be a difficult area to harmonize given the variety of corporate regimes across the union. In some countries by virtue of historical development or corporate law, hostile take-overs are virtually unknown whereas other nations, including the UK, have an active take-over market.

In July 2001, the European Parliament voted on and rejected a compromise text for a proposed Directive on Take-overs (the 13th Directive on Take-overs).

The Proposed Directive, if enacted, will, in the panel's opinion, put at risk the advantages of the current non-statutory system of take-over regulation in the UK, but without providing compensating benefits.The Directive contains (in Article 4.5) provisions that are designed to limit the damage that would be caused to the existing UK system of regulation by increased litigation. It would allow the UK to retain an administrative process of bid regulation, as presently provided by the Panel.The courts would be able to dismiss tactical litigation and prevent litigation affecting the outcome of a bid, thereby continuing the approach adopted by the Court of Appeal in the *Datafin* case in 1986. Further, in implementing the Directive, the UK government could ensure that the supervisory authority could not be sued for damages and that no new grounds for litigation would be created between the parties to a bid.These provisions should minimize the scope for litigation. But the risk of increased litigation can be eliminated only by having no Directive at all.

From the start the Panel was suspicious of the harmonization process, believing that it would inevitably lead to a statutory system that would undermine the efficiency of the Panel and bring regulation down to the lowest common denominator. The Panel further expressed that the introduction of statutory control would slow the process down and thereby make take-over activity in the UK less appealing and more costly.

Notwithstanding this, the draft Directive stipulated a minimum level of protection that is, in the Panel's opinion, far inferior to that currently provided by the Code in the UK. Even though many of the Articles (for example those on general principles and mandatory bids) have taken the Code as their starting point, the text agreed in the Council reflects the lowest common denominator of what is capable of agreement between the member states.

The future of the Take-over Directive has become increasingly uncertain due to an argument regarding whether target companies may take action to frustrate a bid. The initial draft of the Directive effectively prevented a company from taking defensive action during a hostile bid without the prior approval of the shareholders.

Many EU countries were distinctly unhappy with this provision, especially as US take-over regulation allows it. The Legal Affairs Committee concluded that if member states were required to prohibit frustrating action, it would have the effect of making it easier for US companies to take-over EU companies. However, the UK is vehemently opposed to the use of frustration. At the time of writing, EU ministers are struggling to put together a proposal for a way forward.

24.1 EU Merger Regulations – EC Council Regulations 4064/89 and 1301/97

These EU Regulations give the European Commission jurisdiction over mergers that have an effect on a number of member states. The Regulations provide that a 'Concentration with a Community dimension' is one where either:

(1) the aggregate worldwide turnover of all parties concerned is more than €5,000 million; and

(2) the aggregate Community-wide turnover of each of at least two of the parties involved is more than €250 million,

or

(1) the aggregate worldwide turnover of all the parties concerned is more than €2,500 million; and

(2) the aggregate turnover of all of the parties in each of at least three member states is more than €100 million; and

(3) in each of the same three member states as in (2) above, the aggregate turnover of each of at least two of the parties involved is more than €25 million; and

(4) the aggregate Community-wide turnover of each of at least two of the parties involved is more than €100 million.

Concentration under the Regulations is envisaged to arise in one of two ways:

(a) two or more independent undertakings merge, thus becoming one new independent undertaking; or

(b) one or more undertakings (or a person(s) already controlling an undertaking) acquire(s) direct or takes indirect control of the whole or parts of some other undertaking.

The operation of these Regulations for cases having a cross-border impact is at present being examined.

24.2 EU v UK merger regulations

The take-over of the Midland Bank by the Hong Kong and Shanghai Banking Corporation is a good example of the impact of both EU and UK merger regulation. After Hong Kong had made its initial offer for Midland Bank, Lloyds Bank stepped in with a rival bid on the basis that it would make an offer if the two rival bids were treated alike by the merger authorities.

The Hong Kong bid did amount to a Concentration with a community dimension under the above regulations but was cleared by the EU Commission. Hong Kong and Midland competed in only a few sectors and, if they merged, intense competition in those sectors would remain. The proposed Lloyds bid did not, however, fall within the EU Merger Regulations. The Lloyds bid was not referred to the then Monopolies and Mergers Commission and Lloyds withdrew its offer.

Fourteen

Secured finance and guarantees

1 Security in assets

A lender may decide to seek security over the company's assets, in preference to enforcing a default. This could have implications regarding the negative pledge and *pari passu* clauses. However, as with other types of documentation, the rights of the parties, and the terms and conditions, would need to be specified.

Assets pledged (and registered as such) could be itemised, or a floating charge of assets to the value of a specific amount would be detailed. The latter would allow the company to sell assets, or interchange assets, without seeking the lender's permission each time.

As previously stated, secured borrowing is unusual in today's environment, but companies such as property developers do tend still to borrow on a secured basis. In these instances the documentation will obviously also include the details of the security. The negative pledge is likely to have specific exclusions to property already charged, and some form of exclusion for future charges, such as to a monetary value, or replacement of existing charges, or in support of the purchase of the asset, such as in a financial lease.

2 Purposes of security

(1) The lender can sell security in the event of default and has priority over unsecured lenders.

(2) Insulation from sovereign states by the use of external security such as bullion, investments, etc.

(3) Control especially in project finance transactions whereby the lender is able to exercise operational control over assets rather than by sale.

(4) Protection against other creditors, especially if borrower has given security already to domestic lenders.

3 General conflict rules on security over assets

One must consider the various problems posed by conflict of laws and securities and, in particular, the law that will apply to the security where such security is taken over assets in a foreign jurisdiction. For instance, under English rules of private international law there is the fact that different rules govern different types of assets and may be categorized into immovables (land), tangible movables (goods) and intangible movables (debts). Land is an available security extensively in most states.

The general rule (at common law) regarding the proper law governing security is the *lex situs* (ie where the asset is situated). Many countries have adopted the *lex situs* doctrine as the paramount influence in relation to security and this approach is confirmed by the Rome Convention (which applies to the EU countries) in Article 4, part 3 which provides that the law that applies will be the place where the immovable property exists. As regards moveable property the general rule (at common law) is that the proper law will be the place where such assets are located at the date the security is created. A problem will occur with movable property in that different laws could govern the security taken if such security were located in different countries. The *lex situs* of securities is the place of incorporation of the issuer and was confirmed by the English courts in the case of *Macmillan Inc v Bishopsgate Investment Trust plc* (1996). Another approach in the case of shares or bonds is that the *lex situs* is the place where the securities are situated or registered or where they are being negotiated, as in the case of negotiable instruments.

Charges on tangible movables or chattel mortgages require registration if not protected by possession, actual or constructive (warehouse key). International registers exist for a ship and aircraft mortgages. In the case of stationary goods, the applicable law is the *lex situs*, eg the *Scotch whisky in Inglis v Robertson* (1898). In the case of ambulatory goods, the *lex situs* may apply or the law of the flat (ships or aircraft). If the goods are moved to a new place, it will depend upon whether there has been a further dealing in them or not. If not, the original *lex situs* should apply except, of course, an external forum may impose its own registration rules as a public policy requirement. If there has been a further dealing in the new state, that *lex situs* will determine the validity of the new dealing, eg the Quebecan car in *Century Credit Corpn v Richard* (1962).

There is little certainty as to the rules that govern the taking of security over intangible assets. Although some jurisdictions, including England, recognize the ability to take a security interest over such assets, there are also a number of jurisdictions that acknowledge that it is conceptually impossible to take a security interest.

It would therefore be crucial to obtain appropriate legal opinions covering the question of whether or not an effective security interest could be taken in the property; the formal requirements that must be satisfied in order to create an effective and binding security interest; the nature and extent of any perfection requirements.

Questions of priority should also be covered in any legal opinion that is obtained.

The most common form of a charge over an intangible moveable asset is assignment of a debt. The law of the debt contract determines whether it may be assigned. The law of the place where the assignment occurs determines what formal requirements apply, although it should be valid if it complies with the requirements of its *lex causae*. Article 12 of the Rome Convention 1980 establishes that the validity of an assignment and the form of notice is determined by the proper law of the debt assigned and not by the *situs* of the debt. The assignment's proper law also determines the validity and interpretation of the assignment. If there are successive assignments, that law also should determine priority and notice of assignment whereby the debtor brings the right to receive payments from the debtor and priority over subsequent assignees, *Dearle v Hall* (1828).

Also consider difficulties with recognition of appropriate security interests. For example, the fact that many jurisdictions will not recognize a floating charge and that many civil law countries (for example Germany, France and Italy) have a very restricted approach towards the type of security that can be created over assets where a proprietary interest is not passed in those assets to the chargee.

4 General considerations and principles with regard to security

A bank should raise the following questions before making the loan available:

(a) does the borrower have good unencumbered title to the assets over which security is proposed to be taken? Investigate the effect of retention of title clauses;

(b) other creditors may have priority under local rules, eg preferential creditors ahead of a floating charge, liquidator's costs in an insolvency;

(c) are there restrictions on the nature of the security that can be taken? For example, many civil law jurisdictions do not recognize anything other than a fixed security interest whereas others, for example the UK, may recognize securities over future (after-acquired) property. After-acquired property may escape the charge;

(d) will the granting of the security conflict with a contrary contractual agreement, for example, a negative pledge?

(e) A maintenance of value clause which provides for automatic topping up if the asset value deteriorates may be ineffective as a fraudulent preference or there may be no available assets;

(f) a roll-over (eg on currency conversion) may discharge the security or lose the lender his priority, eg *Clayton's Case* (1816);

(g) second or junior mortgagees may exercise rights to the disadvantage of a first or senior mortgagee, eg to realize the security, and priority for further advances will be lost unless there is an obligation to tack;

(h) some jurisdictions insist that the mortgage debt be expressed in local currency, exposing the lender to adverse movements in exchange rates;

(i) any prohibition or penalty on prepayment may constitute a clog on the equity of redemption;

(j) government consent may be required for the grant of security to an alien;

(k) there may be stamp duty to pay;

(l) the security may not be recognized in other jurisdictions;

(m) a trustee may not be allowed to hold the security, eg an agent bank;

(n) an external court may not have jurisdiction to enforce the security;

(o) in enforcing the security, the lender may have to follow a specific procedure in exercising a power of sale, and may be liable for selling too cheaply (*Standard Chartered Bank v Walker* (1983) CA) or may face restrictions on whom he may sell to;

(p) if he enters into possession, he may be liable for negligence, *White v City of London Brewery Co* (1889);

(q) the security may be void for want of registration, which may be a multiple requirement;

(r) will the proposed security interest require to be registered in order to perfect the interest and if so are significant costs attached to such registration requirements? Will non-registration make the security interest void and or will it affect priorities?

(s) Should the security be held by a trustee in order that the bank will be able to bring some flexibility into the advancing of the facility in the event that the bank at some stage in the future decides to sell all or part of its loan to the borrower? Are stamp duties or other similar taxes payable in respect of the taking of security in any of the three jurisdictions and will the documentation in respect of the creation of the security required to be notarized?

(t) What is the position on enforcement of the appropriate security interest? What remedies are available on a default? Will the assets over which security is to be taken be capable of being sold and are particular restrictions applicable in the event of any sale post-enforcement?

(u) Are there restrictions on the currency of the security and if so will these present problems upon enforcement?

(v) There is also the need to obtain an appropriate opinion in each of the jurisdictions, covering many of the points raised above and any additional points, which will invariably depend upon the specific security interest proposed to be taken by the lending bank.

5 Registration of security

The purposes of the requirement to register security include the protection of intending creditors by advertising the existence of charges, the provision of an unarguable system of priorities based on date of registration or a more arguable system of constructive knowledge as in England. Registration may be by asset (eg the Land Registry) or by debtor (eg the Companies Registry and the Land Charges Registry). Different registers can and do overlap.

In the USA, Article 9 of the Uniform Commercial Code, adopted by most states including New York, offers a comprehensive system of resolving conflicts over registration. It does not deal with land. Other assets are divided into 'goods, documents and interests', 'accounts and general intangibles', 'mobile goods', 'chattel paper' and 'minerals'. The first category includes charges over non-mobile goods, over documents of title and over negotiable instruments. The applicable law will be that of the state where the asset is when the 'last event' occurs. This 'last event' is the latest to happen of (a) the asset being in the mortgagee's possession or the mortgagor signing the charge form, (b) the mortgagee granting the loan and (c) the mortgagor having rights in the asset. Signatory states require that non-possessory charges be protected by filing (registration). The second category includes book debts and intellectual property, conflicts rules determine the relevant law to be that of the debtor's place of residence which also applies to the third category. Generally, priority is determined by chronological order of filing (if required). Filing expires automatically after five years but may be extended.

In England, section 396 of the Companies Act 1985 sets out which charges over company assets must be protected by registration on the companies register. They include – charges created by an instrument that would require registration as a bill of sale if executed by an individual, charges on land, on book debts, on ships or aircraft, any floating charge and any charge to secure an issue of debentures. This applies to all English registered companies and to all overseas companies having an established place of business in England, where the property being charged is in England, *Re Oriel Ltd* (1985) CA and section 409. If the overseas company has an established place of business it should already be registered as an overseas company. The Registrar of Companies will not register a charge if the company is not registered but sending him particulars should preserve the lender's position following the decision in *Slavenburg's Bank NV v Intercontinental Natural Resources Ltd* (1980). Failure to register within 21 days of the creation of the charge renders it void against a liquidator and creditors who acquire rights in the property concerned. It is not void against the company and the chargee will in any case remain an unsecured creditor. Until the twenty-one days have expired the charge is fully valid against any charges taken later even if registered first. Since the *Slavenburg* case banks must attempt to register such security at Companies House that is over security situated in Britain that is owned or being charged by an overseas company. Possessory pledges over goods and charges over insurance policies including an ECGD policy do not require registration at Companies House.

A banker taking a charge should be alert to the possible need for registrations in several registers in one country and in other countries. The countries concerned include the place of incorporation of the borrower, the borrower's established place of business, the places where he does business, the place where the asset is and places where it may go to, eg the Australian bus in *Lucking v Highway Motel (Caernarvon) Pty Ltd* (1975). Obviously there is a better chance of escaping a local registration law if action is taken in an external form.

6 Floating charge

This is an equitable security (available only to companies) over the assets of a company as subsisting from time to time, not attaching to any particular asset until the charge is crystallized, when it becomes an equitable fixed charge. Meanwhile the company is free to deal in the assets concerned without reference to the chargee, *Re Yorkshire Woolcombers Association Ltd* (1903). Its advantages are that it can catch all the assets, including after-acquired ones, and allows the company to continue trading freely. Its disadvantages are lack of priority over preferential claims such as employees and liquidation expenses in an insolvency, any judgment creditor completing execution before crystallization gets priority (although an automatic crystallization clause may assist), a fixed charge takes priority (although a *pari passu* clause assists), the company can run down its assets, goods may be subject to retention of title clauses, and it may be void as a fraudulent preference or under section 617 of the Companies Act 1985.

Under the Enterprise Act 2002, preferential creditors other than employees have been eliminated. Consequently the floating charge will be in terms of security and be better than the previous position in that it will no longer (except employees) be eroded by the preferential creditors. A floating charge will though still suffer if any assets are subject to a fixed charge and any retention of title clauses, known as Romalpa clauses (see below).

Banks and other lenders prefer a fixed charge because this ranks before floating charges and unsecured creditors and they are paid before preferential creditors (such as employees). The issue whether it is possible to have a fixed charge over property that is changing all the while as debts are paid off and new ones incurred was considered in the case of *Agnew v Inland Revenue* [2001] All ER (D) 2 (known as the *Brumark* case).

The case concerned Brumark Investments Ltd in receivership, its only distributable assets were the proceeds of book debts that were outstanding when receivers were appointed and which they collected. But who did the proceeds belong to: a lender with a fixed charge over them or the Inland Revenue and other preferential creditors?

The Privy Council (basically the Law Lords) decided that it was possible to have a fixed charge on book debts but the degree of control over them by the lender was crucial. Here the debts were released from the charge as soon as the company received them. This was not enough said the court. The charge must be regarded as a floating charge and was therefore postponed to preferential creditors.

If a bank or lender is concerned to achieve a fixed charge on book debts following *Brumark* it seems essential to open an account for proceeds at the bank as a trust account and name it as such and pay only the proceeds of the charged assets into it. The borrower should also undertake not to overdraw the account and give undertakings to the lender to obey such instructions as the lender may give in connection with the funds in the account. The appeal came from New Zealand and although the Privy Council's decisions are not binding here they are strongly persuasive and the decision is likely to be followed in the UK.

In the international context a floating charge may fail for lack of recognition by another state. In *Carse v Copper* (1961) a Scottish court held that a floating charge created by a Scottish domiciled company over its English assets was invalid because the proper law of the charge was the law of the chargor's domicile, which did not recognize floating charges. It has been argued that the *lex situs* should have governed validity. In *Re Anchor Line Ltd* (1937) an English court held that a floating charge granted by an English company over assets in Scotland to a Scottish bank was valid as the proper law was English law. The courts of the *situs* may invalidate the charge for lack of compliance with local formalities, eg *Re Maudslay Sons & Field* (1900) where an English court upheld an assignment of French debts (invalid under French law for want of procedure) to English creditors. The cynical view would be that in each case the forum is applying its own security law, upholding devices familiar to it and knocking down those that are unfamiliar.

Under the Enterprise Act 2002, under their floating charges, banks will generally no longer be able to appoint administrative receivers. Banks will be given the chance to appoint an administrator of their own choice should they wish to overrule the company's choice. Holders of floating charges taken before the implementation of the Act will still be able to appoint administrative receivers.

The administrator will be under an express obligation to act in the interests of all creditors and not just the bank by way of the floating charge. Under the Enterprise Act 2002, preferential creditors other than employees have been eliminated.

The floating charge is accepted in most common law jurisdictions; the USA's Uniform Commercial Code Article 9 conceives of a similar charge.

A receiver appointed under floating charge should be recognized in a foreign court when he sues to collect in the assets because his powers should be governed by the place of incorporation, but US courts have raised objections.

7 Retention of title clauses

These are sometimes known as *Romalpa* clauses after one of the early cases in this rapidly developing are of law, *Aluminium Industrie Vaassen BV v Romalpa Aluminium Ltd* (1976) CA.

A clause that seeks to retain ownership of goods in the supplier until paid for will be effective inasmuch as the goods remain in an unaltered state in the buyer's possession and it is even possible to claim rights over the proceeds of sale of unaltered goods (*Romalpa*). Where the goods are converted in a manufacturing process, there can be no claim by the seller either for the produced goods or proceeds of their sale, eg the resin used in the manufacture of chipboard in *Borden (UK) Ltd v Scottish Timber Products Ltd* (1981). Any attempt to retain equitable ownership in the supplier while the buyer converts the goods will be void for want of registration of a floating charge, *Re Bond Worth* (1980). Severable assets may remain claimable by the supplier, eg the engines attached to generator units in *Hendy Lennox* (1984).

Retention of title clauses can come in different forms but all seek to cover both stock and debtors. It may not be easy to establish the full extent to which assets are subject to retention of title because borrowers take little notice of it. *Romalpa* clauses are also so prevalent that it may not be practical to carry out a full stock check where a large number of suppliers are involved.

The situation over work in progress is not clear cut because for a retention of title clause to be enforced the goods supplied must be identifiable as belonging to the supplier. This is not case where they become mixed with other materials as part of the manufacturing process.

The situation on debtors has not been tested in the courts but a banker could be in danger where goods remain readily identifiable while passing through the borrower's hands to his debtor. Businesses like wholesaling could be at risk from such an attack.

8 Corporate guarantees

8.1 Introduction

Companies tend to have set guideline policies for the giving, or not, of guarantees. Most companies will guarantee only the portion of a subsidiary company's indebtedness for which the (ultimate) parent is responsible. In other words, if a company owns 100% or 70% of the shares in a subsidiary, it will guarantee only 100% or 70% of the indebtedness, respectively.

In the UK, guarantees are noted in a company's annual report, as contingent liabilities. Analysts may add these into the borrowings figure to calculate gearing. However, in reality, only guarantees given in respect of the performance of third parties should be added in, because guarantees of inter-company indebtedness would already be included in the total borrowings figure, as shown on the balance sheet. The difference lies in the guarantor obligation falling on the company, not the consolidated group. It is therefore the gearing level of the company that is affected by the contingent liabilities – a fact that is sometime miscalculated.

The policy to guarantee or not will vary by company, and industry type. Many companies will wish, for management purposes, to ensure that subsidiaries are viewed on a stand-alone basis, and will maintain the subsidiary's capital base to that effect. Other companies will take a group approach, seeing the subsidiaries or divisions forming a part of the whole, and therefore be more 'relaxed' about giving guarantees to lenders as support for indebtedness.

8.2 Purpose of guarantees

1. To ensure if principal debtor does not pay then recovery can be from another person.

2. To ensure a supervisory function, ie parent and subsidiary. It may also bind a director to the company.
3. To secure non-interference, ie in the case of a central bank with power to impose exchange controls.

8.3 Forms of guarantee

1. Guarantee – an obligation of secondary liability where demand must be made on the principal debtor or borrower first before making demand on the guarantor.
2. Primary – indemnity liability. No consideration is needed with an indemnity obligation as opposed to a guarantee in as much as the indemnifier must pay even if the underlying transaction is void or unenforceable. Thus as with an indemnity the liability of the indemnifier does not depend upon the liability of the principal debtor.
3. Letter of comfort – not necessarily legally binding but can vary in wording as to be guarantees or indemnities. This is discussed in more detail below.

8.4 Inter-company guarantees

In large international companies with many subsidiaries and associated companies the pattern of financing can often be very complex. The fact that Subsidiary A requires funds does not necessarily mean that it is the best vehicle through which the group should obtain the relevant finance. On the other hand, it may be that Subsidiary B, which is highly liquid, will nevertheless be the most economic unit through which to source a new group borrowing. For the most part, decisions in this area are tax-driven but there are other considerations, such as access to domestic markets, which might cause the corporate to route a borrowing indirectly. Looked at on a unilateral basis, it is not to be expected that all the units in a group will have the same credit standing and it is accordingly normal for such transactions to be supported, where necessary, by inter-company guarantees. The bank will want to look very closely at the implications of these while, in turn, the corporate must ensure that it does not agree to anything that might constrain the corporate's ability to finance itself in the most satisfactory way in the future.

8.5 'Upstream', 'downstream' and 'cross-stream' guarantees

The credit strength of a group of companies lies where the assets are. If the group is structured with a parent company that is merely a holding company, the various subsidiaries will be the only assets to which a bank can look if it is lending to the parent company. Any guarantee given by one of those subsidiaries will result in the relevant creditors ranking ahead of the parent company in the event of that subsidiary's liquidation – they will thus rank ahead of the bank that has lent to the parent company. A banker must be alert to the problems of lending to holding companies against the security of upstream guarantees that in effect may be worthless and banks should lend direct to the asset-holding subsidiaries instead. In the case of corporate guarantees a bank must ensure that the issue of consideration is duly addressed in the taking of any guarantee.

Accordingly, the bank would require an extension of the restrictions of the negative pledge to the subsidiaries in which the real strength of the company lay. Where the bank is lending to one of the subsidiary companies, the need for protection may be equally acute. One particular danger that the bank will perceive is that the subsidiary might give what are known as 'upstream' or 'cross-stream' guarantees for indebtedness of the parent company or of a fellow subsidiary. The existence of such guarantees can change the order or ranking in a liquidation situation to the disadvantage of the bank and in an extreme situation could possibly be used to defraud it. Thus, the parent company lends money to Subsidiary A under the guarantee of Subsidiary B that has, in turn, borrowed from the bank. The parent then deliberately strips all assets out of Subsidiary A and forces it into liquidation using the upstream guarantee to rank ahead of the bank in the consequent liquidation of Subsidiary B. You will find it instructive to review the matrix of possibilities in this area. Banks therefore should lend money directly to subsidiaries where the assets are held and not through a layer or structure of guarantees.

When negotiating these points, the corporate's concern must be to ensure that none of the constraints that have been introduced into the loan agreement to protect the bank will, in turn, place unacceptable constraints on the company's financing flexibility. In particular it should not agree to any prohibition of 'downstream' guarantees (that is, parent guarantees of subsidiary or associate company borrowings) even though it is possible to demonstrate that, in certain circumstances, the bank could be disadvantaged thereby. Such a restriction could prevent the use of borrowing-vehicle companies to achieve a tax advantage or circumvent foreign exchange control restrictions. Similarly it could impede the financing of a joint-venture operation, with adverse commercial consequences.

8.6 Possible problems for the guarantor

Dependent again on the credit status of the parties, the bank may wish to obtain similar covenants from the guarantor that it has required from the borrower. This will be the case particularly if the borrower is a vehicle company so that it is only in the guarantor that credit of any substance lies. In such a situation the bank will be negotiating directly with the guarantor and will behave much as if it were making a direct loan. The borrower's position in all this should be to ensure that the covenants his company accepts in the capacity of guarantor are no stronger than those he would accept were the company itself borrowing. While it is prudent financial management to regard a guarantee as a real, rather than as a contingent liability, for purposes of internal housekeeping, it is certainly not sensible to allow the company's financing flexibility to be reduced in order to obtain off-balance sheet finance.

Any guarantee given for a loan will be required to cover not only its capital value but also outstanding interest charges and any other payments due by the borrower under the loan agreement. Where the borrower is not a wholly-owned subsidiary, this could put the guarantor into a situation in which it was compelled to continue supporting the borrower even though it did not wish to do so. It is therefore advisable to specify, in the guarantee agreement, a limit to the amount of interest to be covered, such as one year's interest or one period's interest. What the guarantor does not want is to be forced, against its will, to continue to meet routine interest payments because the bank has elected not to call a default and the guarantor has no powers to force the bank to do so. This is an unlikely situation but one which should be guarded against when the borrower is a joint-venture company. While the bank will not normally fail to call a default if the guarantor asks it to do so, it could be in a difficult situation were it to receive conflicting requests from two parent guarantors which could not agree on how to treat their failed associate.

8.7 The effect of time-limited guarantees

In this connection you should note that, while it is possible to write a time-limited guarantee, its only effect is to bring the bank to a point at which it must either call the underlying loan or insist on the guarantee being renewed. In all normal circumstances it will do the latter, but it will certainly insist that the agreement specifies that expiry of the guarantee constitutes a default, so that it is in a position to do the former should it be appropriate. More important, the existence of such a covenant will give it the leverage to obtain a continuing guarantee. Thus the commonly-heard statement that there is no such thing as a time-limited guarantee, while not strictly true, is a sensible axiom for the treasurer to work to.

8.8 Joint or several guarantees

Particular care needs to be taken where a guarantee is given in association with a third party, as may frequently occur when the borrower is a joint-venture operation owned by two or more otherwise unconnected parents.

A company should not normally be willing to guarantee more of a subsidiary or associate company's debt than is properly attributable to its share of the ownership. If it owns only 50% of the associate then it should guarantee only 50%, unless there are specific reasons for doing otherwise – perhaps the existence of a separate profit-sharing agreement. Where the guarantee is to be given by more than one party it can be given in one of three forms:

- joint: the guarantors are jointly responsible for the whole debt in the event of default by the borrower. The effect is that, if for any reason one of the parties is not able to meet the liability, the guarantee becomes unenforceable against the others. This situation is, understandably, unacceptable to the banks – were one partner to fail then the bank would become dependent on the goodwill of the others to recover anything;
- several: the guarantors are severally or individually liable for a specific amount, regardless of the actions of the others. Clearly no partner should ever give a several guarantee for more than its appropriate proportion of the debt, nor will it be necessary to do so. This is the normal form in which guarantees should be given. The effect is that the guarantor has a clearly-defined obligation which is restricted in any eventuality to the proportion of the borrower's debt properly attributable to it;
- joint and several: under this form of guarantee each guarantor becomes individually liable for the whole amount of the debt. In the event of the guarantee being called the co-guarantors will share equally in the obligation because the guarantee is joint. However, in the event that one of them is, for any reason, unable to unwilling to pay, the bank can turn to the others that are individually liable for the whole of the debt. Banks will frequently seek joint and several guarantees, particularly in situations where one guarantor is stronger than another. The corporate should think hard before agreeing to such a proposal which has evident dangers, the most obvious being that the 'strongest' guarantor is required to make full payment and seek contribution form its co-guarantors afterwards... an unsatisfactory situation.

9 Guarantor's rights

Where a guarantor has met its obligation to the bank under a guarantee in full, it would automatically be entitled under the doctrine of subrogation to stand in the bank's position as regards recovering all or some part of its resultant loss from the borrower and be entitled to any security that the bank holds. The right of subrogation can be varied in the guarantee and in the case of joint or several guarantees, whatever its form, the situation should be specified to this effect in the terms of the guarantee.

- In the normal course, the bank will expect to maintain its full rights against the borrower unless and until it has recovered the whole of its debt. Thus if companies A and B each guarantee one half of a $100 million borrowing by company Z, which subsequently defaults, the position will be as follows:

9.1 Under a joint guarantee

A and B will each be liable for $50 million but, if one fails to pay, the other may be able to avoid its obligation at law. Note that the consequences of doing so would be so severe as to make such action unthinkable in any but the most critical circumstances. If A pays and B does not, then the bank will normally claim against the liquidator of Z for $100 million even though it has already recovered $50 million under the guarantee. Only if it should recover more than $100 million will it reimburse company A in respect of the excess.

9.2 Under several guarantees

A and B will each be liable for $50 million. Failure of one to pay will not affect the position of the other. The situation as regards subsequent claims against the liquidator of company Z is the same as in the case of a joint guarantee.

9.3 Under joint and several guarantees

Should A fail to pay, then B becomes liable for $100 million and vice versa. Given that the bank has recovered in full, A and B (or whichever of them has paid) can rank against the liquidator of company Z for whatever they have paid in meeting their respective guarantees.

It is not within the scope of this course to discuss the advantages and disadvantages of joint ventures. However, it will be clear to students that one of the considerations for an intending partner must be the credit standing of the other parties. Such operations do not usually make good borrowing vehicles and there is usually much to favour the financing of new ones at least with equity.

10 Guarantee documentation

Guarantee wording will differ in each instance, and it is, therefore, difficult to generalise about it, but standard clauses should include:

- the names of the guarantor and the debtor;
- the amount, or reference to a loan schedule, in order to limit the guarantor's obligation;
- the situations covered by the guarantee, such as non-payment of principal and interest (after grace periods) or liquidation of the company;
- a clause stating that the guarantee is continuing, ie is not time limited;
- protection clauses which allow the lender to modify the obligation of the debtor without discharging the guarantor, otherwise the guarantee would be discharged;

- clauses enabling the lender to receive sums from the guarantor into a suspense account;
- the terms of cancellation of the guarantee;
- the rights of remedy of the lender;
- the provision of no variation without written consent of the guarantor; subrogation rights;
- the rights of the company to sue its subsidiary in competition to the bank if it has paid up under the guarantee;
- identification of the governing law – the jurisdiction should be same as that governing the transaction; and
- the consideration to be stated – consideration is a vital part of the contract in England, not so in Scotland. The consideration is, of course, provided to the debtor not the guarantor and can sometimes be the continuation of an existing facility (if previously in default) and not always the generating of new funds.

Additionally, the guarantor in a term loan may give similar covenants to those given by the borrower, including negative pledge, undertaking to give financial or other information, reps and warranties, grossing up clauses and *pari passu* and sharing clauses.

11 Legal problems

1. If the debtor is not liable then under English law then neither is the guarantor unless he is indemnifying or the guarantee contains an indemnity clause.

2. The problem of capacity of the guarantor with the possibility of the guarantee being held to be ultra vires. This is especially true of non-corporates or entities in other jurisdictions. Section 35A of the Companies Act 1985 in England provides that in favour of a person dealing with a company in good faith, the power of the board of directors to bind the company shall be deemed to be free of any limitation under the company's constitution. It is expressly provided that a person shall not be regarded as acting in bad faith by reason only of his knowing that an act is beyond the powers of the directors.

   In section 35B it is stated that a party entering into a transaction with a company is not bound to enquire as to whether the transaction is within the company's memorandum or whether it is within the powers of the directors acting on behalf of the company.

   Under these rules, a bank lending to a company need not be concerned to look at the company's memorandum and articles of association to determine whether the company or its agents are acting properly. Nor will it be put on notice of lack of capacity by having seen these documents. In order to be free from doubt as to whether the persons representing the company have authority to do so, however, it is necessary that the bank deals with the board of directors or some other person authorized by the board.

3. Like any other contract in English law a guarantee requires consideration if it is to be valid, ie some benefit or promise given by the lender to the guarantor in return for the guarantee. Consideration in this sense is that there must be some commercial benefit to the guarantor for giving a guarantee which should be stated, such as if the guarantee is being given in consideration of the bank lending the borrower a sum of £5m and the bank in the event lends only £4m, the guarantee may be ineffective.

12 Letters of comfort

12.1 Introduction

A letter of comfort is a letter, usually written by a parent company, to a lender giving comfort to a lender about a loan made to a subsidiary. Parent companies will often argue strongly with lenders to give a letter of comfort as opposed to a full guarantee. A letter of comfort, or letter of awareness, is not legally binding on the giver of it, unlike a guarantor of a guarantee. However, in dealing with relationship bankers there can be said to be a moral obligation attached to such a letter. As such, therefore, they should not be given lightly, and should be negotiated as would any formal, legally-binding agreement. However, views vary from company to company on this. They are given because the person giving them does not intend legally to be bound by them but perhaps want to give approval to a proposed loan or transaction.

12.2 The terms of comfort letters

English law presumes that a commercial agreement is legally binding unless otherwise clearly stated (*Edwards v Skyways Ltd* (1964)). Under English law the courts construe that letters of comfort are intended to create a contract but lean against converting comfort letters into guarantees and construe them against a lender. However, some letters of comfort may be binding but this will depend on the drafting of such letters and different jurisdictions react differently to letters of comfort.

Most letters of comfort can be classified into three types, which are (a) a letter of awareness, (b) a commitment to maintain ownership interest and (c) the degree of support required by the lenders.

The weakest form of wording is commonly called a letter of awareness, where the parent company acknowledges its relationship with another group company, and its awareness of a loan being made to the company by the lender.

In the case of *Kleinwort Benson Ltd v Malaysian Mining Corpn* [1989] All ER 785 it was held that that the parent company was not liable because the parent had stated in its comfort letter that 'it is our policy to ensure that the business of our subsidiary is at all times in a position to meet its liabilities to you'. It was not held binding because it merely stated its present policy which could thus be changed at any time. A letter of comfort therefore tries to state a policy or intention to do something but if it contains a promise or guarantee it may well constitute a legally binding agreement.

However in the case of *Chemco Leasing SpA v Rediffusion plc* (1987), the parent gave an 'assurance' that it would inform a third party of any disposal of its interest in its subsidiary in certain circumstances. This was held to create a binding obligation upon the parent because of the specific language used, indicating that an obligation upon the parent was created.

It was held in the case of *Banque Brussels Lambert v Australian National Industries Ltd* (1989) that the parent was liable to the bank because the parent company stated in its comfort letter to the bank that 'it is our practice to ensure that our affiliate... Will at all times be in a position to meet its financial obligation as they fall due', including repayment of obligations to the bank.

Although, as stated, letters of comfort do not have a legal standing in English law, the corporate should be aware that in other countries the use of certain wording does raise what is, in English law terms, a comfort letter to a guarantee under the foreign jurisdictions. Legal advice through a legal opinion should therefore be sought in such instances.

A comfort letter in its stronger form will, in addition to acknowledging the situation, indicate the company's willingness to accept some responsibility to honour the borrowing obligations of the subsidiary, without legally binding itself so to do. Such wording as using 'its rights as a shareholder', or 'best endeavours' so that the company conducts its business in a prudent manner shall be used. There are many variations on the theme, but the letter should refrain from making positive statements that the company 'will ensure' etc, which could then transform the letter to being a guarantee. Legal advice should be sought on the matter.

A letter of comfort can be created in addition to a guarantee. From a banker's point of view, if the bank is lending to a subsidiary, it should preferably take a formal guarantee rather than a letter of comfort from the parent company. This would ensure that the document creates a binding obligation upon the parent should the subsidiary default in repayment. It would be more preferable to lend direct to the subsidiary if there are substantial assets in that subsidiary and not to rely on any guarantee.

Fifteen

Swaps

1 Interest rate swaps

Although there is a degree of mystique surrounding swaps, the concept really is quite simple.

1.1 Definition

An interest rate swap is an agreement between two parties who agree to exchange differing interest commitments on a notional sum throughout a pre-deferred period. Essentially, interest rate swaps are most commonly used as a method of converting fixed-rate debt to floating-rate debt, or vice versa. The transaction involves no exchange of principal, but simply transfers the interest obligations between the parties involved.

The backbone of the market is the concept of 'comparative advantage'. This is because some companies can command their finest rates in, say, the fixed-rate market, whereas others are best placed in floating. So a company can raise funds in the cheapest possible way, say fixed rate, and then, if necessary, swap with a counterpart in a similar situation but whose comparative advantage is in floating.

The benefit can be shared between the two and in this way both have raised finance cheaper than they could have achieved themselves direct from the market.

Protection is given to the counterparties because a bank will act as intermediary and put the swap transactions together, assuming the credit risk of both parties.

1.2 Swaption

A swap is a binding agreement that all parties are obliged to see through. A swaption is where the buyer has the right but not the obligation to site into a swap transaction at some future date, like a typical 'option', and an up front premium is payable.

1.3 Features

Amounts: Minimum £1 million, no maximum.

Term/Period: Minimum one year, maximum usually ten years (longer subject to availability of counterparty).

Documentation: A swap agreement – standard terms have been established by ISDA (International Swap Dealers Association).

Fees: Arrangement fee may be taken by the bank acting as intermediary, ie matching counterparties, although most commonly the fee is 'hidden' in the spread of rates quoted.

Currencies: The bulk of the interest rate swap market is in US$ and sterling; other currencies are subject to availability.

Availability: Financial institutions (particularly merchant banks).

Protection: Provides the opportunity to switch from fixed to floating and vice versa, to suit requirements and perception of future movements.

1.4 Benefits

(a) A means of managing existing debt, ie by swapping if necessary.

(b) Access to cheaper finance through comparative advantage.

(c) The swap market is sufficiently liquid to enable reversals of positions if necessary.

(d) Counterparty risk is assumed by the bank acting as intermediary (the underlying loan does not have to be with the latter).

(e) Discrete, ie not made public.

(f) Flexible as to amount and period, subject to intermediary's ability to match terms or otherwise hold a mis-match position itself.

1.5 Disadvantages

(a) Having said above that positions can be unwound, it may be more expensive than in the case of alternative hedging techniques.

(b) Other alternatives may be more flexible and less expensive.

(c) A swap involves 'locking in' and therefore loses the benefits of the option-type products.

(d) Can appear to be complex.

2 Currency swaps

2.1 Definition

A currency swap involves two parties (counterparties), usually through a bank acting as intermediary, who agrees to:

(a) exchange at the outset a principal sum denominated in one currency for another at a specified rate; and

(b) to reverse the transaction, at the same rate, as a predetermined date; and

(c) in the meantime, cover each other's interest commitments during the term of the swap.

A swap is a legally binding exchange which both parties are committed to, unless by mutual consent (including the intermediary bank). A currency 'swaption' (see above) may be obtained, on an individually tailored basis.

As in the case of interest-rate swaps, the essence of the market is 'comparative advantage' and the benefits companies can obtain in different markets.

2.2 Operation

There are two companies. Company A is British and Company B is an American operation. Company A is well known in the UK and can therefore raise sterling cheaper, although it requires US$ finance. The opposite is the case for Company B. In order to take advantage of their relative strengths in their home currencies Company A borrows in sterling and Company B in US$.

Company A has borrowed £50 million. It is agreed that A and B will enter a swap transaction whereby A receives US$ and B sterling. The current spot rate is 1.80 and this is the exchange rate that is agreed between both parties. Thus Company B receives £50 million and Company A US$90 million. During the term of the swap, Company A pays the interest costs relating to the US$90 million and Company B does likewise in connection with the finance arranged by Company A. These payments are made in the respective currencies.

At the end of the swap the principal sums are repaid. Most textbooks explain this by a series of boxes and arrows, as follows:

Day 1

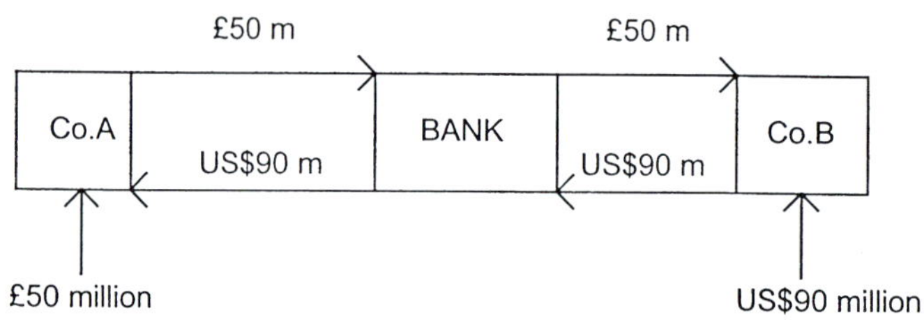

(a) During swap (interest)

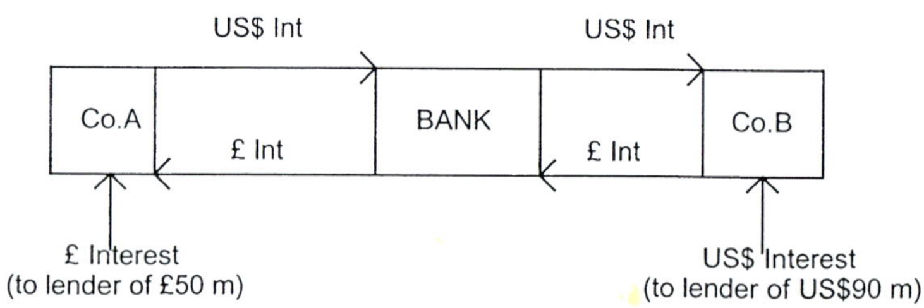

(b) Expiry of swap

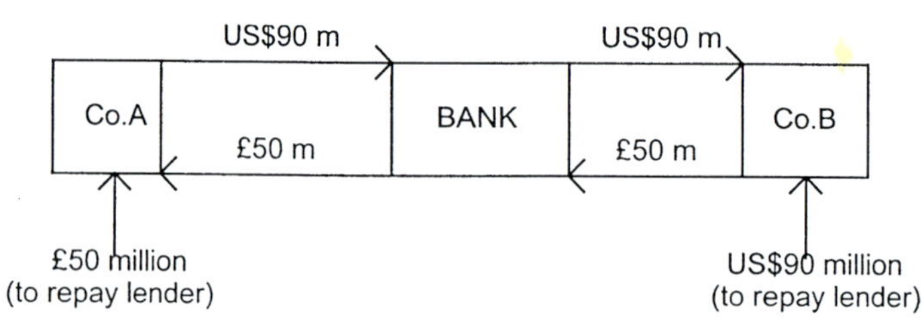

(In reality, the bank will cover any loss by way of its fee.)

Thus it is possible to obtain currency finance at competitive rates by raising in the 'cheapest' and then swapping to the currency required.

2.3 Features

Accounts: Generally a minimum of £3/£5 million, or currency equivalent, but smaller amounts may be accommodated on an individual basis. No maximum, subject to counterparty availability.

Term/Period: Usually minimum two years, maximum 10–12 years.

Documentation: swap agreement, generally ISDA (International Swap Dealers Association) terms used.

Fees: Intermediary bank may have taken an arrangement fee, although most commonly this is achieved by way of a loss on the rates allowed between counterparties.

Currencies: All major currencies.

Availability: Financial institutions (particularly merchant banks).

Flexibility: Subject to counterparty availability, or desire of intermediary bank, the swap market provides a flexible means of raising currency finance to suit a varied range of needs.

Protection: A means of establishing a rate to apply now, for the initial exchange, and on expiry of the swap.

2.4 Benefits of swaps

(a) Cheap currency finance is possible by using 'comparative advantage'.

(b) A useful means of managing 'translation' exposure by converting foreign currency items into 'home' currency.

(c) Flexibility of the market enables a wide range of needs to be met.

(d) Establishes exchange rate at outset.

(e) Off balance sheet.

(f) Private, ie no publicity.

(g) Generally no up-front fee payable.

(h) Terms clearly established through standard documentation and counterparties have the comfort of the standing of a bank as intermediary.

(i) Available to meet medium-/long-term needs.

2.5 Disadvantages of swaps

(a) A definite commitment (may be difficult/impossible to break).

(b) Not available for short-term purposes.

(c) Can appear complex.

(d) Security depends on the standing of the intermediary bank.

3 Legal position of swaps

Before effecting a swap one must ensure that each party has the legal power to enter into a swap. In the case of companies that are incorporated in England and Wales the power is given under section 35 of the Companies Act 1989 that companies have the necessary power to enter into a swap transaction. In the case of unincorporated bodies or companies or bodies incorporated overseas it is imperative that the legal position is checked and that a legal opinion is taken from a competent lawyer.

Section 35 of the Companies Act 1985 does not apply to local or public authorities, which do not have the legal powers to enter into swaps and whose powers are set down in statute. This was held in the cases of *Guinness Mahon and Co Ltd v Kensington and Chelsea Borough Council* (1998) and *Westdeutsche Landesbank v Islington BC* (1994).

The decision of the House of Lords in *Hazell v Hammersmith and Fulham LBC* (1988) held that swap transactions involve speculation in future interest trends with the object of making profits and such transactions are inconsistent with local authorities, authorized functions of borrowings and could not be justified in those terms. Swap contracts are therefore not capable of being lawfully entered into by the Council and were ultra vires.

There was a distinction in the approach taken by the Court of Appeal (which made a distinction between transactions that were incidental to the function of debt management and those that were incidental to the function of borrowing) and that of the House of Lords, which made no such distinction.

In another case of *Credit Suisse v Allerdale* (1996) a local authority was held to be unable to guarantee a transaction, because the actual transaction was outside its powers. In such a situation, a company would be able to bring a restitutionary claim seeking a return of any funds that it had transferred to a local authority under a swap transaction, as in the case of *Kleinwort Benson v Glasgow City Council* (1997).

The question of ultra vires is clearly relevant to other business entities in the United Kingdom as follows:

(i) Building societies – under section 23 of the Building Society Act 1986 swap contracts may be entered into by building societies but subject to certain limitations, and therefore a bank must make sure that it has full board minutes and representations before it enters into swap transactions with such entities.

(ii) Universities – the charter of such bodies should be carefully reviewed before banks enter into swap contracts with such entities.

4 The 1992 and 2002 ISDA Master Agreements – Documentation Provisions

4.1 Master agreements

The International Swaps and Derivatives Association (ISDA) published in January 2003 the 2002 ISDA Master Agreement to replace the 1992 master agreement. The impetus for the new agreement arose from the difficulties affecting various Asian markets in the late 1990s over distressed counterparties and markets. Some of the changes that the new ISDA 2002 Master Agreement from that of the ISDA 1992 Master Agreement are commented upon late in the text.

ISDA has published much standard swap agreement documentation for use in connection with swaps and other forms of derivative products, by way of a Master Agreement that includes a Schedule and Confirmation, to be exchanged between the parties. One of the main purposes of the Master Agreements is to provide a single document that can easily be used in relation to a much wider range of derivative instruments. The objective of a Master Agreement is to make subsequent swaps part of same transaction and that the Master Agreement takes the net position by netting of all payments due in same currency on same day.

ISDA has produced two forms of Master Agreement, one for use where both counterparties are in the same jurisdiction and conduct a transaction in the local currency of that jurisdiction – the local currency – the Single Jurisdiction Master Agreement and the other, the Multicurrency Cross-Border Master Agreement, for use in connection with transactions where payments are to be made in differing currencies, between parties in different jurisdictions. The Local Agreement is in substantially the same form as the Cross-Border Agreement, save for the tax provisions. There is also a form of amendment to enable a 1992 Master Agreement to be updated to the 2002 ISDA Master Agreement.

4.2 1992 ISDA Master Agreement (local currency – single jurisdiction)

This agreement is used to document transactions between parties located in the same jurisdiction and transactions involving one currency. The Agreement is designed, among other things, to facilitate cross-product netting and may be used to document a wide variety of derivatives transactions. The 1992 Agreements were prepared to accommodate transactions that could be documented under the 1987 Agreements with their 1989 and 1990 Addenda. ISDA also prepared a User's Guide to assist in the understanding and use of this document.

4.3 2002 ISDA Master Agreement (multi-currency – cross border)

This Agreement updates the 1992 ISDA Master Agreements and is used to document transactions between parties in different jurisdictions and/or transactions involving different currencies. The Agreement adds several new provisions, including: a new measure of damages provision, close-out amount, which replaces market quotation and loss in the 1992 ISDA Master Agreements; a set-off provision in section 6(f); force majeure termination event in section 5(b)(ii); and consolidated interest and compensation provisions in section 9. In addition, several provisions are amended, including a shortening of grace periods associated with some of the events of default in section 5(a).

4.4 Form of Amendment to 1992 ISDA Master Agreement

This Form of Amendment, published in March 2003, allows firms to amend on a bilateral basis various sections of the 1992 ISDA Master Agreement (multi-currency-cross border). The Amendment adds a close-out amount, the new measure of damages in the 2002 ISDA Master Agreement, and deletes market quotation and loss as well as making other corollary changes.

4.5 Master Agreements – generally

ISDA has stated that parties from the same jurisdiction contemplating transactions involving only the local currency are unlikely to require the additional tax provisions contained in the cross-border agreement. Accordingly, such parties may prefer the Local Agreement unless a relevant jurisdiction in question imposes withholding taxes on domestic payments. ISDA has recommended the use of the Master Agreements for new contractual relationships between parties and that, where feasible, parties should implement the new Master Agreement architecture into existing contractual relationships, especially where derivative products are included. ISDA believes that, in most jurisdictions, the most efficient means through which the new Master Agreements can be implemented for existing contractual relationships is to replace any existing 1987 Agreement with a Master Agreement. A form of Amendment Agreement that may help to effect such replacement is set out in the User's Guide to the Master Agreements, which has been published by ISDA.

In the Schedule to each of the Master Agreements parties may alter or amend the provisions of a Master Agreement as they wish through specification of additional or alternative provisions.

Once the parties have chosen the appropriate Master Agreement and negotiated the Schedule, they must then select the appropriate confirmation for documenting the economic terms of a contemplated transaction. Separate booklets of definitions and confirmations for equity index options, commodity derivatives, foreign exchange and currency options, and swaps with US municipal counterparties have been published. The 2000 ISDA Definitions (the '2000 Definitions') are intended for use in confirmations of individual transactions governed by agreements such as the 1992 ISDA Master Agreements.

By extending the number of derivative products that can be documented under each Master Agreement users can extend netting of payments to cover a wide range of transactions entered into with a single counterparty. This will reduce transaction costs and the level of credit exposure that one counterparty has to another.

4.6 Delivery

The Master Agreements now contemplate settlement not only by way of payment but also by physical delivery as a result of the inclusion of transactions relating to commodities. They also provide that where settlement is by delivery it will be made for receipt on the due date in the manner customary for the relevant obligation, unless otherwise agreed.

4.7 Netting

The parties may now elect in respect of two or more transactions that a net amount will be determined in respect of all amounts payable on the same date in the same currency in respect of such transactions, regardless of whether such amounts are payable in respect of the same transaction; provided that in such case such provisions apply separately to each pairing of offices through which the parties make and receive payments or deliveries. Such election in the Schedule or a Confirmation may also be made for different groups of transactions.

In the case of interest rate swaps it is usual to try to make payment dates coincide, ie pay and receive, because the aim is to NET OFF against one another. Netting is safer from a credit point of view and avoids problem of conditionally. In the case of a cross-border swap there is also the reduction or elimination of payments subject to withholding tax.

In the case of a currency swap the payments will be gross, but netting can be achieved by conversion of one currency with only the excess over the smaller being paid by the larger party. However, payments are conditional upon the other party receiving/making payment.

There is also the practical problem of time differences. For example dollar/yen swaps escrow arrangements are used to instruct the escrow bank of the amount payable by the counterparty on such payment dates.

The advantage to be gained from netting is that it reduces settlement risk (ie the risk that one of the parties, having received the sums due to it in a particular currency on a particular day, will not in turn honour its own obligations). This is often known as the Herstatt-risk and where netting takes place the exposure is only the net difference and not the entire amount of the swap. There is also the administrative advantage of reducing the number of payments that have to be made between the parties. Importantly, for bank counterparties netting is also increasingly significant in the context of capital adequacy requirements. The netting arrangements also aim to prevent possible 'cherry picking' (ie selection of profitable and disclaiming unprofitable transactions) by a liquidator or administrator because under a Master Agreement all swaps are part of the same transaction and the Master Agreement takes the net position by netting of all payments due in same currency on same day.

4.8 Close-out netting

The ISDA agreement provides for contractual netting of mutual payment obligations and for 'close-out netting', which specifies that on the termination of an ISDA Master Agreement, the parties agree to set-off the values of each swap or other financial product documented under the Master Agreement so that a single amount would be owed by one party to another. One does need to consider the effect of contractual netting provisions under English insolvency law and in particular the effectiveness of netting provisions under rule 4.90 of the Insolvency Rules 1986.

The decision in *British Eagle International Airlines Ltd v Compagnie Nationale Air France* (1975) may prevent contractual netting in an insolvency situation. However, the subsequent case of Carreras Rothmans (1985) and general market practice suggest that provided the contractual arrangements do not confer greater rights than provided in Rule 4.90 of the Insolvency Rules, they are likely to be upheld.

There are also difficulties in interpreting Rule 4.90 in terms of what is meant by 'mutual credits, mutual debts and other mutual dealings' should be given credit.

It is necessary to consider the precise moment at which an executory contract is terminated under English law, ie whether such a contract is terminated and therefore available for set-off prior to insolvency or post-insolvency. If the various debts entered into under a Master Agreement 'mature' upon or immediately following an insolvency such arrangements may fall out of the contractual netting-out provisions and make the swap transaction vulnerable to 'cherry-picking'.

4.9 Inclusion of set-off provision

The 1992 ISDA Master Agreement did not include a set-off provision but the 2002 ISDA Master Agreement does so. Set-off provisions are important in default situations because they allow the non-defaulting party to attempt to garner assets of the defaulting party other than the amounts it is owed. Thus, with a set-off provision, the non-defaulting party can explore whether there are other assets such as a deposit account that can be attached and then set-off against the amount the defaulting party owes the non-defaulting party.

4.10 Representations and warranties

The ISDA agreement contains standard representations and warranties that are as follows:

(i) Both parties are in good financial and legal standing.

(ii) By entering into the transaction, both parties are not in conflict with any law or judgment of any court.

(iii) Both parties have obtained any necessary consents, including government consents.

(iv) Both parties will be legally bound by the swap transaction.

(v) Any information provided by either party to the other is accurate.

(vi) Neither party has committed an event of default or potential event of default.

4.11 Events of default

Events of default are more limited in the ISDA agreement vis-à-vis a loan agreement because in a swap both parties have continuing obligations. In a swap both parties provide that any failure to pay amounts owing under the swap, by either party, will constitute an event of default. Broadly, this will enable the innocent party to terminate the swap agreement. Inadvertent situations that are caused by external events such as imposition of withholding taxes or illegality are discussed in greater detail further in the text.

The following events of default are standard in the ISDA agreement.

(i) Breach of the swap agreement by either party.

(ii) A material representation by either party to the other.

(iii) The cross-default provision applies only if a specification to that effect is made in the schedule. The cross-default clause does not catch swaps prematurely terminated as a result of a non-fault related event such as withholding taxes. The non-defaulting party can sue the other counterparty for breach of contract. It is usual to have a credit event upon merger default if one of the counterparties does undergo a merger.

Scope has now been provided for events of default to relate to a 'credit support document', eg guarantee, pledge agreement or letter of credit, and a 'credit support provider', eg a parent company guarantor. Default under specified swaps has been extended so as to include repudiation, rejection, disaffirmation or disclaimer (in whole or in part) of 'specified transactions' which include, in addition to swaps, bond options and any other transaction that the parties may specify in the schedule.

(iv) The bankruptcy insolvency of either party or of a party providing credit support to either party. The clause also applies to distress, execution, or other legal process levied against a counterparty by a mortgagee, if such proceedings are not dismissed, discharged etc within 30 days.

(v) The merger, consolidation or amalgamation of either party or a party providing credit support to either party.

One of the primary initiatives in publishing the new definitions was to amend the menu of consequences available to parties when a merger event occurs. Merger events and other such extraordinary occurrences will result in the stock underlying the equity derivative transaction disappearing or assuming an economically different value. Thus, the options available to parties have been expanded in order to offer more customized provisions. In addition, tender offers are also addressed in the new Definitions. Tender offers were not as common in 1996, but in the intervening years have become more standard. Thus, the new definitions define a tender offer as an offer for more than ten percent, but less than 100% of the outstanding shares of a company.

4.12 Event of default – changes in ISDA 2002 Master Agreement

Under the ISDA 2002 Master Agreement the following changes have been made to the events of default vis-à-vis the 1992 ISDA Master Agreement:

(a) the grace period in respect of a failure to pay or deliver has been reduced from three business days to one;

(b) the breach of agreement Event of Default has been expanded to include repudiatory action by a party;

(c) the Default Under Specified Transaction event of default has been amended to take account of any default or repudiatory action in respect of any credit support arrangement;

(d) the cross-default provisions have been amended so that the amount of borrowed moneys accelerated may be aggregated with the amount of any indebtedness in respect of which there has been a payment default for the purposes of determining whether the applicable threshold amount has been exceeded;

(e) the bankruptcy Event of Default has been amended to distinguish between action taken by a regulator and any other party instituting a proceeding seeking a judgment of insolvency or presenting a winding-up petition which is subject to a 15-day grace period as opposed to 30 days in the 1992 ISDA Master Agreement.

4.13 Additional termination events

A new concept of 'additional termination event' has been introduced in order to accommodate those parties who wish to include additional termination events, eg downgrading by a credit agency, in their schedule or any confirmation and any affected party shall be specified for such additional termination event in the schedule or such confirmation.

The 2002 ISDA Master Agreement introduces a new Termination Event permitting the close-out of transactions affected by force majeure or an act of state (which is beyond the control of the relevant party and cannot be reasonably overcome) occurring after such transactions were entered into. It includes those transactions that have given effect to any appropriate fallback, prevent the applicable office of a party from making or receiving a payment or delivery or complying with any other material provision relating to the affected transactions, or which prevents a party (or any entity providing credit support in respect thereof) from making or receiving a payment or delivery or complying with any other material provision of any related credit support documentation.

This new provision is intended to ensure that force majeure events such as natural or man-made disasters, labour riots, acts of terrorism and other unanticipated events that prevent the performance of a party's obligations under the contract are considered. Once such an event occurs, a party is obligated to show that the event is beyond its control and that it could not overcome the event by using all reasonable efforts and that a waiting period of eight local business days has expired. At that point, a party may move to terminate the transactions affected by the event.

4.14 Automatic early termination

On the occurrence of a bankruptcy event of default, the parties now have the option to elect in the schedule for there to be an immediate early termination. If no election is made the normal procedural process of giving notice will apply.

4.15 Payments on early termination

The payments on early termination provision has been amended to provide two alternative measures of payment, either based on market quotation or actual loss, and two alternative methods of payment, either the first method (one-way payments) or the second method (two-way payments). This is perhaps the most important feature of the Master Agreements. In the event that no option is selected, the second method and market quotation will apply.

There are now four options available to the parties for calculating compensation payments on early termination resulting from an event of default:

- First Method and Market Quotation
- First Method and Loss
- Second Method and Market Quotation – this is the normal method
- Second Method and Loss

These elections regarding the payment method and payment measure required under the 1992 ISDA Master Agreement do not apply under the 2002 ISDA Master Agreement. The 2002 ISDA Master Agreement prescribes the procedures as being commercially reasonable. Also under the 2002 Master Agreement, where termination occurs as a result of a termination event (as distinct from an event of default), the amount payable is required to be calculated by reference to mid-market values, which do not take account of the creditworthiness of the determining party.

4.16 Set-off

Early termination payments are subject to set-off. Appropriate set-off provisions can be included in the schedule to the Master Agreement. The user's guide to the Master Agreement contains various suggested forms of wording.

4.17 Taxation

Any reductions in amount received by either party to a swap would adversely affect the viability of the swap. The obligation is to gross-up in the event of withholding tax imposition but each party has the right to terminate the swap in such case. The agreement may have a negotiation clause to substitute the basis for making payments and if the parties are unable to agree on this affected party may terminate.

A counterparty is now obliged to supply any form or document that would enable the other party to make payments without any deduction or withholding for or on account of any tax, or at a reduced rate of tax, on reasonable demand by the other party (unless it can show that to do so would materially prejudice its legal or commercial position).

The only change of substance to the payee tax representations is an additional representation that the counterparty is a recognized UK swaps dealer for the purposes of the United Kingdom Inland Revenue Extra Statutory Concession C17 on interest and currency swaps, dated 14 March 1989. Where the counterparty is a recognized swaps dealer the other party is entitled to make payments under the swap without withholding or deduction for UK tax.

A termination event will now arise (by reason of a tax event) where a party will, or where there is a 'substantial likelihood' that it will, on the next succeeding scheduled payment date, be required to gross up a payment or to receive a payment, net of tax, by reason of any action taken by a revenue authority or proceedings brought by that authority, as well as in relation to a change in tax law.

4.18 Illegality

In the ISDA Master Agreement there is provision that in the event of the swap becoming illegal either or both parties are entitled to terminate the swap. Illegality gives rise to a direct right of termination rather than an event of default.

In *Nuova Sfim SpA v Sakura Bank Ltd* (1998), NS entered into a swap with SB. NS was a wholly owned subsidiary of EPIM. EPIM was dissolved by presidential law decree made in Italy. This decree also prevented NS from making any payments under the swap. The swap was made under the standard ISDA Master Agreement and was expressly made subject to English law and jurisdiction. If there is some illegality, which affects some other party not specified in the agreement, the situation will not constitute illegality.

The High Court held that the prevention of NS from making payments under the swap constituted illegality. Under the terms of the swap, illegality gave SB the right to terminate the swap. Similarly, in the case of *Australia and New Zealand Banking Group Ltd v Societe Generale* (1999), a banking moratorium was imposed upon

Russian banks, preventing them from performing certain hedging contracts that were made under standard ISDA Master Agreement terms; this entitled them to terminate such agreements.

4.19 Other provisions

(a) Covenants: usual to have *pari passu* ranking of swap agreement obligations.

(b) Assignment: usual to restrict without consent of the other party.

(c) Governing law: either English/New York law, plus submissions to jurisdiction, process agent and waiver of immunity clause if applicable.

4.20 Legally binding

A statement has been included in each of the Master Agreements that the parties intend to be legally bound by the terms of each transaction from the moment they agree to those terms (whether orally or otherwise).

5 The impact of the euro

The introduction of the euro in the UK would mean that a cross-currency swap that was originally between sterling and euro would in effect be rendered nugatory in practical terms. Cross-currency swaps though will not be frustrated or otherwise terminated because they continue to have meaningful payment obligations, so there is no scope for the application of the doctrine of frustration. In practical terms though the introduction of the euro for any sterling/euro swaps would lead to their likely termination by mutual consent. The ISDA did, however, publish their EMU continuity provision that will not allow either party to terminate or modify the swap.

Cross-currency swaps that involve non-euro currencies, or where only the sterling component is converted into euros, will continue to fulfil their original commercial function and there will be no basis upon which the contract may be said to be frustrated or otherwise terminated.

Interest-rate swaps, by the substitution of the euro for both of the currencies in which the contract is expressed, will be unaffected by the euro and continue to insure against movements in the comparative value or cost of money. The interest-rate swap cannot be said to be frustrated or otherwise be terminated.

In 1997 ISDA published the EMU continuity provision, intended for use in existing and future ISDA Master Agreements where the parties wish to document their intention that European economic and monetary union ('EMU') should not affect the continuity of their contract. The provision enables parties to confirm in their ISDA Master Agreement that the EMU will not give either party the unilateral right to walk away from, or modify the terms of, any transaction governed by the agreement.

Currencies of member states of the European Union that adopted the euro as their new currency on 1 January 1999 ceased to exist as currencies in their own right. Instead, for a limited transition period prior to their final disappearance, these currencies existed as distinct units of the euro ('national currency units').

ISDA in 2001 published its Euro Protocol that addresses payments, rate fixings, redenomination of notional amounts for payments and payment netting relating to the end of the euro transition period on 31 December 2001.

The EMU Protocol is ISDA's innovative approach to providing parties with a structure that will permit them to multilaterally amend existing transactions governed by an ISDA Master Agreement in light of European Economic and Monetary Union. The structure, which is supported through ISDA's website, will allow parties to effect adjustments on a collective basis, instead of through time-consuming and costly bilateral negotiations. There is no charge for the document itself, but there will be a charge for utilization of the Protocol process.

Sixteen

Legal aspects of contract guarantees and performance bonds

1 Introduction

There are occasions when a corporation finds that in certain circumstances, its own willingness to enter into a contractual (or otherwise legally binding) obligation to make a payment, to one of its customers or to some other organization is not sufficient. The other party wants the corporation to provide it with absolute assurance through the introduction of a third party of undoubted financial strength. This is normally an organization – a bank or an insurance company – which will substitute its promise for that of the company and which can be trusted to make the payment if the circumstances arise. Often these contracts are so large that the corporation is using syndicated finance.

To that extent, bonds and guarantees are very similar to the letters of credit used as a payment mechanism in the course of international trade. Indeed, the letter of credit form is often used where bonds and guarantees are called for (the letter of credit form clearly describes the circumstances in which the paying bank is to make payment. This has the benefit of a set of standard conditions of practice that are recognized throughout the world – the International Chamber of Commerce's Uniform Customs and Practice for Documentary Credits). The letter of credit form is often used where there is a requirement for issuance by a US bank, such banks being constitutionally unable to issue guarantees.

Most commonly, a corporation finds itself involved with bonds and guarantees if its business involves it in large long-term contracts. For this reason, bonds and guarantees are frequently referred to as 'contract bonds'. Similar arrangements may, however, arise in any number of areas that may involve corporations other than those involved in contracting. Two examples are given below.

(i) Customs bonds. Where goods have been imported temporarily into a country in which duty would be payable if the importation were permanent, the customs department may require a bank guarantee under which the import duty can be claimed if the goods are not re-exported within a certain time limit.

(ii) Guarantees in lieu of payments into court. In some jurisdictions, where a payment into court is required, or desirable, in the course of litigation, it may be possible to substitute a bank guarantee for the actual payment.

These two examples demonstrate an important principle, which will be easily recognized by corporations: it is better to keep one's hands on the money, even if one has to pay it over later. In all normal circumstances the interest saved through possession of the money will outweigh the cost of providing the bond or guarantee.

2 Types of contract bonds

The main types of contract bonds are outlined below.

2.1 Tender (bid) bonds

Tender bonds are intended to ensure that the customer's time is not wasted, during the tender process, by bids frivolously submitted even though the bidders have no intention, or capability, of carrying out the work. Each contractor responding to a tender request will be invited to submit a tender bond for a small percentage of the bid value (usually 1–5%). If he does not do so, his bid will be invalid and will be ignored. When the customer has selected the winning bid, unsuccessful bidders will have their bonds returned. The winner, however, will be expected to proceed to sign the contract and undertake the work. If he does not, the customer will be entitled to claim the amount of his bond.

Because one of the contract conditions that has to be fulfilled will be the provision of other contract bonds, the bidder will be well advised to line up the issuers of those bonds before submitting his tender.

2.2 Advance payment bonds

On large contracts, particularly overseas, significant advance payments are often made on the contract becoming effective. These payments, which can be for as much as 15% of the contract value, may be intended to help with the contractor's mobilization costs. In exchange, the contractor provides advance payment guarantees under which the customer can reclaim the advance payments if the contractor fails to proceed with the contracts.

2.3 Performance bonds

Performance bonds are given at the start of contracts, normally for 10% of the contract value if the 'bank' bond (see below) is being given. They remain in force unreduced through the construction period and sometimes to the end of the maintenance period. The purpose of performance bonds is to give the customer an instrument for obtaining quick and clear redress for damage suffered because the contractor's performance has been poor.

2.4 Retention bonds

As an additional protection for the customer, contract terms normally allow for retentions, whereby 5% or so of all contract payments are held back by the customer and are paid to the contractor only at the end of a maintenance period, when all the defects that inevitably arise on major contracts have been identified and corrected. The contractor will normally press for contracts to allow retention bonds to be provided instead. Ideally, such bonds will be issued at the time that the first retention would have been made, and automatically increase in value as each subsequent payment is received. Some clients, however, may decline to accept the bond and to release the retention until the maintenance period starts to run.

3 The structure of bonding arrangements

There are two basic forms in which contract bonds may be issued. These must be carefully distinguished because they have very different effects.

3.1 'Bank' bonds

These simply lay down that, in certain clearly-defined circumstances, the provider of the bond will pay a sum of a defined maximum amount to the beneficiary of the bond. All tender bonds, advance payment guarantees and retention bonds will take this form, as will many performance bonds. We call them generically 'bank' bonds but, in practice, this type of bond may be issued by an insurance company. The key feature is that the bond is purely a financial arrangement. If the laid-down conditions for payment are met, the bond provider will have no choice but to make the payment. In deciding whether to provide a bond for a contractor, the provider of the bond will be concerned primarily with the contractor's financial standing, ie his ability to reimburse the bond provider for the amount of any money paid out under the bond.

3.2 Surety (default) bonds

These are a traditional form for the provision of performance bonds by surety or insurance companies. They are particularly common in North America. The bond may have no set financial value (though it usually will have a limit), because the surety is guaranteeing to the customer that, should the main contractor fall down on his performance under the contract, he will complete the contract himself (by employing another contractor) or will pay whatever expense the customer is forced to incur in putting the faulty work right. Before deciding to issue this type of bond, the surety company has a wider range of concerns than the provider of a bank bond. He will want to examine the contract itself to see whether it is likely to go wrong, and to look at the contractor's expertise in performing that type of contract – as well as his financial resources.

Most of the problems concerned with contract bonds arise under the 'bank' bond form of arrangement. The rest of this chapter therefore deals exclusively with that type of arrangement.

3.3 Legal structures

The provision of contract bonds creates a legal structure that is separate from, but parallel to, the underlying contract that lays down the necessity for the bonds. Figure 1 shows how the provider of the bond enters a relationship with the contractor's customer. This relationship, if the bond is later called, involves the bond provider in making a payment to the customer. There is also an agreement – the counterindemnity – between the bond provider and the contractor, under which the contractor undertakes to reimburse the bond provider should the payment be made under the bond. There are essentially two categories of bonds, namely first demand, or on demand, bonds that are called by simple request or breach and conditional bonds that are discussed in detail below.

Figure 16.1: The relationship between the bond provider, contractor and customer

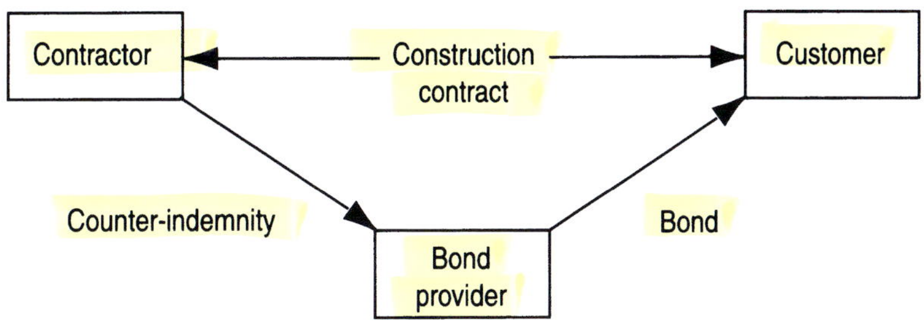

The structure may, in practice, be considerably more complicated for any of several reasons.

3.4 Requirement for a local bank issuer

On overseas contracts, particularly in the third world, the contract conditions may lay down that the bonds have to be issued through one of a strictly limited number of local banks. The contractor probably has no previous relationship with this bank which might have neither the skill, nor the inclination, to assess the credit implications of its taking a counterindemnity direct from the contractor. The contractor is then forced into using a double bank structure whereby he makes arrangements, with an international bank, for that bank to instruct the local bank to issue the bond against the international bank's counterindemnity. This latter document is in a standard format requiring automatic reimbursement of the local bank if it makes payment (see Figure 16.2).

The structure is inevitable but it has disadvantages:

- it is more expensive. Unfortunately the local bank being isolated from the pressures of the marketplace tends to charge heavily for its services (often over 1% pa) even though it has the benefit of an undoubted counterindemnity;
- it is difficult to control the form of bond being issued. It is not unknown for a contractor, having carefully negotiated a bond wording in a special form, and having instructed his international bank to instruct the local bank to issue the bond in that form, to find that the local bank has issued a standard form anyway;

- it is difficult to control the situation if the customer calls the bond. Where the bond has been issued by a friendly international bank it will always, in practice, discuss the situation with the contractor before making any payment. Where the bond has been issued by local bank, payment may well have been made to the customer before the contractor hears about it.

Figure 16.2: Double bank structure

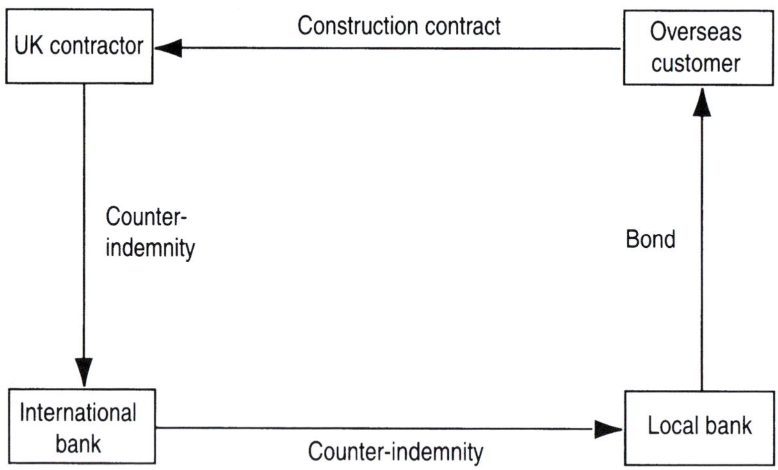

3.5 Requirement for 'several' counterindemnifiers

Joint ventures between a number of contractors are common in the world of international contracting. In such circumstances the contractors often want to split the responsibility for the counterindemnity into their several shares so as to control their total bond exposure. In this case they ask the bond provider to accept one 'several' counterindemnities from each joint venture member for its joint venture share. As long as the bond provider considers each joint venture member to be equally creditworthy there is no problem. If, however, one is weaker than the others, the bond provider will probably insist on a single counterindemnity under which the joint ventures take 'joint and several' liability.

Figure 16.3: A single counter-indemnity with joint and several liability

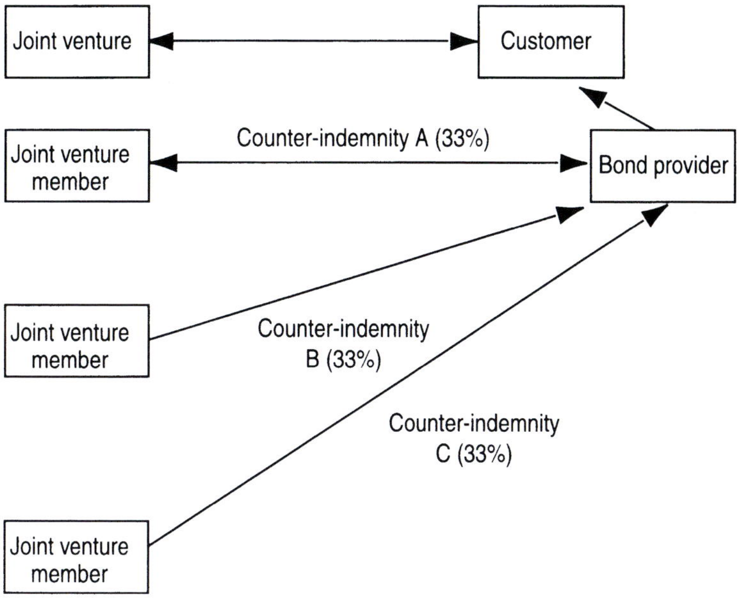

3.6 Building in the requirement for sub-contractor bonding

On a large contract, a contractor always employs a number of sub-contractors who undertake particular parts of the work on the contract. Plainly the bonds provided by the main contractor cover the work undertaken by the sub-contractors as well as his own work. He will, therefore, seek to obtain bonds from the sub-contractors framed in precisely the same terms as those he has to give. Then, if the sub-contractor's failure to perform leads to a call on the main bond, the main contractor can claim in turn on the sub-contractor's bond.

Figure 16.4: Sub-contractor bonds

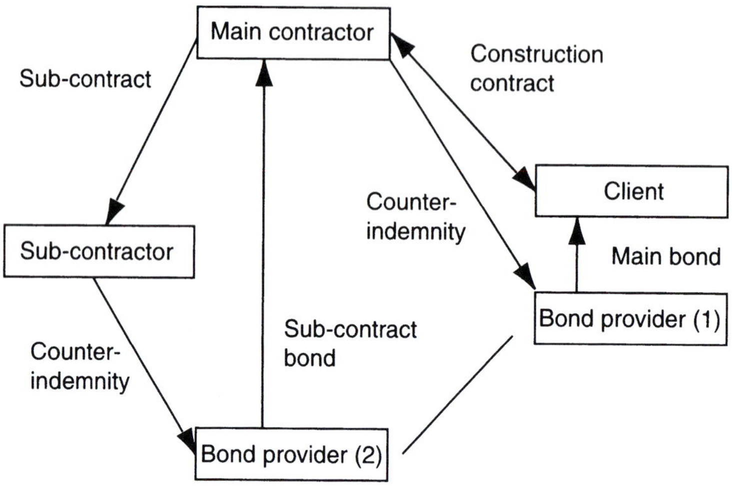

3.7 The relationship between the bonds and the underlying contract

The bonding arrangements provide a set of legal agreements that can survive independently of the main contract. Even if the contract is terminated by the contractor in accordance with its terms, the bond and the counterindemnity may survive and the bond may be called if the conditions for call laid down within the bond are capable of being satisfied.

This does not mean, however, that the main contract does not cover the provision and calling of the bonds. Indeed the contract will ideally lay down:

- what bonds are to be provided;
- their precise format; and
- the circumstances under which the customer is able to make a call under the bond.

It is very important that the contract is clear on these points – not because the contract is brought into consideration when a call for payment is made by the customer on the bond, but because the contractor may retain rights under the contract if the customer can be shown to have departed from the procedure laid down by contract.

4 On-demand bonds

4.1 Definition

These are bonds whose wording states that the bond amount is payable to the beneficiary of the bond on his first demand, without the need for any evidence of a breach of the underlying contract. The corporate will readily appreciate that providing such a bond is the same as providing his customer with a banker's draft, which he may cash whenever he chooses.

In English law the nature of an on-demand bond and of the obligations undertaken under it are determined by construing the guarantee as a whole, as held in the case of *Trafalgar House Construction (Regions) Ltd v General Surety and Guarantee Co Ltd* (1996) AC199. In the case of *Wada Bank v Arab Bank* (1994) the Court of Appeal stated that both the performance bond and the counterindemnity should be governed by the same system of law to achieve uniformity in result. This means to try to ensure that the bank that paid under the performance bond would receive repayment form its customer under the counterindemnity.

First demand, or on-demand, bonds may be called by the buyer (beneficiary) by simple request or request backed by a specified document without any evidence of breach by the supplier or judgment of the merits of the claim. In *Esal (Commodities) Ltd v Oriental Credit Ltd* (1985) CA, the terms of the bond read 'on your written demand in the event that the supplier fails to ship...in accordance with the terms of their contract with you'. The court held that a bare demand was insufficient but the beneficiary merely had to assert that the supplier was in breach. The court further held that there was no implied condition obliging the bank to notify its customer supplier either before or after the bond was paid out. The triggering mechanism for bank bonds is that they are frequently accelerated by production of simple documents where the bank issuing the bond has no legal right to prevent payment once the underlying document in question has been delivered. In terms of legal analysis such bonds are more akin to indemnities than true guarantees. On-demand performance bonds can be contrasted sharply with true guarantees that require a failure on an underlying obligation before payment can be triggered. In the case of an on-demand bond no such secondary commitment needs to be triggered unless the bond is drafted in conditional terms. The distinction between on-demand bonds and guarantees is in relation to rights of subrogation and contribution that apply in the case of a guarantee but not in the case of on demand bonds.

In the case of first demand bonds there is no connection between the bond obligation and the underlying contract. The bank is in a similar position to having issued an irrevocable letter of credit, *Edward Owen Engineering Ltd v Barclays Bank International Ltd* (1978) CA. The bank must pay out on the bond if the event stipulated in the bond has occurred, eg demand by the beneficiary and his assertion of the supplier's breach as in the *Oriental Credit Ltd* case. The recent case of *Potton*

Homes v Coleman Contractors focused on the primary obligations of a bank that issues an on-demand commitment in a performance bond. The significance is the wording of the instrument and the fact that such instruments can be couched in either conditional or documentary form.

4.2 Unfair calls

The risk of an unfair call always exists when a contractor has agreed to the issue of an on-demand bond. Fortunately, such an event is not as common as might be expected. Most clients in the public sector – even in politically volatile countries – are sensitive to the effect on their future business arrangements of the cynical calling of bonds without justification. If, however, the contractor hears from his bank that a purported call on a bond has been received but which he thinks is not justified, what does he do? This is considered below.

4.3 Possible action against the bank

First, the contractor would be wise to consider the detail of the purported call. It is remarkable that a high proportion of calls do not take the form laid down in the bond. The bank should not, of course, have to be reminded that, if the bond says that a call has to be made in writing signed by a specific individual, then it is not in order for it to pay out against a call by telex. If the bank can be persuaded politely to reject the call on the basis of its incompatibility with the bond, it can provide valuable breathing space for the contractor.

Eventually, however, the customer may find that a call in the correct form has been made and he has to consider taking legal action against the bank to prevent it making payment. Unfortunately, he will then find the English courts extremely reluctant to interfere and stop the bank making payment in accordance with what are seen as irrevocable obligations undertaken by the bank.

The only chink of light for the unhappy contractor whose bond has been unfairly called is that payment may be stopped where there is clear notice of fraud on the part of the caller of the bond. To take advantage of this the contractor has to prove that the bond beneficiary is, with fraudulent intent, presenting what he knows to be an invalid claim. Unfortunately, major contracts inevitably involve complex situations. Even if the call seems obviously unfair (at least to the contractor) it is only in extreme cases that he can prove fraud. If he cannot, the courts will inevitably allow the bank to make payment.

The fraud exception

The only ground upon which the court will prevent a bank from making payments is in cases where the demand for payments is fraudulent. Several cases have reached the English courts in the last ten years where suppliers have sought to restrain their banks from paying out. Every case has failed and each time the court has asserted the exclusiveness of the 'fraud exception'. Were the courts to do otherwise, of course, the commercial attraction of the first demand bond would diminish. In *State Trading Corpn of India Ltd v ED and F Nan (Sugar) Ltd* (1981) CA, an attempt by the supplier to restrain the buyer from giving notice of default and claiming on the bond was unsuccessful.

In both the *Edward Owen case and in RD Harbottle (Mercantile) Ltd v National Westminster Bank Ltd* (1978) there was evidence that the buyer had himself been in default under the sale contract by not opening the necessary letters of credit, but the courts made it clear that this did not amount to fraud and, even where the supplier had no hope of succeeding in a separate action against the beneficiary, the court would not intervene. In *United Trading Corpn SA v Allied Arab Bank* (1984) CA the court suggested it would not order a bank not to pay on a bond unless the beneficiary was made a party to the proceedings so he has an opportunity to deny fraud on his part

Only in *Potton Homes Ltd v Coleman Contractors (Overseas) Ltd* (1984) CA did any indication appear of an extension to the fraud exception. Everleigh LJ (but not the other members of the bench) said he would be prepared to restrain the bank from paying on a bond if the supplier could prove the underlying contract had been avoided or there was a total failure of consideration.

In *Kvaerner John Brown Ltd v Midland Bank plc* (1998) there was procedural fraud by the beneficiary in its actual claim. The beneficiary had fraudulently alleged that it had given notice of its claim to the seller when in fact no such notice had been given. Where there is a procedural fraud then the bank is able to refuse to pay the beneficiary. In such a case, the bank will have irrefutable evidence of fraud.

The *United Trading Corpn SA v Allied Arab Bank Ltd* (1985) case further establishes that if the only realistic inference to draw from the facts is that of fraud and the beneficiary has failed to provide an adequate answer to questions which demand one then, and only then, will the courts issue the injunction sought by the supplier. In that case Ackner LJ said a bank could be liable in negligence to its customer if it paid on a bond when it had actual knowledge of fraud.

Particular issues that arise out of these cases include the fact that evidence of fraud must be clear both as to the fact of fraud and to the knowledge on the part of the bank. It must be shown not only that the caller is fraudulent, but that the bank knows of this, *Deutsche Ruckversicherung v Wallbrook Insurance* (1994).

A bank cannot draw inferences of fraud simply because breach of the contract is alleged, *Turkiye Is Bankasi v Bank of China* (1996). It will not be sufficient for an assertion or allegation of fraud to be made. The courts will require strong corroborative evidence (frequently in the form of contemporary documents), particularly those emanated from the buyer, in order to prevent payment. In addition it would be necessary for the party against whom fraud is alleged to be given an opportunity to answer the allegation of fraud, and either to give an unsatisfactory response or to give no response at all when one could be expected in the circumstances.

In the case of *Czarnikow-Rionda Augar Trading Inc v Standard Bank London Ltd* (1998) the High Court stated that the reason why an injunction would not be (and has not been) given is that it was important that banks carry out their contractual obligation to make payment under the performance bonds.

There was one Court of Appeal decision in the case of *Themehelp Ltd v West* (1996) that suggested that a principal could circumvent this approach by obtaining an injunction not against the bank, but against the beneficiary, thus preventing the beneficiary from making a demand under an on-demand bond. This case is exceptional in that the injunction was granted against the beneficiary and not against the bank. This decision was inconsistent with legal principle and was subsequently disapproved of in the case of *Group Josi Re v Wallbrook Insurance Co Ltd* (1996). This case also confirmed that illegality would give the bank a defence to non-payment to a beneficiary by the bank in relation to a documentary credit. By analogy, such an approach could and should apply to a performance bond.

In the case of *Solo Industries UK Ltd v Canara Bank* (2001), the Court of Appeal stated that the mere appearance of a valid instrument does not commit the bank; if it can establish that there is a real prospect of success on this basis, it is unjust for the court to give summary judgment to the beneficiary in an action against the bank for payment.

It is also necessary to examine the contractual link, particularly in the case of an overseas bond where it frequently has no relationship with the underlying beneficiary because the bond may be issued in a bank based in the jurisdiction of that beneficiary. In many cases the English bank will simply be providing a counterindemnity in respect of the bond that is being issued by the issuing bank. In such a case it will be necessary not only to show fraud on the part of the beneficiary, but also on the part of the bank that is triggering the claim on the counterindemnity with the English bank.

The position in the USA

In the USA, there is a prohibition on banks acting as sureties for the debts of third parties, which makes the issue of performance bonds there impossible. As a result, the stand-by letter of credit has evolved from the documentary credit and serves an identical function to that of the performance bond. The only requirement need be the presentation to the bank of some form of document that may be a simple written assertion by the beneficiary that the supplier is in breach. The stand-by letter of credit in this form is thus just as separate from the underlying contract as is the first demand bond. The US courts have established an identical approach to any attempt to restrain payment under the stand-by letter of credit as the English courts have to first demand bonds, ie the only exception to automatic payment is 'active fraud' on the part of the beneficiary (*Sztejn v J Henry Schroder Banking Corpn* (1941)). The bank will also be liable to the supplier if it does pay when it has knowledge of fraud.

Whenever legal action is taken by a customer to restrain his bank from paying out on a bond, the bank must fight this through the courts because the international consequences of meekly agreeing not to pay out on its bond will be more harmful to the bank than losing the goodwill of any individual customer.

4.4 Possible action against the customer

The other option open to the contractor is to proceed in some way against the bond beneficiary. In practice, UK-based banks receiving calls on bonds will normally delay payment long enough to give the contractor time to contact his customer and to try to smooth over whatever real or imagined problem led to the call. The contractor may be able in this way to get the customer to withdraw the call on the bond. He may also consider legal action in the customer's own country to force the customer to follow the conditions of the underlying contract and to drop the bond call. Regrettably, however, if the customer's country has a legal system that is slow or undeveloped in commercial areas, or courts that tend to favour local nationals, the expense of such action will be wasted.

Even after the bank has finally made payment under the bond, the contractor's right of action against the customer is not over. It is clear that, at least under English law, where a customer has received payment through a call on an on-demand bond that is not justified under the underlying contract, the contractor can seek repayment under a claim under the contract. Again, however, it would usually be hard to succeed in such a claim outside the UK and even if the contract was under English law and subject to the jurisdiction of the English courts, it might be hard to find any conveniently-sited assets of the customer against which to enforce judgment.

4.5 Practical and legal considerations to mitigate the effect of on-demand bonds

Even when a contractor is forced into providing an on-demand bond he should pay very careful attention to the wording. In spite of various attempts the world's banks have not managed to agree a uniform commercial practice on which a bond issuer can rely for protection. He must therefore try to provide his own. Points to look out for, in order of importance, include the following.

(a) There should never be a (top-up) clause whereby, after a call, the amount of the bond is automatically reinstated so that the full bond amount can be called again.

(b) The amount of advance payment guarantees should reduce gradually over the life of the contract as the advance payment is recovered by the customer by deduction from payments.

(c) There should always be a set expiry date after which valid calls may not be made. In practice the benefits of such a protection may be obviated since:

 (i) The law of some countries disregards expiry dates and allows bond beneficiaries to claim indefinitely. It is very easy for a bond beneficiary to get the expiry date extended by making an 'extended or pay' call, saying that he will call the bond unless the customer and the bank extends the validity of the bond.

 (ii) All calls should be required to be in writing and to be signed by someone in a specific position of authority in relation to the contract. This is to ensure that the bonds are not called prematurely (or fraudulently) by some over-zealous junior official.

(d) There should be a notice period after the call before the bank is obliged to make payment. This will give time to the contractor to approach the customer to convince him to withdraw the call.

(e) The law under which the bond is issued and the courts that have jurisdiction should be made clear, if they are not to be those of the customer's country. It will be appreciated that in some countries having bonds issued under the local law may allow very little protection even when the contractor is clearly in the right.

(f) Also, it is possible to draft conditions that effectively restrict the beneficiary's right to call (outlined below).

5 Conditional bonds

5.1 Definition

These are bonds that provide that the beneficiary must meet some condition before being able to claim payment under the bond. The introduction of this condition is plainly designed to protect the contractor against calls when he has not in fact breached his contract. It should be noted, however, that an attempt to make direct reference to a breach of the underlying contract will probably be doomed to failure. The bank issuing the bond will want clearly defined the circumstances in which it is to make payment under the bond. Wording that says that the bond is payable 'only if there has been a failure by the contractor to perform under the contract' will not be acceptable to the bank. It will not want to have to go deeply into the situation on the contract to make a subjective judgment as to the state of play between the parties.

Plainly, the contractor will try to negotiate bond wordings in a conditional form. In the UK it is generally accepted as unreasonable for the customer to expect on-demand bonds. Overseas the position is different. In some countries, where contracts for public sector customers are involved, on-demand bonds in a set format are a non-negotiable requirement of doing business. It is for the contractor to consider his attitude to on-demand wording of bonds on a country-by-country, customer-by-customer, basis. He may choose to set himself stronger rules against providing on-demand bonds to private sector than to public sector clients. Even here, however, he may find himself limited in his ability to negotiate by the fact that on-demand bonds are laid down in the documents provided at the time of tender. At such time he will have limited negotiating ability, being only one of several tenderers. If he qualifies his tender on the subject of the form of the bonds, he may be disqualified from the tender. If he does not, he will be considered to have accepted the bonds.

5.2 The conditionality

Conditional bonds are paid out only if a condition is justified; usually that the beneficiary's claim is backed by an arbitral award. Alternatively the bond may be expressed to be void if the supplier performs his obligations under the contract or if the surety compensates the beneficiary for all his actual loss, up to the value of the bond.

Unlike the first demand variety, conditional bonds involve the surety in judging the validity of the beneficiary's claim, although this is less apparent when an arbitral award is the only evidence required. Insurance companies are more involved in the provision of conditional guarantees than are banks.

Nonetheless, it is possible to draft conditions that effectively restrict the beneficiary's right to call. Examples are where the bond can be called only if:

(i) the contractor gives his consent; or

(ii) a certificate stating that the contractor is in default is provided by an independent third party (eg a consultant engineer); or

(iii) the beneficiary provides a copy of a judgment from an arbitrator in his favour.

6 Form of counterindemnities

When a bank issues a first demand bond it will require a counterindemnity, from its customer, irrevocably authorizing it to pay on the bond without any reference to the customer and to debit the customer's account if it does. Frequently the buyer will insist on the bond being issued by a local bank, in which case two or more banks may be involved; the customer's bank counterindemnifies a local correspondent bank which issues the bond.

Where a correspondent bank is involved, the *United Trading* case suggests that a customer has a direct right of action against this bank but this is not clearly established and, in any case, it may be difficult to enforce. Otherwise the customer is faced with establishing fraud on the part of both the beneficiary and the correspondent bank when he seeks to restrain his bank from paying out. The customer would do better to have an overseas branch of his bank issue the bond locally.

The purpose of the counterindemnity provided by the contractor to the bank issuing a bond on his behalf is simply to have a legal structure in place under which the bank can claim reimbursement from the contractor if he has to pay out under the bond. The counterindemnity will have to provide for this reimbursement immediately that payment has been made under the bond. It will include the authority to debit the amount of the call directly to the contractor's account if it happens to be held by the bank concerned. Unfortunately the standard forms of indemnity used by many banks extend this principle too far. Careful reading will show that the bank is seeking protection even if it has paid out under the bond when it need not have done. Nothing will be more frustrating for the contractor than to have negotiated a conditional bond with the client which can be called only in clearly defined circumstances and then to find that the client succeeds in calling the bond without meeting the condition and that the bank is able to claim reimbursement under the counterindemnity. It is sensible always to insist that the counterindemnity provides for reimbursement only when payment by the bank following a call is made 'in accordance with the terms of the bonds'.

7 Insurance against unfair call

It is possible for the contractor to obtain insurance against the unfair calling of on-demand bonds and, indeed, the justified calling of bonds where the contractor is in default under its contract for political reasons outside its control. The principal sources of such insurance are described in the following sections.

ECGD bond risk insurance cover offers reimbursement of 100% of the loss arising from the unfair calling of bonds, for a premium – normally of 0.5% pa of the bond amount. This insurance enables a contractor, when the issuing bank has made payment under the bond and obtained reimbursement from the contractor under the counterindemnity, to reclaim the amount paid to the bank from the ECGD. In order to assist the contractor's liquidity, ECGD will pay this claim immediately, provided the contractor warrants that the call on the bond was unfair. Thereafter the contractor has six months to prove the unfairness of the call to the ECGD's satisfaction.

ECGD bond risk insurance cover is a useful protection for a contractor/exporter, although its value is limited by its restriction to bonds issued to public-sector clients and, more importantly, to situations where the contractor has taken out one of the ECGD's credit insurances in relation to the underlying contract with the customer. If the contractor would not otherwise have taken that insurance, the extra cost of doing so just to get the bond risk insurance cover cannot be justified.

Private-sector insurance is available to cover on-demand bonds issued in some foreign markets. There is the advantage that no credit insurance of the contract is required as a precondition of the availability of the insurance, and there is no limitation to public-sector buyers. However:

- the premium rates may vary widely and can be very expensive;
- some risks, notably major wars, are excluded;
- claims will not be paid at least for six months after the call and then are limited to 90% of the loss;
- there may be restrictions on the amounts available in individual markets and on the periods for which the cover is available.

7.1 The effect of providing bonds

The contractor has to decide on the presentation, in the notes to its published accounts, of the potential liability under counter-indemnities given in support of contract bonds. In particular the question arises as to whether the giving of performance bonds amounts technically to a contingent liability, which should be quantified in the published figures. Most contractors take the view, with their auditors' agreement, that the potential liability under a performance bond is not a contingent liability, because it will arise only as a result of a failure of the contractor's own trading performance. A contractor's accounts will normally, therefore, simply contain at the end of the contingent liabilities note a phrase saying that, in addition to the quantified contingent liabilities, certain obligations may arise under guarantees given 'in the ordinary course of trade'.

This treatment is very important when assessing the impact of outstanding bonds on a contractor's borrowing capacity. Plainly, an individual bank that has given a bond for a contractor will treat the value of the bond as a credit risk taken on the customer and therefore decrease the total value of other facilities that it is prepared to make available to that contractor. By contrast, however, any other bank, preparing its own analysis of the contractor's overall liability structure, will take some consideration of quantified contingent liabilities but none of outstanding bonds. The conclusion is that the giving of a bond does not generally affect the contractor's borrowing capacity.

The main exception is where the contractor is limited in the number of banks it can use. The most frequent reason for such a limitation is that a relatively small company may have given a floating charge to its clearing bank. In this situation the reduction of that bank's willingness to extend credit because of the bonds issued assumes extra importance. The contractor may not have alternative banks to whom to turn. Such a contractor may well turn to a form of cover available from ECGD known as the 'ECGD bond support cover'. This is specifically designed to enable exporters to obtain bonds on contracts with public-sector clients without eating into their credit limit with their banks. In exchange for a premium of 1.25% pa of the value of the bonds (1% pa for tender bonds), ECGD unconditionally undertakes to reimburse the issuing bank if the bond is called. ECGD does have a right of recourse against the contractor in the event that the contractor cannot prove that the call is unfair (it will be noted that payment of the premium thus effectively also establishes insurance against unfair calling), but the bank's limit is unimpaired.

ECGD bond support cover is available only to contractors who have taken out ECGD credit insurance in relation to the underlying contract.

The giving of bonds – particularly in an on-demand form – can seriously impede a contractor's ability to take advantage of the rights of termination afforded to it by the contract. The contractor will normally set out to ensure that the payment terms of major contracts in politically volatile areas are such that it is always paid sufficiently in advance to cover all its expenditure to date, plus outstanding commitments. Provided that the contract gives the right to the contractor to terminate the contract on significant non-performance by the customer (particularly non-payment) the contractor will then be able to walk away without risk of loss other than future profit.

If, however, the contractor has provided on-demand bonds in support of the contract, it may lose this flexibility. The threat of the bonds being called when it walks away disturbs the whole payment balance. It is worth noting that, even though the contractor plainly would think that its action in walking away was justified, it would probably not be able to use the concept of fraud by the customer to stop the bank from paying out on a subsequent call on the bond. The very fact that the contractor had abandoned the contract would make fraud very difficult to prove.

It is important for the contractor to exercise control over the bonds that have been issued on its behalf. It should always have lists of the bonds issued by bank and by country. Every effort should be made once a bond has passed its expiry date, or the condition that gave rise to the need for the bond has passed, to recover the bond, or at the very least to obtain a letter confirming that the customer regards its rights under the bond as being at an end. Banks tend to want to continue charging for bonds issued until they receive them back or have notice of cancellation. This may be true even if there is an expiry date and it has passed.

It would appear that most banks have not in the past felt the need to allocate any element of their capital to off-balance sheet contingent liabilities such as the giving of bonds and guarantees. Any income that they have been able to generate from such activities has, therefore, been a total addition to bottom line profit. No matter how many bonds were issued, there would be no effect on the bank's ability to write other business. In the circumstances it is not surprising that recent years have seen competition among banks to provide bonding facilities, and a consequent depressing effect on the cost of those facilities.

In January 1987, however, the authorities regulating the banking systems in the USA and the UK agreed common standards for judging the quality of banks' balance sheets by applying weightings representing the inherent riskiness of different types of assets. Those weights stretch from 0% for cash and claims on the domestic central banks to 100% for normal commercial loans. Off-balance sheet items are also brought into the equation for the first time, with performance bonds and other commercial guarantees receiving a 50% weighting. This can be expected to bring forward the day when banks will feel that they must allocate capital to such off-balance sheet commitments. That capital will have to be rewarded if its allocation is to be justified. The result may well be to reverse the downward trend in bonding costs in the near future.

8 ICC Uniform Rules

The International Chamber of Commerce (ICC) has published 'Uniform Rules for Contract Guarantees' 1978 (No 325), the ICC Uniform Rules of Contract Bonds of 1993 (No 524) and the Uniform Rules for Demand Guarantees (No 458), which set out internationally applicable definitions of terms of liability expiry dates and a system for resolution of disputes. The following is an extract from the ICC home page in the light of the physical introduction of the euro:

> The International Chamber of Commerce (ICC) is the world business organization, based in Paris. The ICC Commissions on Banking Technique & Practice, International Commercial Practice, and Insurance, develop and maintain uniform rules for international trade, including the Uniform Rules for Contract Guarantees (URCG 325), Uniform Rules for Demand Guarantees (URDG 458), Uniform Customs and Practice for Documentary Credits (UCP 500), Uniform Rules for Collections (URC 522), Uniform Rules for Contract Bonds (URCB 524), and Uniform Rules for Bank-to-Bank Reimbursements (URR 525) (hereinafter referred to collectively as 'ICC Rules'). The Introduction of the European single currency (euro) shall not have the effect of altering, discharging or excusing performance under any instrument subject to ICC Rules. This Decision emphasizes the need to correctly interpret and apply ICC Rules. Consequently, ICC

national committees and associated organizations are strongly urged to distribute this Decision as widely as possible to help to ensure the future smooth running of the instruments issued under ICC Rules. This Decision does not amend any articles of ICC Rules in any way, but merely indicates the correct interpretation thereof that has been adopted unanimously by the ICC Commission on Banking Technique and Practice on 6 April 1998.

8.1 Consequences of the introduction of the euro on practice under various ICC rules 2.1 UCP 500 for Documentary Credits (including standby letters of credit)

Below are the different possible cases and the relevant rules of interpretation:

Documentary credits issued in a national currency unit before 1 January 1999 and payable on or after 1 January 2002. Payment must be made in euro, but documents issued between 1 January 1999 and 1 January 2002 may be presented either in the currency of the credit or in the euro equivalent or in the equivalent cross-value in the national currency unit of the beneficiary's place of business; documents issued on or after 1 January 2002 must be denominated in euro.

Documentary credits issued on or after 1 January 1999 but before 1 January 2002 in a national currency unit or in euro and payable on or after 1 January 2002. Payment must be made in euro, but documents may be presented either in the currency of the credit or, as the case may be, in euro or in the national currency unit of the beneficiary's place of business, provided always that documents issued on or after 1 January 2002 must be denominated in euro.

For purposes of examples above, documents (including insurance documents mentioned in UCP Art. 34 f) are not considered as being inconsistent with one another if, within a single presentation of documents, any documents are denominated in the currency of the credit and/or in euro and/or in the national currency unit of the beneficiary's place of business.

Documentary credits issued and payable on or after 1 January 2002. Credits cannot be issued in a national currency unit and must be issued in euro and payment must be made and documents (issued on or after 1 January 2002) denominated in euro.

The guidelines set forth in this decision apply equally to transferable credits. With regard to transferable credits issued in a national currency unit and to be transferred during the transitional period, the transferring bank may convert the currency and amount of the credit into the euro equivalent. The principles set forth above also apply to guarantees and bonds.

You must be aware of the following specific uniform rules. Article 20 of UCP 458 provides that any demand for payment under a guarantee 'shall be in writing and shall be supported by a written statement', stating:

(i) that the principal is in breach of his obligation(s) under the underlying contract(s) or, in the case of a tender guarantee, the tender conditions; and

(ii) the respect in which the principal is in breach.

In addition, any demand under the counter-guarantee relating to the on-demand bond shall be supported by a written statement that the guarantor has received a demand for payment under the guarantee, in accordance with its terms and article 20 of UCP 458.

Article 20 shall apply to an on-demand bond issued pursuant to Uniform Customs and Practice (458) unless it is expressly excluded by the terms of the guarantee. This article is intended to address one of the most significant problems experienced with the issuance of on-demand bonds, namely capricious triggering. Article 20 requires a positive statement to be made relating to breach of the underlying contract or, as the case may be, triggering of the underlying bond prior to a claim being made. It is hoped that this will significantly reduce the incidence of unfair calling, both of guarantees and counter-guarantees.

The requirement for a statement to be made that the underlying contract has been breached is stated to be in addition to any other documentary requirements that are set out in the bond itself. The fact that Article 20 applies unless it is expressly excluded reinforces the importance that the ICC has placed upon this particular article.

In short, the requirements are:

(i) the demand must be in writing;

(ii) there must be a written statement of the breach;

(iii) the beneficiary must furnish any further documents specified in the guarantee;

(iv) taken together with Article 9, all documents presented in connection with the demand must be consistent with one another and conform to the guarantee.

Article 4 stipulates that the on-demand guarantee is not assignable unless expressly stated to be so. This is obviously contrary to the general provision of English law that permits assignment unless otherwise stated. Article 4 does not prevent the ability to assign the proceeds of a guarantee, however.

Some of the articles in UCP 458 cover the liabilities and responsibilities of the issuing bank. Article 9, for example, provides that the guarantor shall examine the documents submitted to it with reasonable care. This is to ascertain whether on their face they appear to conform with the terms of the guarantee. If the guarantor decides to refuse a demand, he is required to give notice to the beneficiary immediately. It was not clear that this was previously the case, and this article obviously improves the position of the beneficiary, who will know as soon as reasonably possible that the demand has been refused.

Article 17 requires the guarantor to inform the relevant party of receipt of a demand, and must be read with Article 21. This requires that the guarantor transmits the demand and any related documents to the relevant party without delay in the event that the demand is paid.

Articles 19 and 22 taken together require that demands be made prior to the expiry date of the guarantee. This shall be either upon a specified calendar date, or upon presentation of the guarantor of the document specified for the purpose of expiry, or whichever of the two appears first.

Irrespective of any expiry provision contained in the guarantee, it shall be cancelled on presentation to the guarantor or the beneficiary's written statement of release from liability under the guarantee, whether or not the actual guarantee itself is returned (this requirement set out in Article 23 clarifies the previous situation, where guarantees in some jurisdictions were held to continue to be enforceable, notwithstanding their expiry terms, until they were returned, either to the issuing bank or the underlying account party). Procedures relating to the extension of guarantees are also covered by the new rules; reference should be made to Article 26 – and to amendments in respect of demand guarantees – Article 3.

The uniform rules have also clarified the situation with regard to periodic stand guarantees in Article 26, and to the governing law and jurisdiction of demand guarantees, which are comprehensively covered in Article 27, and this is considered further below.

9 The position with regard to conflicts of laws

The proper law of performance bonds, like any contract, will be determined by normal conflict rules and it is open to the parties to express a choice in the bond itself. A supplier would obviously prefer an external law to govern and jurisdiction in the external courts but the buyer often insists on his law and his courts

Article 27 of the ICC Uniform Rules provides that the parties to a performance bond are able to specify the law that applies. The primary rule laid down by Article 3(1) of the Rome Convention is that a contract is to be governed by the law chosen by the parties. If the proper law is one of an EU country then the Rome Convention applies.

Under Article 4 of the Rome Convention in the case where there is no proper law specified the law will be that of the country in which there is the closest and most real connection. In the case of *BCCI Hong Kong Ltd (in liquidation) v Sonali* (1995), involving a letter of credit, the closest connection test was used at common law.

The court held that as the place of payment was Hong Kong, the proper law was Hong Kong law.

Article 4 (2) of the Rome Convention goes on to provide a presumption that the test of closest connection will be the country where the party that is to carry out the characteristic performance of the contract is based. This is of course payment and was held in the cases of *Sierra Leone Telecommunications Co Ltd (Sierratel) v Barclays Bank plc* (1998) and *The Bank of Baroda v The Vysya Bank* (1994).

There was no express nor tacit choice of law to a letter of credit in *Offshore International SA v Banco Central SA* (1976) and the court applied the 'closest and most real connection' test. As the credit was opened through a New York bank, payment was in US$ against documents presented in New York and performance was undertaken by the New York bank, New York law governed. The court in the *Edward Owen* case reiterated the closest and most real connection test in the absence of express or implied choice. Where the bond is issued in England this would probably lead to English law but if it is issued locally through a correspondent bank it may lead to the local law. Some countries have rules on bonds which may override an expiry date expressed on the bond, eg under Turkish law all bonds have a ten-year life irrespective of specified duration.

Seventeen

Documentary credits

1 Introduction

These are usually called 'letters of credit' (LCs). LCs are very formal instruments: the issuing bank (that of the payer) agrees to honour the detailed terms of the credit, provided the payee submits exactly the documents required by the terms of the credit; the issuing bank is thus a party to the LC, and within these limits guarantees its payment.

An importer can arrange for his banker to establish, with an overseas bank, a credit in favour of a third party upon which payment is to be made, when certain specified documents are presented. If a complete set of documents is insisted upon, a good title to the goods can be obtained and the bank will therefore have the goods as security.

If an importer is unable to get the goods shipped to him on open account, he may have to establish documentary credits, and these involve him in a liability to his banker. The importer has some protection, because the money is not paid away until documents showing shipment are produced. However, the documents purport to represent certain goods, and the goods have not been examined. An importer will, for his own protection, have to assure himself of the integrity of the exporter. Also, if a banker is relying upon the goods in any way as security, he will have to satisfy himself that the importer has ability and experience of the trade. If other security is not available, a banker would have to decide to what extent he would rely upon the goods and ask for any shortfall to be deposited in cash on a margin account, before the documentary credit is opened. By issuing an irrevocable letter of credit therefore, a bank is conditionally guaranteeing a customer's trade debt.

The issuing bank can undertake only what it has the power to do. For example, it cannot produce foreign currency if its local central bank does not make it available. In any case, the issuing bank could itself become insolvent.

The issuing bank is not normally in direct contact with the payee, but with his bank that, in doc credit language, is called the 'advising' bank.

The worst pitfall with all LCs, however, is that the payee must produce exactly the documentation required by the terms of the credit. This is often not just difficult, but impossible.

LCs can be:

- revocable;
- irrevocable (ILC); or
- confirmed and irrevocable (CILC).

A revocable LC is, of course, not safe at all because the customer can revoke it. An ILC is safer in that it cannot be revoked.

A CILC has to be confirmed by a first-class bank in the exporter's country, and is therefore bomb-proof, as long as the exporter can produce the required documentation, for the confirming bank guarantees both the credit risk on the issuing bank and the transfer risk on the availability of currency from the foreign central bank.

Everything therefore turns on the detailed terms of the credit, especially its expiry date and the documents specified. To name but one important issue, the pre-credit risk (repudiation of contract before delivery) is covered only if the terms enable the exporter to produce the required documents, even when he has been unable to ship or get the goods accepted by the customer.

LCs often require among the documents either a sight or a tenor bill of exchange.

Figure 17.1

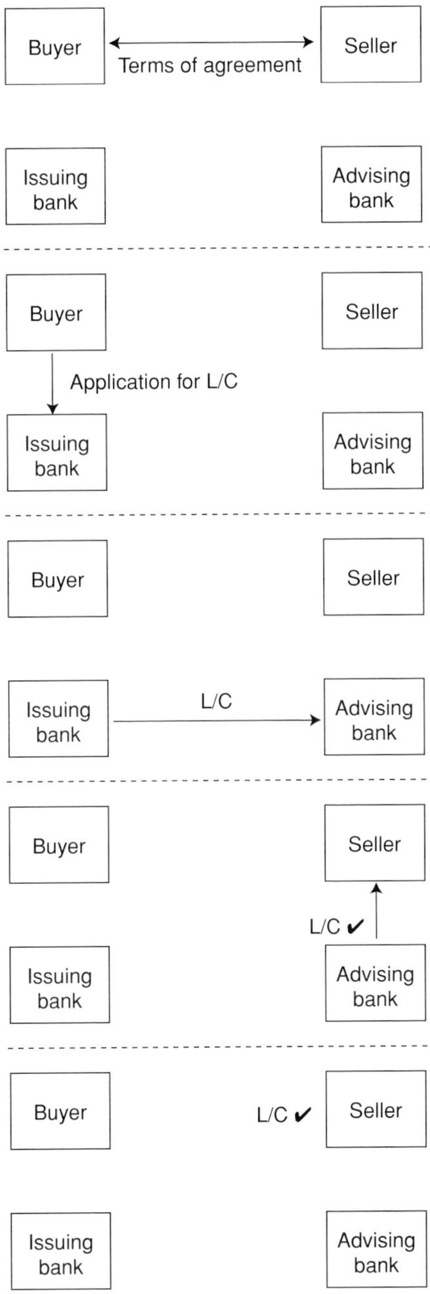

Buyer and seller agree terms, including means of transport, period of credit offered (if any), latest date of shipment, Incoterm to be used.

Buyer applies to bank for issue of letter of credit. Bank will evaluate buyer's credit standing, and may require cash cover and/or reduction of other lending limits.

Issuing bank issues L/C, sending it to the Advising bank by airmail or (more commonly) electronic means such as telex or SWIFT.

Advising bank establishes authenticity of the letter of credit using signature books or test codes, then informs seller (beneficiary). Advising bank MAY confirm L/C, i.e. add its own payment undertaking.

Seller should now check that L/C matches commercial agreement, and that all its terms and conditions can be satisfied, (e.g. all documents can be obtained in good time.) If there is anything that may cause a problem, an AMENDMENT must be requested.

Figure 17.1 continued

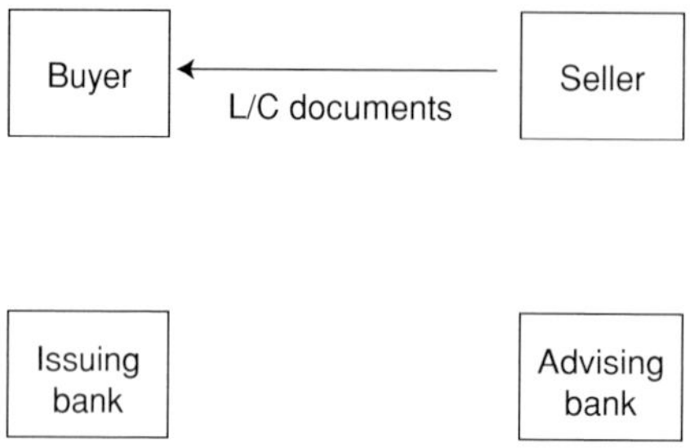

Seller ships the goods, then assembles the documents called for in the L/C (invoice, transport document etc.) Before presenting the documents to the bank, the seller should check them for discrepancies with the L/C, and correct the documents where necessary.

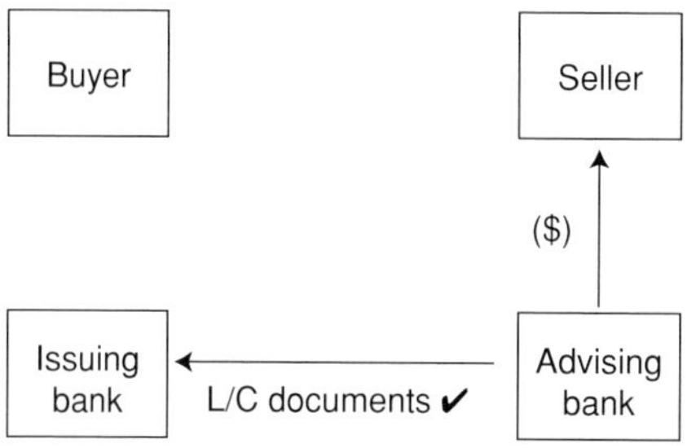

The documents are presented to a bank, often the Advising bank. The Advising bank checks the documents against the L/C. If the documents are compliant, the bank pays the seller and forwards the documents to the Issuing bank.

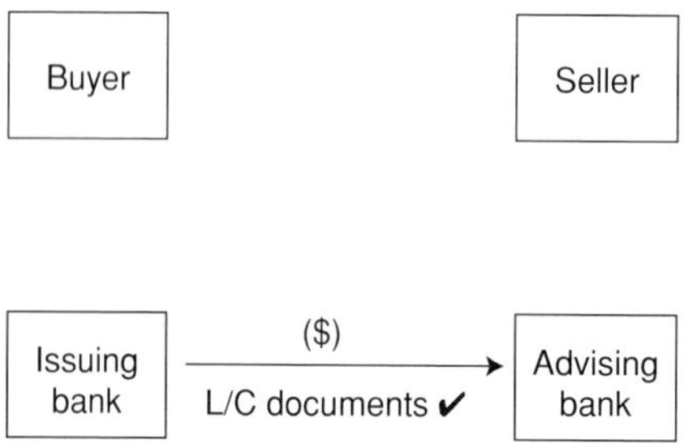

The Issuing bank now checks the documents itself. If they are in order (and it is a sight L/C), it reimburses the seller's bank immediately.

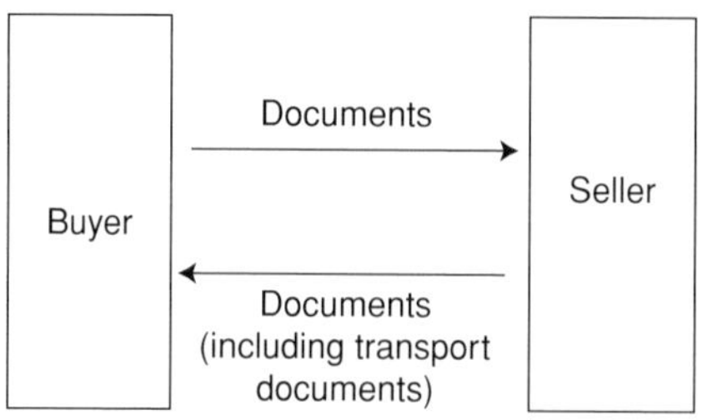

The Issuing bank debits the buyer and releases the documents (including transport document), so that the buyer can claim the goods from the seller.

2 Uniform Customs and Practice for Documentary Credits (1993 Revision)

The Uniform Customs and Practice for Documentary Credits (UCP) is a set of internationally accepted rules and definitions that cover the liabilities and duties of all parties to documentary credits. All bank authorities and advices of documentary credits will state that the credit is subject to UCP 1993. Where the terms of the credit contradict UCP, the terms of the credit will prevail and where national laws conflict with UCP, national laws will prevail.

The main provisions of UCP 1993, as they affect exporters and their banks, are as follows

2.1 Article 3

Banks are concerned only with the documents presented under the credit. Even when the underlying sales contract is mentioned in the credit (eg where the invoice stipulates the Incoterm), the bank's decision to pay depends solely on whether the documents presented conform to the credit.

Comment

The issuing bank should ensure that a credit is logical and workable when it is set up (eg if the sales contract is 'free on board', do not call for an insurance document) and beneficiaries should ensure that the credit meets their requirements as soon as it is advised to them.

However, once the credit has been set up, the bank's decision to pay or not depends solely upon whether the documents presented conform to the credit. The only way payment can be made against the wrong documents is if the applicant agrees to accept the documents despite the discrepancies and authorizes the issuing bank to debit the account.

2.2 Article 4

Banks are concerned only with documents, neither goods nor the performance of the underlying contract.

2.3 Article 6

Credits should clearly indicate whether they are revocable or irrevocable. In the absence of any such indication, the credits are deemed irrevocable.

2.4 Article 7

The advising bank must take reasonable care to check that the credit is genuine, if it elects to advise the credit. If the advising bank cannot establish authenticity, it must inform the bank from which the instructions appear to have been received, without delay. The advising bank may advise an unauthenticated credit but if it does so it must inform the beneficiary that authenticity has not been established. In all cases, there is no obligation on the part of the advising bank to advise a credit, but if it elects not to do so, it must inform the issuing bank without delay.

Comment

If a credit is received by the beneficiary directly from the issuing bank, the beneficiary should ask his own bank to check its authenticity.

2.5 Articles 13 and 15

Banks must examine all documents with reasonable care to ensure that on the face of it they appear to be in order. Documents that, on the face of it, appear to be inconsistent with one another will be considered as not appearing to comply with the credit terms. Any documents that are not called for by the credit will not be examined by banks.

Banks shall have a reasonable time, not to exceed seven banking days following the day of receipt of documents, to examine the documents and determine whether to take up, or refuse, the documents and to inform the party from which the documents were received of the decision.

If the credit contains terms and conditions without stating the document(s) to be presented in compliance with such conditions, banks will disregard the conditions.

Banks assume no liability for the genuineness of documents.

3 Reasonable care – material discrepancies versus trivial discrepancies

In discussing discrepancies in documents with the terms and conditions of documentary credits there are often differences of opinion between what are considered trivial discrepancies and material discrepancies. The question is often asked whether documents presented under a documentary credit may be rejected only if they are discrepant in some material respect with the requirements and stipulations of the letter of credit.

3.1 Background

Despite a number of legal rulings from the courts over a long period and despite helpful guidelines over the years from the ICC, the issue of material discrepancies versus trivial discrepancies continues to be a source of disagreement between bankers and beneficiaries. For the purposes of the discussion in this section, in its simplest terms the issuing bank's undertaking on its documentary credit is to pay against the 'pieces of paper' that the issuing bank has stipulated in the credit. If the pieces of paper submitted by the beneficiary are not strictly as indicated in the documentary credit instrument, then the obligation to pay does not arise.

Nevertheless, practitioners are aware that if banks were to insist on crossing every 't' and dotting every 'i' this could damage their reputation. Conformity does not mean that there has to be a microscopic exactness in the documents submitted and bankers do not insist on this. Bankers are concerned to see:

(a) their name in the marketplace is not damaged by refusal to pay on the grounds of 't's and 'i's not having been crossed or dotted;

(b) the purpose of documentary credits as a method of payment in international trade is not undermined.

3.2 The legal position

Reference is made to ICC Publication No 511 entitled 'Documentary Credits – UCP 500 and 400 compared'. This is a publication authorized by the ICC that comments on the changes of the Articles of UCP 500 from the Articles of UCP 400. The first paragraph of page 39 comments on the meaning of 'on their face', an expression that is common to UCP 400 and UCP 500. It indicates that:

(a) the decision as to whether to accept or reject is based exclusively on the banker's examination of the documents and not upon someone else's understanding;

(b) there is a method of examination of documents under documentary credits that is peculiar to bankers.

It is considered helpful to point to some observations that have been made by judges in cases connected with the compliance of documents, and these are shown below.

1. *Glencore International AG Bayerische Vereinsbank AV v Bank of China*, AC, per Sir Thomas Bingham MR:

   'The banks are not required to familiarize themselves with any of the infinitely various terms, conventions or esoteric understandings of the sales transactions themselves: their role is limited to the demanding, but essentially clerical, task of scrutinizing the documents tendered under the credit to establish that they conform to the terms of credit.

Banks are generally careful not to refuse payment on grounds of non-conformity unless non-conformity is clear.'

2. *Seaconsar Far East Ltd v Bank Markazi Jomhouri Islami Iran*, CA, 28 October 1992 per Lloyd LJ:

   'He argues that the absence of the letter of credit number and the buyer's name was an entirely trivial feature of the document. I cannot regard as trivial something which, whatever may be the reason, the credit specially requires.'

3. *Equitable Trust Co of New York v Dawson Partners Ltd* (1926) L>I>L. Rep 49 at 52 per Lord Sumner:

   'There is no room for documents which are almost the same or which will do just as well.

   Business could not proceed securely on any other lines. The bank's branch abroad, which knows nothing officially of the details of the transaction just financed, cannot take upon itself to decide what will do well enough and what will not.

   - If it does as it is told it is safe;
   - If it declines to do anything else it is safe;
   - If it departs from the conditions laid down it acts at its own risk.'

4. *Banque de l'Indochine* (1982)

   In his judgment in *Seaconsar v Markazi*, Mr Justice Lloyd made the following comments in relation to the above case:

   'But in that case Mr Justice Parker was dealing with an argument that the tender was bad because some of the documents could not be linked with each other. He was not saying that the deficiency in one document could be cured by reference to another.'

5. *Commercial Banking Co of Sydney Ltd v Jalsard Pty Ltd* [1973] AC 279 PC Lord Diplock:

   'This is the reason for the rule that where the banker's instructions from his customer are ambiguous or unclear, he commits no breach of his contract with the buyer if he has construed them in a reasonable sense, even though upon a closer consideration which can be given to questions of construction in an action in a court of law, it is possible to say that some other meaning is to be preferred.'

The question posed in the first paragraph of this section was whether documents presented under a letter of credit may be rejected only if they are discrepant in some material respect with the requirements and stipulation of the letter of credit.

The banker's position should be that:

(i) The document examiner does not make a distinction between material discrepancies and trivial discrepancies.

(ii) The terms and conditions are as shown on the credit and the document examiner is not concerned as to why a particular document is required in a particular form.

(iii) The document examiner is not required to take on the role of an amateur investigator and one who does, does so at his or her peril.

(iv) The document examiner has to decide whether to honour or refuse to honour the bank's undertaking – it is the bank's money involved and accordingly as long as the decision is made on the method of examination that is peculiar to bankers, the question of trivial and material discrepancies do not arise.

Article 20

Unless otherwise stipulated in the credit, banks will accept as an original document a document produced or appearing to have been produced by photocopier, carbon systems or computer, provided such a document is marked as original, and where necessary, appears to have been signed.

Any symbol executed or adopted by a party with the intention to authenticate should be accepted as a signature. One example of such a signature is the traditional chop mark used in Asia that is a legal and valid signature.

Unless otherwise stipulated in the credit, a condition calling for a document to be authenticated or certified will be satisfied by any signature, mark, stamp or label that appears to satisfy such conditions.

Articles 21 and 22

When documents other than transport documents, invoices and insurance documents are called for, the credit should stipulate by whom the documents are to be issued, and the required wording or data content.

If no such instructions are received, banks will accept such documents as tendered.

Banks will accept a document bearing a date of issue prior to that of the credit, subject to such a document being presented within the time limits set out in the credit and in other parts of UCP.

Article 42

All credits must stipulate an expiry date and a place for presentation of documents for payment. Where a credit is freely negotiable, the implication is that the documents can be presented to any bank.

Article 43

Banks will reject any transport document presented more than 21 days after its date. Such documents are considered to be stale.

Article 44

When the expiry date of a credit falls due on a non-business day, banks will accept presentation on the following business day. However, the transport document must be dated on or before the expiry date of the credit, or on or before the last date of shipment if the credit stipulates such a date.

3.3 Fraud and court injunctions in relation to documentary credits

The overriding concept of the autonomous nature of the documentary credit is covered in UCP 500 and in particular how that concept is conveyed in Articles 2, 3 and 4 of the UCP. The fundamental principle is that banks' undertaking on a documentary credit is separate from the underlying contract. Banks are in no way concerned with, or bound by, such contracts. Consequently a bank undertaking to pay on a letter of credit is not subject to any claims or defences that the applicant for the credit such as the buyer might have against the supplier, or indeed the bank itself.

A second fundamental principle with documentary credits is that banks deal in documents and not with the goods, services or performances to which the documents relate. The duty of the bank is to make payment against documents that comply strictly with the terms of the letter of credit.

The autonomy of the credit and the fundamental concept that credits 'must be allowed to be honoured, free from interference by the courts' are best demonstrated in the judgment of Kerr J in *RD Hardbottle (Mercantile) Ltd v National Westminster Bank Ltd* (1978) as mentioned in the previous unit on performance bonds.

'It is only in exceptional cases that the courts will interfere with the machinery of irrevocable obligations assumed by banks. They are the life-blood of international commerce. Such obligations are regarded as collateral to the underlying rights and obligations between the merchants at either end of the banking chain. Except possibly in clear cases of fraud of which the banks have notice, the courts will leave the merchants to settle their disputes under the contracts by litigation or arbitration...The courts are not concerned with their difficulties to enforce such claims; these are risks that the merchants take. In this case the plaintiffs took the risk of the unconditional wording of the guarantees. The machinery and commitments of banks are on a different level. They must be allowed to be honoured, free from interference by the courts. Otherwise, trust in international commerce could be irreparably damaged.'

The only circumstance in which courts should intervene is 'in clear cases of fraud of which banks have notice' and in such cases the courts will take into account evidence apart from the documents tendered under the credit and the terms and conditions of the credit. Proof of the fraud, by the buyer seeking to restrain its bank from paying will rarely be possible. In the case of *Czarnikow-Rionda Augar Trading Inc v Standard Bank London Ltd* (1998) the High Court stated that the reason why an injunction would not (and has not) be given is that it was important that banks carry out their contractual obligation to make payment under the performance bonds.

In the case of *Niru Battery Manufacturing Co v Milestone Trading* (2002) EWHC 1425, Milestone presented a fraudulent document under a letter of credit issued by Bank Sepah. Because the document looked genuine, Bank Sepah paid the sums due under the letter of credit to Milestone's bank, CAI, which, on Milestone's instructions, then paid the monies away.

Bank Sepah sued CAI to recover the money in restitution on the basis that Bank Sepah had paid under the letter of credit as a result of mistake, namely the belief that the document was genuine. CAI's only defence was that it had changed its position in reliance on the payment, namely it had honoured Milestone's instructions to pay the monies away. This defence requires the change of position to be in good faith. The judge decided that this requirement had not been met. The case therefore decided that irrespective of the fact that the documents appear to meet the requirements of the letter of credit does not men that a bank can turn a blind eye to everything else. If a bank knows sufficient facts to question whether its customer has acted honestly and fails to do so then it has not acted with good faith and cannot therefore rely on the defence of payment by mistake.

Article 9

R.76 Bill of Lading – Forgery

The Commission was invited to comment on the following problem raised by a bank in Bangladesh. 'A bill was negotiated under an irrevocable documentary credit by a bank in due course. The negotiating bank obtained reimbursement. The L/C opening bank on receipt of shipping documents from the negotiating bank telexed that the relevant bill of lading was forged. Kindly intimate to us whether the negotiating bank is liable to refund the money.'

The Commission expressed its opinion that the negotiating bank passing forward what proved to be a forged bill of lading was protected by Article 9 unless it was itself a party to the fraud, or it had knowledge of the fraud prior to presentation of the document, or unless it had failed to exercise reasonable care, eg if the forgery were apparent 'on the face' of the document. The commission noted that this was in line with various court rulings.

[(Meeting on 9 December 1980) (ICC Documents 470/371, 470/373)]

The test should be that clear and obvious fraud must be established to the knowledge of the bank before it makes payment under the credit. The dictionary definitions of 'clear' and 'obvious' are a good starting point.

'Clear' – unambiguous, easily understood, manifest, not confused or doubtful.

'Obvious' – easily seen or recognized or understood, palpable, indubitable.

From existing case law, it may be gathered that the following standards need to be applied in considering alleged fraud as a ground for preventing payment under credits:

1. The evidence of fraud must be clear and plain.
2. If the evidence is confused, conflicting or indeed ambiguous as to whether there is fraud, then the fraud exception will not be made out.
3. Uncorroborated assertions or statements by one party are not enough.
4. Strong corroborative evidence of the allegations in the form of contemporary documents is necessary.
5. The conclusion of fraud must be plain; if there is conflicting yet seemingly reliable evidence, the fraud exception will not be made out.
6. There must have been an opportunity to answer allegations and a failure to provide any adequate answer where one could be expected.
7. Bankers will not be imputed with any special knowledge or expertise in fields outside their operation.

Bankers will not be required to act in the role of an amateur investigator.

In the case of *Derry v Peek* (1889) it was stated that fraud is proved where it is shown that a false representation has been made knowingly, or without belief in its truth, or recklessly, without caring whether it is true or false. There must be an intention to deceive or reckless disregard of truth. It is insufficient to establish negligence or pure incompetence.

It is opportune to consider the observation of Sir John Donaldson, MR, in the Court of Appeal in *Bolivinter Oil SA v Chase Manhattan Bank* (1984) which was as follows:

> 'Before leaving this appeal, we should like to add a word about the circumstances in which an *ex parte* injunction should be issued which prohibits a bank from paying under an irrevocable letter of credit, or a performance bond or guarantee. The unique value of such a letter, bond or guarantee is that the beneficiary can be completely satisfied that, whatever disputes may thereafter arise between him and the bank's customer in relation to the performance or indeed existence of the underlying contract, the bank is personally undertaking to pay him provided that the specified conditions are met...If, save in the most exceptional cases, he is to be allowed to derogate from the bank's personal and irrevocable undertaking, given be it again noted at his request, by obtaining an injunction restraining the bank from honouring that undertaking, he will undermine what is the bank's greatest asset, however large and rich it may be, namely its reputation for financial and contractual probity. Furthermore, if this happens at all frequently, the value of all irrevocable letters and performance bonds and guarantees will be undermined.
>
> Judges who are asked, often at short notice and ex parte, to issue an injunction restraining payment by a bank under an irrevocable letter of credit or performance bond or guarantee should ask whether there is any challenge to the validity of the letter, bond or guarantee itself. If there is not or if the challenge is not substantial, prima facie no injunction should be granted and the bank should be left free to honour its contractual obligation, although restrictions may well be imposed on the freedom of the beneficiary to deal with the money after he has received it. The wholly exceptional case where an injunction may be granted is where it is proved that the bank knows that any demand for payment already made or which may thereafter be made will clearly be fraudulent. But the evidence must be clear, both of the fact of fraud and as to the bank's knowledge. It would certainly not normally be sufficient that this rests on the uncorroborated statement of the customer, for irreparable damage can be done to a bank's credit in the relatively brief time which must elapse between the granting of such an injunction and an application by the bank to have it discharged.'

The problem for the documentary credit specialist is not academic because he or she has to decide on the documents and the allegations of fraud made by applying the standards shown above if the document checker is to prove fraud at any subsequent trial.

If the document checker pays and fraud is established in any subsequent trial, there may be a claim for a refund, plus interest, and there may also be a claim for damages – for any resulting loss that the applicant may have suffered.

4 The position with regard to conflicts of laws

The proper law of documentary credits, like any contract, will be determined by normal conflict rules and it is open to the parties to express a choice in the bond itself. A supplier would obviously prefer an external law to govern and jurisdiction in the external courts but the buyer often insists on his law and his courts.

Article 1 of the UCP provides that the parties to a Documentary Credits are able to specify the law that applies. The UCP governs Documentary Credits primarily, but not solely. Courts often apply the UCP because it is the most universally followed set of customary Documentary Credit rules and because it is perceived as being quite close to the level of perfection permitted by the 'laws' of international compromise. However it must be recognized that incorporation of the UCP into the Documentary Credit does not prevent a court from applying its country's national law.

As with performance bonds, discussed earlier, the law chosen is one that is an EU country then the Rome Convention applies. Under Article 4 of the Rome Convention in the case where there is no proper law specified then the law will be the country in which there is the closest and most real connection. *BCCI Hong Kong Ltd (in liquidation) v Sonali* (1995) was a case involving a letter of credit where the closest connection test was used at common law. The court held that as the place of payment was Hong Kong, the proper law was Hong Kong law.

Article 4(2) of the Rome Convention goes on to provide a presumption that the test of closest connection will be the country where the party that is to carry out the characteristic performance of the contract is based. This is of course payment and was held in the cases of *Sierra Leone Telecommunications Co Ltd (Sierratel) v Barclays Bank plc* (1998) and *The Bank of Baroda v The Vysya Bank* (1994)[1].

There was no express nor tacit choice of law to a letter of credit in *Offshore International SA v Banco Central SA* (1976) and the court applied the 'closest and most real connection' test. As the credit was opened through a New York bank, payment was in US$ against documents presented in New York and performance was undertaken by the New York bank, New York law governed. The court in the Edward Owen case reiterated the closest and most real connection test in the absence of express or implied choice. Where the documentary credit is issued in England this would probably lead to English law but if it is issued locally through a correspondent bank it may lead to the local law being applied.

Notes

1. Paragraphs reproduced from ***ifs*** Examiner's Report, May 2000 (Corporate Banking – Practice and Law).

Eighteen

Asset securitization

1 Introduction

Securitization is a financing technique that involves the conversion of usually illiquid assets, with predictable cash flows, into marketable securities. Essentially it is the process of creating securities backed by pools of assets, with the securities then being sold to institutional investors.

Securitization was developed in the USA during the 1960s as part of a public policy initiative to make more funds available for residential mortgage loans. Later on, additional sponsorship has been provided by a certain number of government agencies (GNMA, Fannie Mae, Freddie Mac) carrying implicit US-government guarantees.

Asset securitization came to Europe in the early 1990s, but issues and volumes have increased significantly only since 1997/1998.

Securitization can be defined as the process whereby loans, receivables and other financial assets are pooled together, with their cash-flows, or economic values, redirected to support payments on related securities. For example, risk in project lending is now being securitized and, more importantly, securitization is being employed by banks and finance companies to finance more individualized credits such as corporate loans. These so called 'asset-backed securities' (ABS) are issued and sold to investors who use securitization to finance their business activities. The financial assets that support payments on ABS include any asset that has a reasonably ascertainable value or that generates a reasonably predictable future stream of revenue. Those assets are residential and commercial mortgage loans (residential mortgage-backed securities or RMBS and commercial-backed securities or CMBS), as well as non-mortgage assets such as credit card balances, consumer loans, trade receivables etc.

A typical securitization transaction would involve an entity (the 'seller') selling a pool of assets to a special purpose vehicle ('SPV' – being a trust or a company). Because the transaction is generally structured as an asset sale, the assets are removed from the seller's balance sheet. The SPV, in order to fund the purchase, would issue mortgage or asset-backed securities ('MBS/ABS'), which are sold to institutional investors in the domestic or international capital markets. Investors therefore rely on the cash flows from the pool of assets (and not the seller) for repayment of their investment.

Securitization separates the risks inherent in any corporate finance transaction and transfers these risks from the seller to the purchaser of assets.

2 Benefits of securitization to issuers and investors

Securitization is one way in which a company might go about financing its assets. There are generally seven reasons why companies consider securitization:

- to improve their **return on capital**, because securitization normally requires less capital to support it than traditional on-balance sheet funding;
- to raise **finance** when other forms of finance are unavailable (in a recession banks are often unwilling to lend – and during a boom, banks often cannot keep up with the demand for funds);
- to improve **return on assets** – securitization can be a cheap source of funds, but the attractiveness of securitization for this reason depends primarily on the costs associated with alternative funding sources;
- to **diversify the sources of funding** that can be accessed, so that dependence upon banking or retail sources of funds is reduced;
- to **reduce credit exposure** to particular assets (for instance, if a particular class of lending becomes large in relation to the balance sheet as a whole, then securitization can remove some of the assets from the balance sheet);
- to **match-fund** certain classes of asset – mortgage assets are technically 25-year assets, a proportion of which should be funded with long-term finance; securitization normally offers the ability to raise finance with a longer maturity than is available in other funding markets;
- to achieve a **regulatory advantage**, because securitization normally removes certain risks, which can cause regulators some concern, there can be a beneficial result in terms of the availability of certain forms of finance (for example, in the UK building societies consider securitization as a means of managing the restriction on their wholesale funding abilities).

Establishing the primary rationale for the securitization activity is a vital part of the preparation for a securitization transaction, since it influences the sorts of administrative tasks that need to be developed as well as the transaction structures themselves.

Corporate loans are relatively expensive items, in terms of capital, to hold on a bank's balance sheet. This is because they are risk-weighted at 100%, irrespective of the actual credit quality of the counterparty. Corporate loans are more expensive to hold on the balance sheet than, for example, residential mortgage loans secured by a first-ranking security interest, an asset type that is risk-weighted at 50%, and which has long been securitized. Banks that are focused on increasing return on equity and reducing the cost of capital have been assessing the possibilities of securitizing their corporate loan book for some time. Until very recently, however, very few supervisory authorities had published the criteria that must be satisfied in order for a transfer of assets (or the credit risk associated with assets) to be treated as a clean transfer for the purposes of a bank's capital/risk asset ratio requirement. So new is this technology that securitization structures involving corporate loan assets are still reviewed on a case-by-case basis by the regulator.

The fact that corporate loans are expensive items for a bank to have in terms of capital led National Westminster Bank to become the first bank to sell part of its wholesale corporate loan book in its 'ROSE' (repeat offering securitization entity) loan securitization in 1996 and 1997. Up to US$5 billion of assets, being loans to 200 borrowers, were transferred each time.

3 Benefits to the investor

The main benefits flowing to an investor in acquiring debt securities issued under an asset securitization programme include:

3.1 High credit quality

Asset securitization typically results in the securities issued carrying the highest possible credit ratings afforded by the internationally recognized rating agencies.

3.2 A diversification of investment opportunities

Asset securitization allows investors to indirectly invest in a variety of asset classes.

4 The process and mechanics of securitization

The resulting securitization structures are complicated, primarily as a result of the requirement within a securitization transaction to produce a structure that insulates investors against a multiplicity of risks. Credit risk, market risk and liquidity risk are all possible consequences, and when retained by the original lending institution would be managed on an institutional basis, and supported by the institution's equity base. The more complicated the securitized asset and the less uniform its characteristics, the more difficult it is to achieve the balance required to satisfy investor concerns. Nonetheless, the number and size of asset-backed issuances in the past few years in particular appear to signal another significant move in the on-going process of disintermediation in today's capital markets.

Figure 18.1

Basic structure of securitization

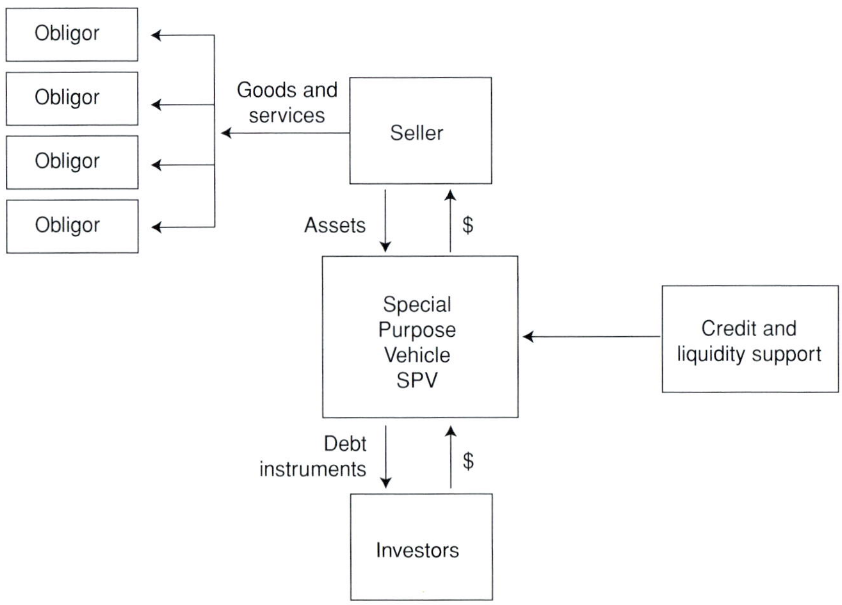

Assets are originated by a company, and funded on that company's balance sheet. This company is normally referred to as the 'Originator'. Once a suitably large portfolio of assets has been originated, the assets are analysed as a portfolio, and then sold or assigned to a third party which is normally a special purpose vehicle company (an ' SPV') formed for the specific purpose of funding the assets. The SPV is sometimes owned by a trust or even, on occasions, by the Originator. Administration of the assets is then sub-contracted back to the Originator by the SPV. The SPV issues tradable 'securities' to fund the purchase of the assets. The performance of these securities is directly linked to the performance of the assets

– and there is no recourse (other than in the event of breach of contract) back to the Originator. Investors purchase the securities because they are satisfied (normally by relying upon a rating) that the securities will be paid in full and on time from the cash-flows available in the asset pool.

A considerable amount of time is spent considering the different likely performances of the asset pool, and the implications of defaults by borrowers on the corresponding performance of the securities. The proceeds upon the sale of the securities are used to pay the Originator. The SPV agrees to pay any surpluses that arise during its funding of the assets back to the Originator – which means that the Originator, for all practical purposes, retains its existing relationships with the borrowers and all of the economics of funding the assets (ie the Originator continues to administer the portfolio, and continues to receive the economic benefits (profits) of owning the assets). As cash-flows arise on the assets, these are used by the SPV to repay funds to the investors in the securities.

Securitization works because rating agencies are prepared to assign ratings to the liabilities of the SPV. As described above, the performance of these liabilities is determined by the performance of the assets that the SPV owns – hence the securities are normally described as 'pass-through' securities (because the cash-flows and credit risks are passed through from the assets to the securities directly). Pass-through securitization is illustrated in Figure 18.2.

As already discussed in Unit 8, there are three methods under English law that can be used to transfer loans or assets from one lender to another. The three methods of transfer are novation, assignment and sub-participation. In the case of novation this is not a practical method in the case of asset securitization because the borrower must consent to such a transfer. In the case of the number of credit card receivables or house mortgages in terms of numbers it is not a practical method in terms of costs. The same will also be true of a legal assignment because the borrower's consent is required. The other reason that a customer's consent is not sought is that it may adversely affect the reputation of the bank if it became known that they were selling their customers' loans.

The normal method of transfer in the case of securitization is that loans are assigned to the issuer by way of an equitable assignment. This method means that no notice is given to the borrower and the assignment does not absolve the bank form its obligations under the loan to make further advances. This is the case with revolving loans or credit cards where further advances can take place. As was seen in Unit 8 an assignment is not suitable where there are continuing obligations, because the transfer of loans, receivables or mortgages by means of an assignment will mean that the bank is still subject to some risk. Because the bank will often still be servicing the loans, by collecting principal or interest before passing it on to the issuer the bank, it is thus still exposed to operational risk.

Figure 18.2

Pass-through securitization

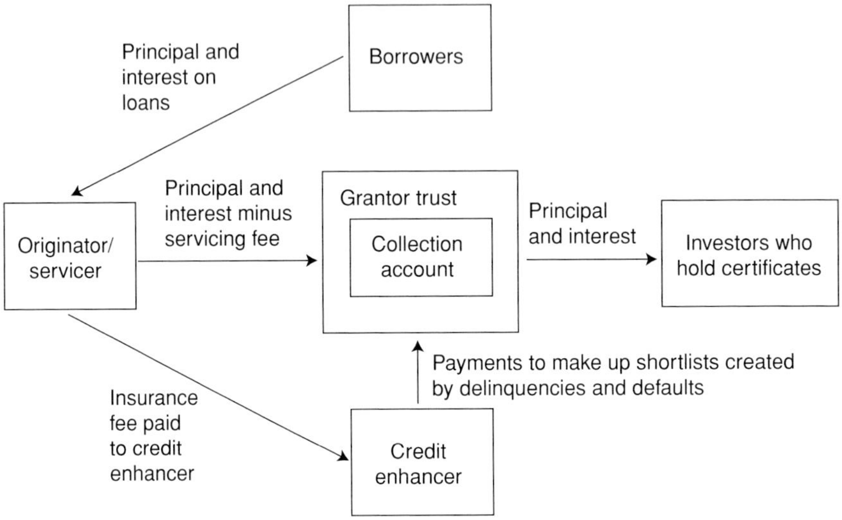

Asset-backed securitization

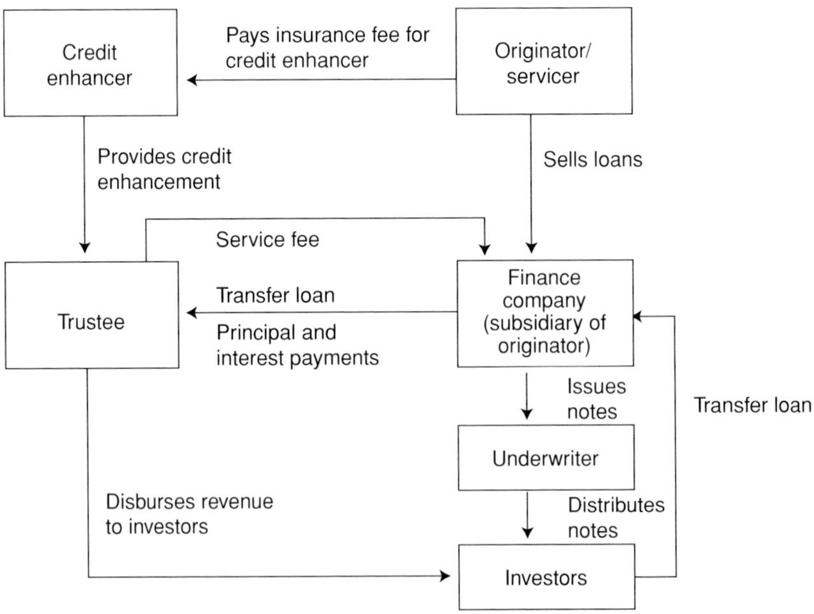

The largest risk to a bank in any securitization is the risk that the borrower fails to repay the loan or credit card advance. If the loans are going to packaged and sold off to investors in a bond then the investors will not want to deal with the aspects of any credit risk that may arise with the assets. There are various ways in which this risk is mitigated in a securitized bond issue.

There may be a put option in that when any mortgage has a default, the SPV has a 'put-option' to sell the mortgage back to the seller such as the bank or building society who then must deal with the credit risk. The bond issue can also undergo a process of credit enhancement whereby there is some sort of 'pool' insurance that covers the eventuality of any credit risk that happens in the SPV. The insurance is provided by an insurance company that may insure a certain percentage of losses in a loan-to-value ratio. Some securitized bond issues are over-collateralized in that more loans are transferred to the SPV than is required to fund payment on the securities, but taking into account that a certain proportion will cause problems.

5 The parties involved in securitization

Securitization normally involves a wide variety of counterparties and advisers. On one particularly complex transaction a few years ago there were six law firms, three firms of accountants, one insurance broker, one investment bank, one consultant and twelve principals (banks, originators, administrators, credit enhancers, underwriters, and so on).

A transaction normally involves the following parties:

- originator and administrator;
- lead underwriter – who purchases the debt issued by the SPV (and sells it to eurobond investors);
- structuring team involving personnel from the lead underwriter and/or other advisers;
- two sets of lawyers, at least one of whom is a securitization specialist;
- trustee and trustee's lawyers – representing the interests of the noteholders in the event that there is (a) an enforcement event (things go wrong) or (b) any requirement to change or amend the documents or procedures after the transaction completes;
- rating agencies required to undertake an analysis of the risks associated with the transaction and to award a credit rating to the debt issued;
- originator's accountants – to agree accounting treatment for the transaction, to verify the analysis and existence of the assets involved and to confirm work undertaken to show solvency;
- credit enhancement providers and their lawyers – transactions often involve a third party fronting some of the risks associated with the assets;
- standby servicer and their lawyers – a third party prepared to administer the assets in the event that the existing servicer fails or is incompetent; this

is now becoming a requirement for all transactions where the administrator does not already have at least an A1/P1 short-term rating;

- clearing bank and its lawyers – running the originator's and the issuer's bank accounts, all of which normally require new mandates, and a bank agreement is also set up to regulate the operation of all aspects of the accounts;
- banking facility providers and their lawyers – often there are requirements for additional banking facilities, eg liquidity facilities or guaranteed deposit arrangements ('GICs');
- hedging providers and their lawyers – assets often need some form of hedging, either using swaps, caps or both;
- paying agents, agent banks, common depositary etc – a whole host of organizations with mysterious Euromarket responsibilities;
- printer – to produce the prospectus (choosing the wrong printers can cause the transaction to fail).

6 Securitization documentation

In terms of documentation for securitization there will be the following agreements.

(i) **Sale agreement:** to sell the assets form the bank or building society to the SPV (the Issuer) or to a trustee to be held on trust for the beneficiaries.

(ii) **Administration agreement:** this governs the on-going administration of the securitized assets and the management of the incoming cash flows.

(iii) **Liquidity facility agreement:** this sets out the terms and conditions on which any liquidity facility can be drawn to cover any late payments or defaults.

(iv) **Guaranteed investment contract:** this sets out the terms and conditions on which the provider of the facility is agreeable to pay a guaranteed, minimum return on amounts invested with it.

(v) **Credit enhancement documents:** this is a document in which the credit enhancement provider gives the bondholders/banks protection against default. This is usually a mortgage pool insurance policy given by an insurance company to insure against non-payment and defaults by the underlying borrowers.

(vi) **Interest rate/currency swaps:** this will be utilized if the debt issued has a different interest basis or currency.

(vii) **Trust deed:** together with the administration agreement the bonds are created and issued by this document, including different classes of bonds and their respective entitlements. The document also provides for the enforcement of security and distribution of enforcement proceeds. The document establishes the trustee's rights and obligations end exceptions from liability.

(viii) **Terms and conditions of the bonds:** these include representations and warranties; events of default and are covered in the unit on capital markets.

(ix) **Security documentation:** this will depend on the nature of the assets and the jurisdiction in which the assets are domiciled or in which any enforcement action may be contemplated. If the security is situated in England (the *situs*) it is normally taken through a fixed and floating charge created over all of the assets of the SPV, including its rights to the mortgages under the transaction documentation.

(x) **Underwriting agreement:** this document establishes the terms and conditions on which the underwriters are prepared to offer the securitized debt. As such it will include conditions precedent relating to the nature of the collateral, the obtaining of all necessary credit enhancement, all relevant consents, authorizations and licences necessary to the issue of the debt and the ongoing administration.

(xi) **Offering circular/prospectus:** this is a selling and disclosure document and the contents will depend on the listing requirements of the stock exchange on which the debt is/are to be listed. Much of this has already been considered in the section on raising capital.

7 Specific legal risks of securitization

This is an area that the lawyers specializing in securitization will be able to advise on more fully. These are normally dealt with by either investigation or by the production of an opinion. However, a thumb-nail sketch follows.

7.1 Title

Nothing must be capable of upsetting the title to the assets that the issuer is acquiring. Dealing with these concerns is often not straightforward. No charges (actual or implied) must be capable of operating so as to restrict the originator's ability to sell the assets, in particular in existing banking facilities. This means a thorough review of any likely source of implied right to the assets is required.

Consequently, if the assets have passed through a number of hands prior to the securitization, each transfer has to be considered. Portfolios purchased from other companies raise particular problems.

The question as to the solvency or insolvency of any company involved at any stage with the receivables has to be addressed.

In the selling of the loans to the SPV the seller such as a bank or building society may have to represent and warrant to the issuer (the SPV) that the quality of the loans being transferred is good and have met the specified lending criteria. In the event of a breach of these representations and warranties the issuer would have recourse to the bank or building society.

7.2 Contractual

All of the agreements must be binding upon all of the parties. The issuer must be properly constituted etc...

7.3 Statutory

The Consumer Credit Act 1974 regulates consumer lending agreements and statutory restrictions can cause problems of their own. A full CCA review of the documents is normal practice.

Similarly, product liability issues need to be analysed out or shown to be *de minimis*.

7.4 Special risks

Each structure has to address different problems. Sometimes the answer to these problems is empirical (ie the risk is included in the analysis of the transaction and quantified). However, some points can be dealt with only by legal analysis and an opinion. The extent to which the law firm involved is prepared (on occasions) to be slightly 'sporting' can be critical.

Set-off and related risks

Set-off can occur in a variety of ways, for instance: lessees could have deposited money with an originator of the assets (who then becomes insolvent), or lessees could have paid for maintenance of equipment (which is then not carried out). Even if there is no legal justification for the set-off (ie the lessor is wrong), it may still have to be taken into account in the structure.

Similar risks relate to the position of the Issuer in the event that there is a liquidation of the administrator. A critical aspect of the structure will be the consideration of the liquidator's rights in this circumstance – can the collection of the Issuer's receivables (and their payment to the Issuer) be interrupted or stopped?

Executory contracts

Contracts that impose obligations upon the lessor are not generally securitizable. An example of an obligation would be procuring that maintenance is carried out, or agreeing to collect funds on behalf of a third party. The concern arises from a view that, were these obligations to be carried out poorly, the lessor would be in default, which could then permit the lessee to avoid his obligations. A lessee may also have the right to reject the replacement of the lessor with a third party. Essentially the problem is that the contract becomes personal to the particular lessor and not generic.

However, there are certain techniques and credit enhancement structures that could be used in these circumstances.

Unsecured creditors

The rating agencies are also concerned to ensure that either the Inland Revenue or HM Customs do not become unsecured creditors to any part of the transaction structure; in other words, that there are no known liabilities to either body that might not be met at any future point. This is considered to give an excuse to 'go after' the Issuer or the structure as a whole to try to recover assets that have been sold to the Issuer and unravel the deal.

A detailed investigation of the deferred tax positions of the originator and any group companies is therefore required. Plans have to be made to show how any resulting liabilities are proposed to be paid, given certain assumptions about origination levels and credit losses.

Contractual failure

Even if a party has committed in contract to do XYZ, will it actually do it? On the Anglo transaction, officers of both the trustee and the clearing bank were required to confirm separately to Moodys that if their respective organizations agreed in contract to do something, they would actually do it.

8 Regulatory framework and regulatory issues

The main regulatory paper for securitization for banks incorporated in the UK, that are regulated by the Financial Services Authority (FSA), is a notice issued 26/6/98 by the FSA called securitization and loan transfers. This is concerned with ensuring that there is a clean transfer of the assets from the balance sheet of the bank and that there is no recourse or redress by the issuer or SPV to the bank. This paper is also supplemented by other provisions within the FSA Handbook and is commented upon below.

However, regulators have been concerned of the underlying risks of securitization that may still be there such as operational, credit or liquidity risks to banks and building societies. The key issues of concern to regulators are the issue of moral hazard, the banker-customer relationship and cherry picking.

8.1 Moral hazard

One of the principal concerns of bank regulators around the world who have examined securitization structures is the question of moral hazard. A bank may transfer the credit risk associated with an asset, but will almost always retain servicing rights and remain as the principal point of contact for borrowers. In most securitization structures, borrowers are not aware that their loan has been transferred to an SPV; in some structures, there is not even a true sale of the loan asset.

The regulators' concern is that a bank will feel obliged to step in and assume responsibility for an asset or customer relationship, notwithstanding the transfer of risk achieved through the securitization. This risk may arise in a number of different circumstances. For instance, a borrower may default and, in order to protect future customer relationships, the Originator would repurchase the defaulted asset, rather than leave the SPV to pursue its own remedies. The Originator will be aware that an SPV will have a relatively rigid funding structure, and will be less able to exercise discretion in favour of defaulting borrowers than the Originator. Alternatively, the Originator may step in to protect investors in securities issued by the SPV if default levels on the underlying assets prove to be higher than expected. An Originator would probably undertake such extreme measures only if it was concerned that the SPV's failure to meet its liabilities would impact its own reputation. Such action would, however, undermine the objectives of securitization.

8.2 Banker-customer relationship

The banker-customer relationship and the spectre of moral hazard takes on particular importance in the regulatory treatment of securitizations of uncommitted lines of credit. On the one hand, it might be argued that such facilities are relatively easy to securitize because undrawn amounts under uncommitted lines of credit, and commitments with a tenor of 365 days or less, have a credit conversion factor of 0%; thus they incur no capital cost. Once drawn, the resultant loan asset will be risk-weighted at 100%, as with other corporate credits. Because there is no capital cost so long as the facility is undrawn, the structure does not have to address the complicated funding and cash collateralization issues alluded to above. Furthermore, because the facilities are uncommitted, or committed only for short time periods, it is simple (theoretically) to terminate the credit line or to wind down the commitment once the time comes for the SPV to amortize and pay down its debt.

8.3 Cherry picking

Regulators have voiced concern that banks are securitizing their best assets, or to put it another way, that they are cherry picking the portfolios identified for securitization. This will cause concern for a number of reasons. The minimum capital/risk asset ratio of 8%, established by the Basle Accord and the EU Directives on capital adequacy requirements for credit and financial institutions, assumes a diversification of assets within a bank's overall portfolio. This is based upon four elements: industry diversification; diversification by the country of the borrower; diversification by economic sectors; and diversification in the types of borrower and credit facility. Without this diversification, it must be assumed that the minimum 8% requirement would be significantly higher.

It is with these issues in mind that the Financial Services Authority (FSA) in the UK has laid down rules in the FSA Prudential Sourcebook (under banks, chapter SE, paras 6.3.7) that require that the association of a bank with a securitization issue must be severely limited and the flowing conditions apply:

(i) any offering circular must contain a highly visible unequivocal statement that the bank does not stand behind the issue or the issuer and will not make good any losses in the portfolio;

(ii) the bank should not have any share capital in the issuer or otherwise have a proprietary interest in, or control over, the issuer;

(iii) the issuer's name should not include the name of the bank or any reference to it; and

(iv) the bank should not provide any general continuing support.

There are no other laws or regulations that protect consumers in any special way with regard to securitization. In the case of mortgages in the UK the Council of Mortgage Lenders issued in 2000 a Statement of Practice, Transfer of Mortgages. It expects its members to comply with this statement in that home mortgages can be assigned to securitization vehicles without the specific consent of the individual borrowers.

Nineteen

Eurobonds and capital debt markets

1 Types of bonds

A bond is a negotiable debt instrument issued in bearer or registered form. It constitutes a commitment by the issuer to pay a specified sum or sums of money to the holder at a predetermined date or dates; and to pay interest to the holder at stated intervals either at a fixed rate agreed at the outset or on a floating-rate basis.

The international debt markets are often thought of in terms of eurobonds only. While the eurobond sector is the most visible, it is but one method of capital finance and but one option for investors. There are many active domestic markets. Banks regularly access these markets to raise capital and are also active in them as lead managers and advisers on issues, as traders, market-makers and investors.

1.1 Domestic debt issues

A domestic debt issue is one that an issuer raises within his own country and is denominated in his own country's currency. A German company raising D-mark in Germany was a totally domestic operation. Domestic issues invariably have a greater attraction to resident investors than investors from elsewhere because most of such securities are subject to withholding tax. Foreign investors may not be willing to take advantage of double taxation agreements that may exist between their own and the issuer's country because of the delay in reimbursement of the amount withheld. Domestic issues, therefore, are placed largely, but by no means exclusively, with investors of the issuer's country.

Domestic issues are usually registered and regulations may require them to be issued at par (for the full face value of the bond, expressed as '100').

A feature of some markets is the requirement by the central bank for issuers to submit to a queue procedure. This is to prevent an oversupply of issues at any one time with the monetary authorities establishing an orderly market through a calendar for new issues. The Bank of England's approach is less formal but the Bank must be pre-advised of new issues in sterling.

1.2 Foreign bond markets

A foreign bond is where a foreign borrower raises funds on a domestic capital market with the paper denominated in the domestic currency. Examples are as follows.

- Yankee bonds: a UK company raising US dollar debt in the USA is a foreign debt issue and is known as a 'Yankee bond'. This is a deep and liquid market.
- Samurai bonds: Issues in the yen public markets by foreign borrowers in Tokyo.
- Bulldog bonds: these are issues of sterling securities in London for sale principally to resident investors. However, the international nature of the London market has meant that new unsecured issues are made as eurobonds and not as foreign bonds.

1.3 Eurobonds

Definition

Eurobonds:

- are unsecured securities. The only security they convey is the unpledged assets and creditworthiness of the issuer;
- are in bearer form. There is no register of holders and ownership passes on delivery to the purchaser;
- are underwritten or bought by an international syndicate of investment houses and banks;
- have interest paid without deduction of tax. If withholding tax were applied, it would effectively terminate any meaningful activity in bonds in that currency;

- are listed on one or more stock exchanges but very few bonds are ever traded on them;
- normally raise a single amount of funds at the outset for the issuer;
- may be issued at a discount or at a premium to the par value;
- can be issued in the most favourable market at the time with the proceeds of the issue swapped to provide the issuer with his desired currency and interest basis;
- are placed with investors internationally and this may exclude nationals of the country of the currency of issue.

There are strict prohibitions on the sale of US dollar eurobonds in the primary market to US citizens until a 40-day lock-up period has elapsed. If sold to US residents earlier than this, the issue would need to be registered with the Securities and Exchange Commission. One reason issuers chose the euromarket route is to avoid registration with the SEC. The sale of eurobonds to UK investors is restricted under the Financial Services and Markets Act 2000 to professional investment firms or those private customers who may be classified as an intermediate customer.

Eurobonds and foreign bonds are known collectively as international bonds.

1.4 Global bonds

The process of offering bonds simultaneously in the USA, Europe and the Far East allows issuers to place the paper at the best possible price. The first global bond issue was issued by the World Bank for $1.5bn. Global bonds combine the features US foreign bonds and eurobonds. The issuer has to register its intended offering with the Securities and Exchange Commission in New York.

The benefit to issuers is that a single world price is established for these bonds whereas yield differentials of up to 10 or 20 basis points may be seen if separate issues are made in the separate markets. To date, issues have been made in US dollars, euros, Swiss francs and Japanese yen but issues in other currencies are less likely because they are not traded widely enough in the international markets.

1.5 Private placements

This unit covers public issues because the information on such issues is widely available. The time and expense involved in making public issues may sometimes be avoided by using private placements. These are issues to single investors or groups of investors rather than in the open market. They permit issuers and investors to match specific interests in terms of currency or maturity. Because of their specific nature and legal restrictions on trading, privately placed securities tend to be held by the original investor until maturity.

In the USA, Rule 144a of the US securities law allows the issue of securities without their having to be registered with the SEC. Such issues can be placed privately with and traded only by large investing institutions. Yankee bonds may be issued under Rule 144a.

2 Features of eurobonds

2.1 History and size of the eurobond market and eurobond issues

The first eurobond was issued in 1963 by the Italian motorway construction industry, Autostrade, for USD 15 million. Eurobond issues in that year totalled 13 in number and the equivalent of USD 147 million in amount.

2.2 Features of eurobond issues

(i) Size of issue: the usual range of issue size is USD 50 million to USD 500 million, although larger issues are frequently made by governments and supranational issuers. The lower limit is dictated by the costs of issue. Floating-rate notes (FRNs) can be much larger and longer term because the interest rate risk for investors is much lower.

(ii) Term: the usual term of eurobonds is five to seven or ten years, although longer terms are seen if market conditions are favourable. Issues for shorter periods are not unusual. There is an occasional market for perpetual floating-rate note issues that have no stated maturity (often issues by banks). Some centenary bonds with 100-year maturities were issued by Far Eastern borrowers in 1996.

(iii) Currencies: eurobonds have been issued in about 35 currencies, although the market in some currencies is very limited and issues infrequent. The main currencies of issue are US dollars, yen and euros. For the more exotic currencies, the windows when issues and a related swap transaction can be made are sometimes not available.

There is no euromarket for Swiss francs owing to Swiss central bank opposition to the development of an offshore Swiss franc capital market. All Swiss franc issues are foreign bonds although they are issued and traded as eurobonds.

(iv) Interest: fixed-rate eurobonds pay interest annually on the basis of a 360-day year. The interest is called the 'coupon' because the printed bonds have coupons attached. The coupons, which have the paying agent's details on the reverse, were traditionally clipped to claim the interest payments. Interest on floating-rate issues is paid according to the terms of each issue with the basis of the rate fixings needing to be defined.

(v) Denominations: the denominations of individual printed bonds within an issue may range from USD 1,000, for retail investors, to USD 100,000 to meet the need of institutional investors. Global printed bonds are printed until the smaller denominations are available. The bonds are normally stored with centralized depositories such as CEDEL or Euroclear.

Among the matters to be addressed before the euro is introduced are:

- the basis for calculating interest;
- rounding and odd-lot arrangements on conversion;
- different holidays and trading days across Europe.

3 Types of issues

3.1 Fixed-rate issues

These are the most common type of issue. The advantages of fixed-rate bonds to the issuer are that financing costs are certain for the life of the bond, and bonds can be issued in a choice of currency. Because eurobonds tap an international investor base, larger and more frequent issues are possible than in domestic markets. Collateral for eurobonds is not required beyond a negative pledge. The disadvantages are that issue costs are heavy and the time of issue may depend on market conditions, not the issuer's preference.

The advantages of fixed-rate bonds to the investor are that he obtains a certain rate of return and normally his the ability to sell his holding in the secondary market before maturity of the bond.

Step-up and step-down bonds allow for increases or decreases in coupon rates during the life of the bond. Deep discount bonds, convertibles and warrants are types of fixed-rate issues.

3.2 Partly-paid issues

It is possible for bonds to be issued on a partly-paid basis with, say, 50% of the bond payable by the investor at the outset with one or more subsequent instalments. Because the issue proceeds will not be received in one lump sum, it is easier for the issuer to employ the proceeds.

The investor may derive a gearing benefit initially because interest is payable on the whole full amount of the issue. It also means that the price volatility of the bonds in the secondary market is proportionately greater until the bond is fully paid. If the investor fails to honour subsequent calls then his holding is forfeit.

3.3 Deep discount bonds

Deep discount bonds are issued at a price well below the par or face value of the bond.The investor receives the par value at maturity, which means that his return is partly or wholly capital gain.

This type of bond is of interest to issuers who do not wish to make interest payment during the life of a bond, but may still be able to claim the annual capital increase as the equivalent of interest payments.

There are advantages for the investor. The bonds will appeal to investors whose income tax rates are higher than their capital gains marginal rate.The bonds are in effect fixed-rate bonds and offer protection against falling interest rates. The effective re-investment rate on coupons is in effect fixed.

The disadvantage to the investor is that the bonds are subject to much greater volatility in the secondary market.This is because the capital value has to reflect interest-rate changes for the whole of the life of the bond.They are more attractive to speculative investors.

3.4 Convertibles

Convertible bonds are equity-linked bonds. That is, the bonds are exchangeable into equity on predetermined terms.They give an option to buy equity and the cost to the investor is that he accepts coupons on the bonds that are lower than current interest rates at the time of issue.

The attractions to the issuer are that lower coupons can be set on the bonds and if the bonds are converted, it is equivalent to a rights issue without the costs. Convertibles are often issued when it is difficult to raise equity directly due to market conditions.

The benefit to the investor is that he has the potential to make a capital gain if the share price rises in line with expectations.

3.5 With warrants

A bond with warrants attached gives the holder of the warrant the option to acquire another asset at a predetermined price.The warrant can be detached and sold separately. The asset may be equity, another bond, currency or an asset such as gold. The warrants are usually exercisable only at defined times or for a defined period.

The benefits to the issuer are that investors will pay a premium to acquire the warrant and that the warrants can be for any asset that the issuer holds and is willing to dispose of.

The benefits to investors are that the bond is repaid at maturity, or can be sold in the secondary market, and the warrant is a highly leveraged option with the potential for capital gain.

3.6 Calls and puts

A call option gives the issuer the right to redeem a bond early at or within set times.

A put option gives the investor the right to early repayment to the bond at or within set times.

3.7 Dual currency bonds

In dual currency bonds, an issue is made in one currency, say sterling, with the issuer receiving sterling. However, redemption is in another currency, say USD, at an exchange rate fixed when the issue is launched. Investors whose assets are USD can avoid exchange risks on their investment.

3.8 Floating-rate notes (FRNs)

The first FRN issue in the eurobond market was launched in 1970. For a short period in the early 1980s it was the fastest growing capital market. However, problems arose with perpetual FRNs. The problem was an excess of large issues by banks who were raising long-term capital, subordinated bonds, but in effect paying short-term rates.

Borrowers who seek a long-term commitment of funds yet feel that interest rates are too high for a fixed-interest coupon may consider a floating-rate note issue. FRNs are suitable for banks to raise capital because the issues can broadly match the assets of a bank.

The interest rate payable on the borrowing will be brought into line with current market rates applicable usually to the three or six-month Libor rates for the currency concerned. FRNs provide investors with a higher rate of return than they could expect to receive from a bank over the same interest period.

Floating-rate notes can be issued incorporating caps and/or floors (maximum and minimum rates payable).

The majority of bonds are issued with repayment in one sum at maturity. Staggered redemption could be in the form of a sinking fund or a note-purchase programme. Redemption is by purchases in the open market or by repayment of bonds whose numbers have been drawn by lot.

4 The role of the rating agencies

A credit rating by one of the credit agencies for a new issue, though not a regulatory requirement, is now essential for market reasons. There are several rating agencies, the major ones being Standard and Poors (S & P), Moodys, IBCA and Thomson BankWatch. The latter two specialize in ratings for banks and publish ratings on an issuer (short and long term) as well as individual issues..

The purpose of a rating for a bank is:

- to assess the likelihood of a particular issue not being repaid in full when it falls due for redemption; or
- to give an indication of the likelihood of future problems arising in a bank and its ability to address such situations.

Ratings are published following examination of a bank's published accounts and in-depth discussions with the bank's management. The following is a summary of the items likely to be considered by a rating agency for a bank issue.

Quantitative factors:

- asset quality (spread of portfolio, bad debt experience, etc);
- capital adequacy;
- profitability;
- liquidity.

Qualitative factors:

- management quality;
- business franchise;
- environment;
- hidden strengths and reserves;
- hidden weaknesses and overvalued assets;
- government ownership and support or support of a major shareholder.

The characteristics of an issue will be taken into account in setting the rating, such as whether an issue is subordinated.

Ratings for long-term issues are consistent between most agencies, as follows:

S & P	Moodys	Interpretation
AAA	Aaa	Extremely strong
AA	Aa	Very strong
A	A	Very strong but more susceptible to changes in circumstance
BBB	Baa	Adequate – minimum to be considered investment grade
BB	Ba	Has some speculative elements
B	B	Assurance of interest and principal payment may be small
CCC	Caa	Poor standing – may be in default
CC	Ca	Highly speculative – may be in default
C	C	Very poor prospects
D	D	In default

These grades may be modified by adding +/- or 1/2/3 suffixes.

5 Parties in involved in a eurobond

(a) **The lead manager**

He is nominated by the issuer, to take responsibility for the issue. He acts on behalf of the issuer in all matters, including preparation and advice. The lead manager is responsible for all aspects of documentation, including distribution, as well as for the selection of all other parties involved in the deal.

(b) **Co-managers**

They assist the lead manager in his duties, particularly in terms of distribution – ie finding the investors. All managers (lead and co-managers) are responsible for underwriting the issue; in this way, the issuer has assurance of funds, and it is the role of the managers to, then, on-sell the notes to investors.

(c) **Underwriters**

Normally, these will consist of the 'management' group, although larger issues may involve a separate 'underwriting' group, the responsibilities of which lie purely in providing the underwritten support.

(d) Selling group

This consists of the managers and other underwriters, together with an additional group of banks with no such underwriting commitment. The selling group is responsible for selling the bonds to investors.

(e) Paying agents

A number of paying agents may be nominated to provide representation in the key international financial centres. A principal paying agent will be nominated. These agents are responsible for the payments made to investors in respect of interest and redemption.

(f) Trustee

The trustee's role is to act as intermediary between the issuer and the investor in terms of monitoring the administrative aspects of the issue and to ensure that respective obligations are fulfilled.

(g) Others

Other key parties are the following.

- The issuer's accountants/auditors, to advise on tax/accountancy aspects and to certify the financial data as revealed in the issue prospectus.
- Legal advisers to advise on all legal aspects involved in the issue and the documentation.
- Printers, to prepare all necessary paperwork, including the bonds themselves that must be prepared by a recognized security printer to eliminate, as far as possible, the risk of forgery.
- The listing agent/sponsor, to arrange for the issue to be listed on the desired exchange(s).
- The guarantor – where the issuer is unable to convincingly justify its ability to meet its commitments under the issue, a third party (normally, the parent company of an issuing subsidiary) may add its name to the issue and, in so doing, accept full liability thereunder. (It should be noted that this is most uncommon.)

6 Eurobond documentation

By far the majority of eurobond issues are in unsecured form. As regards documentation, the following will, usually, apply.

6.1 Prospectus

This is prepared by the issuer in close consultation with the lead manager. Its purpose is to provide detailed background information regarding both the issuer and the issue itself. It is similar in content to the 'information memorandum', which we have seen earlier. A detailed prospectus is a standard requirement of the international stock exchanges. The document will be despatched to the selling group and it will be used by it to promote the issue. Liability for any misrepresentation within such a prospectus has already been explained above.

6.2 Agreements

There are a number of agreements involved to clearly establish the terms of operation and obligations of all parties.

(a) **The subscription agreement** – between the issuer and all the managers. This covers the following points:

- managers' commitment to subscribe for the bonds;
- the issue price;
- commissions/fees payable;
- terms of the issue;
- various undertakings by the issuer as to the accuracy of financial and other information provided;
- undertakings by the issuer that there are no legal conflicts, or otherwise, in any documentation. The documentation in summary follows along the lines of the subscription agreement for commercial paper and medium-term notes as detailed above.

(b) **The underwriting agreement** – between all the managers and any other underwriters/sub-underwriters. This document sets out the terms under which underwriting will take place, including pricing and fees payable.

(c) **The selling agreement** – between all managers and the selling group members, outlining the terms under which the latter agree to market the shares.

(d) **The managers' agreement** – between all participating managers and specifying the basis of their relationship, including the delegation authorities of the lead manager.

(e) **The trust deed** – this outlines/establishes the terms under which the trustees will act as an independent intermediary between the issuer and the investors.

(f) **Paying agency agreement** – between the issuer and the nominated paying agent, outlining the relationship between the two and the pro-cedures regarding payment of interest and redemption of the bonds at maturity.

(g) **The bonds** – in bearer form, representing evidence of the debt owed by the issuer to the investor. The terms of the issue will be clearly stated on the bonds.

7 Commercial paper

7.1 Definition

Commercial paper is a method available to corporates to raise short-term finance by issuing unsecured bearer promissory notes direct to investors, ie bypassing the traditional channels of borrowing (banks). This process of cutting out the middleman is known as 'disintermediation', and through it corporate issuers (ie the borrowers) are able to raise finance more cheaply than through bank lines. Commercial paper is issued in specific denominations/currencies (see below), usually at a discount to the face value as shown on the note itself. The effective interest cost/return is, therefore, the difference between the discounted sum and the face value.

7.2 Sterling commercial paper – features

Introduction

Because of the growing interest in the Euromarkets and increasing use of 'paper' through acceptance credits as a means of raising short-term finance, the Bank of England acknowledged the need for a suitable domestic market to satisfy the needs of the UK's major corporate players.

The SCP market was introduced in April 1986 to meet this need. However, the Bank of England wished to ensure that the market operated with sufficient investor protection and hence it stipulated a series of requirements that must be met by each issuer.

Criteria

In order to issue SCP, the following requirements must be satisfied.

- The corporate issuer must have a full listing on the London Stock Exchange and minimum surplus resources of £25 m, or be the subsidiary of a parent satisfying the foregoing, with the issue being guaranteed by the parent.
- Notes can only be issued with a maturity of between seven and 364 days.
- Minimum denomination of each note is to be £½ million. (Financial institutions that qualify to issue sterling certificates of deposit are not eligible to issue SCP.)

Amount

There are two aspects to consider. First, there is the 'programme' which, to be cost-effective, should not be less than £25m. (In reality, few are at this level, with £50m being the usual minimum seen, and most programmes at the £100/£200m level.) The programme is similar to a limit on a revolving facility, because it sets the maximum level of paper the issuer can have outstanding at any one time. Once the programme is in place, issues can be made as finance is required. As already mentioned, individual notes must be for at least £500,000. This sum and £1m are the usual denominations seen.

Term/maturities

The individual notes may be drawn for any periods between seven and 364 days (inclusive). Most activity is seen in the one-to-two-month range.

Parties involved

The two key parties involved, once the programme is established, are the issuer and the investor. The investor purchases the paper from the issuer in return for the payment at interest and return of the principal sum on a future date. However, there are three other parties involved and these are:

- the arranger;
- the dealer(s);
- the issuing and paying agent (IPA).

The arranger is responsible for coordinating and advising on all aspects of the programme, eg:

- the size of the programme;
- appointment of dealers (to obtain the best spread of investors);
- appointment of the IPA;
- preparation of the information memorandum (see below).

(Quite often, the arranger is the principal dealer, and sometimes also the IPA.)

The dealers will bid for the issuer's paper with a view to placing it with investors, making a turn on the differential between the bid and offer prices. There is no guarantee that the dealer(s) will bid for the paper when it is issued; therefore, the issuer has no assurance of funds, nor at which price the paper will be acceptable to the market. (A group of dealers bidding competitively for the issuer's paper is known as a 'tender panel'.)

The IPA carries out the administrative aspects of the programme.

- He maintains safe custody of the notes.
- He issues the notes and delivers against payment.
- He authenticates the notes on issue.
- He provides the issuer with the issue proceeds.
- At maturity, he receives proceeds from the issue to settle any notes due for payment.
- He pays out on maturity against surrender of the appropriate note(s).

Back-up lines

A supporting back-up line of finance is not a prerequisite, although, as we have seen above, the issuer has no guarantee that his notes will be taken by the market, at the price he wants, at any given time. Therefore, it is common for supporting committed lines to be available for drawing in case of need.

7.3 Modus operandi

The programme will be established through the arranger and in line with the guidelines laid down by the British Bankers Association. Timing consent is not required from the Bank of England, although the latter is to be advised of proposed programme amounts, and it must be advised of outstanding paper.

Once the programme is established, the utilization procedure is quite straightforward. When the issuer requires finance, he contacts the principal dealer to discuss his requirements. The nominated panel of dealers will be invited to bid for the paper and the issuer will accept those that are most favourable. The usual cut-off time for same-day value is 12.00 noon or 12.30 pm.

When the deal is struck, the issuer advises the IPA of the details, and the dealer, in turn, also confirms these with the IPA. The IPA then prepares the notes for collection, or holds them in safe custody, as appropriate. Arrangements are made for funds to be remitted to the IPA and, in turn, on to the issuer's account.

At maturity, the issuer makes arrangements to have funds with the IPA by 12.00 noon, to cover any paper maturing. The IPA will settle with same-day value for the investor, provided delivery of the note takes place by 2.30 to 3.00 pm.

8 Medium-term notes

8.1 Definition

Medium-term notes (MTNs) provide issuers with the means to raise medium-term finance in a way similar to commercial paper, at which we looked earlier. MTNs are issued in unsecured bearer promissory note form and they may carry interest at either fixed or floating-rate, depending on the issuer's requirements.

8.2 Features

Introduction

MTNs have evolved to fill the gap, both for issuers and investors, which historically existed between commercial paper and bonds. Commercial paper maturities are up to one year, as we have seen, with bonds being, in the main, for much longer terms. The secondary market for bonds with a few years outstanding until maturity is very thin and hence presents few opportunities for investors wishing to place funds for such a term. MTNs can, probably, best be described as bonds issued under a continuous programme – the latter aspect being a feature of commercial paper, as you will recall.

The programme gives much greater flexibility, because issues can be made as and when funds are required and in relatively small sums. Bonds themselves are issued individually to raise much larger amounts.

Like bonds, MTNs carry either fixed or floating interest.

Criteria

There are no qualifying criteria, and credit ratings are not a prerequisite. Having said this, non-rated issues will be difficult to place with investors, particularly for relatively unknown names. This is, certainly, the case in the USA, where credit ratings are a virtual requirement, with the exception of the very large, well-known, issuers.

Amount

There are three different aspects as to amount. First, there is the programme size, which would, normally, be for a minimum amount of US$50m. There is no physical restriction as to size, although the cost of announcement/administration would make it unattractive for smaller programmes to be established. There is no maximum restriction. Individual issues, once the programme is set up, can be for quite flexible amounts, raised as and when finance is required. Amounts down to US$5m would, normally, be acceptable, with notes drawn in varying denominations, usually with a minimum sum of US$50,000/$100,000, although some smaller amounts have been seen in exceptional cases.

Term

Historically, in the US market, terms tended to be around three years, although much larger maturities are becoming more frequent, event to ten to fifteen years and beyond, ie entering the 'long-term' maturity band. The Euro market is, essentially, a 12- to 60-month market – although, again, some for longer terms have been seen.

Currency

This is, essentially, a US$ market, both in the case of its domestic and Euromarket MTNs. The Euromarket, however, has seen other currencies, such as sterling and the ECU. Other markets do cross boundaries with MTNs, in the sense that some countries' commercial paper markets allow maturities beyond one year and, hence, certain other currencies may be available over a medium term in this way.

Investors

The US market is dominated by the professional investors, ie banks, pension funds and other such institutions. The Euromarket also consists of such investors but it has also provided an alternative form of investment for other corporates.

8.3 Modus operandi

Essentially, this is the same as for commercial paper. MTN programmes may be established alongside a commercial paper programme to provide full flexibility as to maturity profile.

Paper is dealer-placed to investors and the commitment of the dealers to make a market in the paper provides for adequate liquidity.

9 Commercial paper and MTN documentation

The documentation for CP and MTN programmes is fairly standard and market forms have been developed by the Euronote association. The issues concerning much of the documentation have already been outlined in previous units and you should revise those units where appropriate. This section is largely concerned with the documentation for CP and MTN programmes in how they vary from that of a syndicated loan from which CP and MTN documentation largely borrows.

There are a number of documents involved in commercial paper and MTNs.

9.1 The notes

These must show the following:

- issuer's name;
- amount;
- date of issue;
- maturity date;
- IPA's certificate of authentication;
- authorized signatory(ies) of the issuer;
- a statement to the effect that the note has been issued in compliance with Regulation 15 of the Banking Act 1979 (Exempt Transactions) Regulations 1986;
- a statement whether the issue does or does not carry a guarantee.

9.2 Global or definitive notes

The bond is either issued as a global or definitive note, but global is the predominant issue. But so as an issuer can be sued direct rather than the clearing system a deed of covenant is also entered into. A deed of covenant gives direct rights against the issuer. The reality of the CP market is that they are traded through euro clearing systems by sophisticated financial institutions. Also, because of the use of clearing systems the issues of issuing and paying are resolved and this CP documentation is comparatively simple.

10 The information memorandum

This is prepared by the arranger to 'sell' the issue. The Information Memo in a CP/MTN programme is of greater significance than that of a syndicate loan because of the objective of on-selling the notes to investors, therefore it is much more important as a selling document.

The operational aspects of the programme that will be included in the information memorandum is as follows:

- issuer's name;
- programme/denomination amounts;
- purpose of the programme;
- method of delivery/settlement;

- IPA dealer details;
- date of issue;
- background details of the issuer;
- financial summary of the issuer;
- a brief analysis of the issuer's business activities;
- any other information relevant to the programme.

Therefore issuers need financial statements to distribute to investors. Disclaimers are usually given in memoranda to cover the reliability of the information.The usual exculpation clauses as discussed above are used.

As with the information memorandum under a syndicated loan there is the danger of fraudulent or negligent misrepresentation through omissions of information. Therefore in addition to the information disclaimer there should be further protective provisions that would oblige the issuer to confirm on each occasion the notes are to be issued the accuracy and completeness of the information memo (same as evergreen clause in a loan) plus indemnify any dealer for damages as a result of the information memo containing inaccuracies. The issuer will also limit by specific provision the exact extent of his responsibilities.

11 The dealership agreement

This sets out the terms of the relationship between the dealer(s) and the issuer. It is similar in terms of documentation structure to that of a syndicated loan where the commercial paper and MTN documentation is based and the general structure of the dealership agreement, as follows.

11.1 Administrative and operational provisions

This has clauses that deal with the framework in which the notes are issued under the programme once the issuer and dealer have agreed upon the terms of the issue. This includes the timetable and procedures for the issue and the amount of the issue, details of the dealers, the form of the notes, etc.

11.2 Conditions precedent

These are typically standard and will include the following.

(a) Issuer agrees to procure supply of notes to each dealer.

(b) In relation to each issue of notes it shall be a conditions precedent that the representations and warranties are true and correct on the date of issue.

(c) Memorandum and articles of association.

(d) Legal opinions.

(e) Information memo.

The conditions precedent are important to the borrower and issuer who both want to be assured of having received the funds, but lenders/underwriters will not take unqualified risks such as external factors. The external risk factors that the documentation will cover include illegality, increased costs and withholding tax provisions.

There will also be additional conditions precedent that cover the ability of the banks to sell to potential investors such as:

(a) conditions relating to a change in the issuer (regarding credit worthiness or validating of its obligations), usually cross-referenced to reps and warranties; and

(b) the important warranty relating to the information memorandums which to a CP/MTN issue is more significant because there are additional liabilities to the underwriters.

11.3 Representations and warranties

The following representations and warranties will typically be found in the dealership agreement:

(a) execution, delivery and performance of this issuer is duly authorized;

(b) obligations of issuer are at least *pari passu* with all other unsecured indebtedness;

(c) non-contravention of law;

(d) all approvals and licences have been received;

(e) information memo and other documents do not contain any untrue statement;

(f) no litigation, or government proceeding pending;

(g) no payment or imposition of withholding taxes;

(h) outstanding principal amount of notes will not exceed the maximum amount of the programme.

11.4 Covenants

The following covenants will typically be found in the dealership agreement:

(a) Information, ie report of accounts or other information to shareholders, to be made available;

(b) indemnification of dealers for:

    (i) issuer failure to make due payment under the notes,

    (ii) notes not being issued for any reason,

    (iii) any breach of the representations and warranties or of the information memo,

    (iv) withholding tax,

    (v) stamp duties;

(c) each dealer covenants and agrees it will comply with the selling restrictions.

12 The IPA Agreement

This sets out the terms of the relationship between the IPA and the issuer. The agreement outlines the relationship between the two and the pro-cedures regarding payment and redemption of the notes at maturity. It is thus a largely mechanical agreement to streamline the arrangements pursuant to which notes are actually issued into the market and payments are made under them.

13 The regulatory framework

The main Act concerned with the regulation of securities in the UK is the Financial Services and Markets Act 2000 (the 'FSMA'), which provides that under sections 21–25 of the FSMA no person may carry on investment business in the UK unless exempted or authorized by the Financial Services Authority ('FSA').

The FSMA lays down rules as to the proscribed content of investment advertisements and there is tougher liability for misleading information that is a criminal offence. FSA rules on investment advertisements will commonly provide that the advertisement must be fair and not misleading and certain prescribed information and risk warnings. There are exceptions within the Act that provide for where the advertisement is being offered only to non-private customers or where the advertisement is required by or permitted by the rules of certain investment exchanges. Such exceptions include where the advertisement is only to investment professionals, large corporates and trusts. Also that the advertisement is in the form of listing particulars for the UKLA. The functions of the UKLA and listing requirements have already largely been covered in Units 13 and 14. Sterling Commercial Paper, Euro Commercial Paper, MTNs and eurobonds are all exempt instruments under the FSMA.

Section 98 of the FSMA applies only where listing particulars are or will be published in connection with an application for listing. The Listing Requirements for eurobonds if they are to be listed in the UK are contained in Chapter 23 of the Purple Book. Due to the complex nature of eurobond transactions the UK Listing Authority should be consulted at an early stage. Depending on the nature of any particular issue, the requirements of certain parts of Chapter 23 of the Purple Book may be modified or additional requirements may apply.

The EC Prospectus Directive 89/298/EEC attempts to harmonize the regulations of EU member states with respect to publication of prospectuses for public offers of unlisted securities, and public offers of securities made before their full application for listing. In the case of eurobonds that do not involve an 'offer to the public' the EU Prospectus does not apply nor does the Public Offer of Securities Regulations 1995 (SI 1995/1537) apply.

13.1 Conditions for listing of eurobonds under the Purple Book with the UKLA

The following additions and exceptions to the conditions for listing apply to issuers of asset-backed securities:

(a) the issuer must normally be a special-purpose undertaking for the issuance of asset-backed securities;

(b) paragraphs 3.3(a) (audited accounts for three years) and 3.6 (nature and duration of business activities) do not apply;

(c) where an issue of asset-backed securities is backed by equity securities, those securities must be listed on a stock exchange or traded on another regulated and regularly operating open market, must represent minority interests and must not confer legal or management control of the issuing companies. Where options or other rights relating to equity securities are used to back an issue, this paragraph applies in respect of the equity securities to which those options or other rights relate. If there is a possibility for the noteholders to receive delivery of such equity securities (other than in the case of a default or winding up of the issuer), the issue will also be treated as a convertible issue under paragraph 23.9(d); and

(d) there must be a trustee or other appropriate independent party representing the interests of the holders of the asset-backed securities and with the right of access to appropriate information relating to the assets.

A large amount of other additional information regarding the underlying assets of the eurobond under Chapter 23 of the Purple Book must also be complied with.

Twenty

Glossary

Acceleration
The ability to treat the loan as if default had occurred.

Acquisitions
The take over of control of another company, usually by the purchase of the equity in that company.

Acquisition finance
The finance used to fund acquisitions.

Blue book
The City Code, lays down the rules on acquisitions and mergers, self administered, overseen by the Panel on Takeovers and Mergers. Lays down ten basic principles on takeovers and mergers.

Book (blue)
See blue book.

Book (purple)
See purple book.

Book (yellow)
See yellow book.

Bretton Woods Agreement
Formed at the Bretton Woods Conference, a system of international monetary control, resulting in the setting up of the International Monetary Fund and International Bank for Reconstruction and Development following the end of World War II.

Concert parties
A combination of people (or companies) working together to acquire the shares of a company, to obtain or consolidate control.

Convention countries
Those countries bound by the convention, typically the Rome Convention.

Cross default
The ability of one lender to claim default on their lending due to the default by the borrower on some other lending.

Divestment
The sale or liquidation of assets or part of a company, typically in an attempt to reduce loss-making activities. The opposite of a merger.

Enforcement
Strictly speaking means giving power to, in this context the English court deciding to give power to a decision made by an overseas court. Enforcement is not possibly without firstly the English court recognising the overseas court.

Exculpation
To free from blame, similar to disclaimer clauses.

Expropriation
To dispossess, or take out of the hands of the owner.

Forum shopping
A method of searching to find the most beneficial legal forum to have your case heard. Prevented by deciding upon the applicable (or proper) law at the commencement of the contract.

Free on board
In respect of exports, where the exporter pays for the carriage up to the point where they are loaded on to the ship.

Jurisdiction
The power of a court to hear, and decide upon, a case.

Lex causae
The proper law of the contract.

Lex domicili
The law of the country of residence.

Lex fori
The law of the country whose courts will hear a dispute on the contract.

Lex loci contractus
The law of the country where the contract is entered into.

Lex loci solutionis
The law of the country where the contract is to be performed.

Lex monetae
The law of the currency used.

Lex situs
The law of the country where the security for the loan is situated (if any).

Moratorium
An extended period to repay a loan, or a period during which repayment is suspended, or a period of protection from creditors, granted by the courts.

Prime bank
The original lender in secondary syndication.

Purple book
Listing Rules: details the requirements a company must meet prior to obtaining a full listing on the London Stock Exchange.

Recognition
Typically, the English court accepting the validity of a decision made in the courts of another country. Recognition is seen to be the first step to enforcing, in England, the decision made by an overseas court.

Tort
A civil wrong, such as negligence or conversion. Heard in civil courts and the claimant (if successful) gains a civil remedy, such as damages.

Withholding tax
The deduction of tax on dividends or interest, deducted at source.

Yellow book:
Admission of Securities to Listing, lists requirements of companies making acquisitions and divestments. Aims to ensure the timely announcement of price sensitive information. Defines five classes of transaction (classes 1-5).

Twenty One

List of abbreviations

2BCD	EU Second Banking Co-ordination Directive
3I	Investors in Industry
ABS	Asset Backed Security
ACT	Association of Corporate Treasurers
AIM	Alternative Investment Market
BBA	British Bankers Association
CA	Companies Act
CC	Competition Commission
CILC	Confirmed and Irrevocable Letter of Credit
CJJA	Civil Jurisdiction and Judgements Act 1982 & 1991
CMBS	Commercial Mortgage Backed Security
CP	Commercial Paper
CPR	Civil Procedure Rules
DTI	Department of Trade and Industry
ECGD	Export Credit Guarantees Department
ECU	European Currency Unit (the Euro)

EEA	European Economic Area (EU plus Norway, Liechtenstein and Iceland)
EGM	Extraordinary General Meeting
EU	European Union
EMU	Economic & Monetary Union (introduction of the Euro)
EGM	Extraordinary General Meeting
FOB	Free on Board
FRNs	Floating Rate Notes
FSA	Financial Services Authority
FSMA	Financial Services and Markets Act 2000
ICC	International Chamber of Commerce
ILCs	Irrevocable Letters of Credit
ISD	(EU) Investment Services Directive
IMF	International Monetary Fund
IPA	Issuing and Paying Agent
IPMA	International Primary Marketmakers Association
ISDA	International Swaps and Derivatives Association
ISMA	International Securities Markets Association
LC s	Letters of Credit
LIBOR	London Inter Bank Overnight Rate
LMA	Loan Market Association
LSE	London Stock Exchange
MBI	Management buy in
MBO	Management buy out
MTNs	Medium Term Notes
NY	New York
OFT	Office of Fair Trading
RSCs	Rules of the Supreme Court
RMBS	Residential Mortgage Backed Security
RNS	Regulatory News Service

M